TALIESIN DIARY
A YEAR WITH
FRANK LLOYD WRIGHT

_1_

October 1, 1942

Our first view of Taliesin in daylight after a 6:50 rising. Beautiful view of sloping hills from our guest room. A carved wooden figure in the attitude of prayer outside our bathroom window. Fluffy white feathers on the stairs as we went up to breakfast, escorted by Davy Davison. Feathers are peacocks' — white, gray, iridescent. There are two little pea-chicks — there were five, but they died as a result of being stuck to a newly tarred roof. Met the Fellowship at breakfast — we're 22 with the Wright family. Ruth and Eleanor showed us around. Picked up our luggage at the station. Into Met Mr. Wright — wonderful, warm personality. "A man is no good without his wife." "You must find your own work to do here. No one will give it to you." Olgivanna, his wife, studied at the Gurjeff

FIRST ENTRY OF PRISCILLA J. HENKEN'S TALIESIN DIARY, October 1, 1942.

TALIESIN DIARY
A YEAR WITH
FRANK LLOYD WRIGHT

PRISCILLA J. HENKEN

PHOTOGRAPHS: DAVID T. HENKEN

EDITOR: SARAH A. LEAVITT, NATIONAL BUILDING MUSEUM

CONSULTING EDITOR: ELISSA R. HENKEN

W. W. NORTON & COMPANY

NEW YORK, LONDON

The publication of *Taliesin Diary: A Year with Frank Lloyd Wright* is made possible by

STUDIOS
architecture

Photographs
Cover, pages 17, 27, 30, 33, 43, 69, 70, 102, 107, 124, 145, 146, 158, 162, 170, 172, 270: David T. Henken
Pages 74, 78: Priscilla J. Henken
Page 176: Taliesin Architects Archives, The Frank Lloyd Wright Foundation
Page 218: Pedro E. Guerrero

Unless otherwise stated, all correspondence, photographs, and diary entries are printed here courtesy of Elissa R. Henken, Jonathan T. Henken and Mariamne Henken Whatley.

For information about permission to reproduce selections from this book, write to Permissions, W. W. Norton & Company, Inc., 500 Fifth Avenue, New York, NY 10110

For information about special discounts for bulk purchases, please contact W. W. Norton Special Sales at specialsales@wwnorton.com or 800-233-4830

Manufacturing by Walsworth Print Group
Book design by MGMT. design
Production manager: Leeann Graham

W. W. Norton & Company, Inc., 500 Fifth Avenue, New York, N.Y. 10110
www.wwnorton.com
W. W. Norton & Company Ltd., Castle House, 75/76 Wells Street, London W1T 3QT

Front Cover
Priscilla and others with Wright in the tea circle, undated (1942-43).

Library of Congress Cataloging-in-Publication Data

Henken, Priscilla J., 1918–1969.
    Taliesin diary : a year with Frank Lloyd Wright / Priscilla J. Henken ; photographs by David T. Henken ; diary transcribed by Elissa R. Henken ; with an epilogue by Elissa R. Henken, Jonathan T. Henken, and Mariamne Henken Whatley. — First edition.
        pages cm
Includes bibliographical references and index.
ISBN 978-0-393-73380-8 (hardcover)
1. Wright, Frank Lloyd, 1867–1959—Friends and associates. 2. Henken, David T., 1915–1985. 3. Architects—Education—United States. 4. Henken, Priscilla J., 1918–1969—Diaries. 5. Architects' spouses—United States—Diaries. 6. Architects—United States—Biography. 7. Taliesin (Spring Green, Wis.) I. Henken, David T., 1915–1985 illustrator. II. Henken, Elissa R., editor. III. Title.
NA737.W7H43 2012
720.92—dc23
[B]
                                    2012019148

ISBN: 978-0-393-73380-8

0 9 8 7 6 5 4 3 2 1

CONTENTS

This book represents an unusual and exciting project for the National Building Museum. As America's leading cultural institution devoted to exploring the history of the built environment and its impact on people's lives, we engage the public in ongoing dialogues about architecture, engineering, and design. Typically, we accomplish this through exhibitions and educational programs, some of which are complemented by related publications. This book, however, stands alone.

This is foremost the diary of an erudite and witty young woman who lived and worked with the Taliesin Fellowship in 1942–43. It vividly captures the experience of a New Yorker temporarily transplanted to an isolated intellectual and artistic enclave in the rural Midwest during World War II. Yet it is also a unique contribution to our understanding of Frank Lloyd Wright, offering sometimes surprising new insights into the already complex story of one of America's greatest architects.

Much has been written about Wright, of course—about the scandals in his personal life, his cultural influence, and his unparalleled architectural achievements. His apprenticeship program, known as the Taliesin Fellowship, has been covered in the literature as well: several former fellows—including Curtis Besinger, Cornelia Brierly, and Edgar Tafel—have published memoirs about their time at Taliesin. But never before has the public had the chance to read a *diary* from Taliesin, written not as decades-later reminiscences but as on-the-ground reporting from the scene. Priscilla Henken's candid diary is thus a notable addition to the voluminous scholarship on Wright.

At the National Building Museum, we believe that broadening the knowledge of architectural history will lead to better stewardship of our built world. This diary provides fresh perspectives regarding Wright and Taliesin and, in so doing, it enhances our understanding of their profound architectural and cultural legacy.

— Chase W. Rynd, Executive Director
National Building Museum, Washington, D.C.

It is a privilege to present here the never-before-published diary of Priscilla J. Henken, penned during her year at Frank Lloyd Wright's home and studio in Spring Green, Wisconsin. Written many decades ago, the diary brings us straight into wartime Wisconsin, into the somewhat mysterious world of the Taliesin Fellowship.

Priscilla spent nearly a year living and working with one of the greatest architects of the twentieth century, but, of course, her life spanned more than just that influential period. She grew up in an immigrant community in New York City; she participated in various cultural and political movements of her day; with her husband David she raised three children in a cooperative living community she helped found in New York; and she taught high school English. By reading her diary, we accompany her across the country as she embarks on a personal journey. Her diary is informal and unguarded, observant and thoughtful. It is, on the one hand, simply Priscilla's story. But it is also a broader American story. Along with day-to-day tales about life with Frank Lloyd Wright, the diary brings us a fresh perspective on the 1940s in rural America, with insight on cuisine, debates about the war, and popular culture.

Diaries—personal writings—are some of the best primary sources we have to understand the past. Both intimate and straightforward, diaries can place us within a specific time period, giving us a sense both of the diarist and of the era. As you will discover, Priscilla Henken was eloquent and charming—she had a talent for language and her literary knowledge spanned a spectacular range of materials. We have provided more information to put her references in their historical and cultural context. Her story takes us into the world of Frank Lloyd Wright, letting us be present as the master architect's apprentices cook him dinner, listen to him debate the issues of the day, and entertain him with music in the evenings. The diary gives us history as no textbook can: from the point of view of somebody who was there.

Priscilla's diary is a classic tale: As a traveler in a strange new world, she adapts and faces conflicts, and she struggles and learns. We find in her story our own worries and triumphs, as she navigates the insular and tumultuous camaraderie of the Taliesin Fellowship.

— Sarah A. Leavitt

ACKNOWLEDGMENTS

We would like to thank, most importantly, the children of Priscilla and David Henken: Elissa R. Henken, Jonathan T. Henken, and Mariamne Henken Whatley, for trusting the National Building Museum (NBM) to present their parents' story, for their extensive work in transcribing the diary, and for sharing the diary with the world for the first time.

Led by our executive director, Chase W. Rynd, many members of the Museum's staff took this project on and cleared the way for the book to reach publication: Catherine Crane Frankel, the vice president of exhibitions, led the way with clarity, enthusiasm, and expertise. The NBM 2011 summer intern, Tara Owens, researched many of the people discussed in the diary. Our curatorial team, Chrysanthe Broikos, Stephanie Hess, Sarah Leavitt, Martin Moeller, Susan Piedmont-Palladino, and Deborah Sorensen, all worked on the annotations and essays. This project has been a group effort and we want to thank our thoughtful and supportive NBM colleagues and the NBM Board of Trustees for helping to make this possible.

Research for this project was helped along by many who took the time to find documents, photographs, and answers for our many questions, including Scott Perkins at the Price Tower Art Center; Jeanne Roberts at the Getty Research Institute; Mary Ann Langston, Indira Berndston, and Oskar Munoz at the Frank Lloyd Wright Archives, Frank Lloyd Wright Foundation; Keiran Murphy at Taliesin Preservation, Inc.; and many others along the way.

The essay "A Broad-Acre Project" was originally published in the June 1954 edition of *Town and Country Planning*, a British journal, and was republished in *Realizations of Usonia: Frank Lloyd Wright in Westchester* (Yonkers, N.Y.: Hudson River Museum, 1985). It is published here with permission from Elissa R. Henken, Jonathan T. Henken, and Mariamne H. Whatley.

Thanks also to Sarah Gephart, Tom Wilder, and Marie Grunenberger at MGMT. design and to Nancy Green, our editor at W. W. Norton, for helping us bring this project forward.

— The National Building Museum

We three Henken children are extremely grateful to our mother for leaving in her diary and correspondence such a wonderful record of her observations and of her eager, curious approach to life, and we are also thankful that our parents exchanged (and saved) letters that have provided fascinating glimpses into their early lives. The insights we have gained from their personal writings have given us even greater loving appreciation of how their examples instilled in us strong senses of aesthetics, idealism, and intellectual playfulness. It has been a pleasure to read their words and to have such an intimate portrait of their work, their relationship, their friendships, and their intellectual and political interest.

We also thank the former apprentices who, over many years, shared with us their experiences of Taliesin and working with FLW. We grew up loving to hear their stories and learning to appreciate the complexities of life at Taliesin. We especially thank Marcus Weston, both for his many years of warm and constant friendship with our family and for being so supportive of our work on the diary. We also thank Pedro Guerrero for his friendship with our family and for his beautiful photography not only of FLW and his houses, but also of our father and his work.

We particularly thank Sarah Leavitt who, having seen the potential in the diary, gained interest and support from the National Building Museum, conceptualized the book project, convinced W. W. Norton of its value, and then did the complicated task of editing. She has been a joy to work with—enthusiastic, dedicated, and sharing her strong insights as an historian. Very simply, this project would not have existed without her vision. Indeed, we thank the National Building Museum and its entire staff for supporting this project and working so hard to bring it to fruition.

Various friends and family have encouraged us in our efforts to publish our mother's work, but we especially thank Judith McCulloh for generously giving support and advice since our earliest efforts, and Judith and Lewis Leavitt for suggesting Sarah might be interested in reading the diary, thus giving this form of the project its start.

— Elissa R. Henken, Jonathan T. Henken, and Mariamne Henken Whatley

DAVID AND PRISCILLA HENKEN, 1940s.

Sarah A. Leavitt

In October of 1942, Priscilla Jussim Henken and David Theodor Herzl Henken traveled from bustling, wartime New York City to a communal farm in rural Wisconsin. Young, urban, and optimistic, the couple, who married in 1938, had been inspired by the writings of Frank Lloyd Wright and moved across the country to join his Taliesin Fellowship. At the time, Priscilla was a public high school English teacher with both a master's degree from Columbia University and a seminarian's diploma from the Jewish Theological Seminary. David, who worked as a lighting designer, had a master's degree in mechanical engineering from the City College of New York. The couple was familiar with Wright's architecture but more interested in his thoughts on urban planning. Wright had built an expansive model expressing his utopian ideas, which he called Broadacre City, and which had toured the country in 1935. The Henkens saw the model in New York and also read about Wright's philosophy and about the Taliesin Fellowship in the December 1937 issue of *Coronet* magazine. As Priscilla later wrote, "Mr. Wright's work represented the essence of integrity in architecture."[1] They wanted to learn from him.

The Henkens were second-generation Jewish Americans whose parents had immigrated to New York City from Ukraine. They grew up in the 1920s and 1930s among labor activists, garment factory workers, and socialists, many of whom had big ideas about what America could achieve through cooperative living and progressive government. They were well educated, politically engaged, and cultured young people who were regulars at New York's many restaurants, museums, and concerts. Comfortable everywhere from Yiddish theater to avant-garde art galleries, the Henkens had a wide group of friends and big plans for their future. By 1942, the Henkens had completed their formal education, started careers, and were ready to take the next step toward realizing their goal—formed in discussions with friends and at the Young People's Socialist League—to start a cooperative community of their own. Studying with Wright, who offered architectural solutions to problems of overcrowding, disillusionment, and social unrest, seemed like a good next step.

By 1942, Frank Lloyd Wright (1867–1959) was enjoying what can be described as a second career, hard-earned after some slow years marked by a decrease in commissions and prestige. The *Wisconsin State Journal* noted in 1928 that Wright's work "is probably better known in Europe and the Orient than it is in this country."[2] His fame as America's leading architect dated from several decades earlier, based on his residential work in what he called the "Prairie Style," with a practice based in Oak Park, Illinois, a suburb of Chicago. His houses, often low-slung, with deep overhanging eaves, stained-glass windows, open floor plans, prominent fireplaces, and built-in furniture, among other distinguishing features, could be found from California to New York. His international reputation had been well established through the German publication of the *Wasmuth Portfolio* and with the successful completion of the Imperial Hotel in Tokyo, Japan, which survived the devastating earthquake of 1923. However, the Great Depression, coupled with his often scandalous personal life, had limited his architectural commissions, and he had begun to focus on his legacy, through working on his autobiography and presenting his utopian vision of Broadacre City. Taliesin, the name of his home and architectural studio in Wisconsin, would become, for Wright, not just a place to experiment with his ideas about architecture but, perhaps even more importantly, also a place where he could enact in real life his theories about communal living.

Taliesin, named for the Welsh poet whose name is interpreted as "Shining Brow," was the house Wright first built in 1911 on the brow of a hill as a retreat for himself and his then mistress, Mamah Borthwick Cheney. The house was also an escape from the societal pressures of Oak Park, where he had abandoned his wife Catherine and their six children in order to live with Mamah, whom he never married. Wright rebuilt Taliesin several times, most famously after the massacre in 1914 in which an employee set fire to the house and murdered Mamah, her two children, and four others. In the subsequent years, Wright married—and divorced—the sculptor Miriam Noel, and Taliesin was rebuilt again after yet another fire in 1925. Soon thereafter, the house would take on a greater role in his life, encouraged by his third wife, Olgivanna Lazovich, whom he married in 1928. Built on land that had been in his mother's family for generations, Taliesin was surrounded by rolling hills and neighboring dairy farms. The estate eventually grew to six hundred acres studded with Wright-designed buildings: the main house, Midway Barns, Hillside School, the Romeo and Juliet Windmill Tower, and Tan-y-deri, the house Wright built for his sister Jane Porter. For about twenty years, from its beginnings in 1911 to the start of the Fellowship in 1932, Taliesin itself was a private house. But that was soon to change.

Frank and Olgivanna Wright opened their home and began the Taliesin Fellowship in part to stem the financial disaster caused by the lack of commissions, in part to expand the reach of Wright's architectural proselytizing, and in part to provide a concrete example of the benefits of communal living to the world. Indeed, Olgivanna was instrumental in suggesting the apprenticeship program, running the Fellowship alongside her husband for the next several decades, and directing it long after he died. Wright had welcomed students into his home and drafting studio in the 1920s, but the Fellowship was a more formal apprenticeship program. The

Fellowship officially began in October 1932 with a few dozen men and women who had written to Wright after reading about the announcement in newspapers and magazines around the country, meeting Wright at one of his various lectures, or reading a brochure. In the next few decades, the Fellowship grew to a list of hundreds of people who lived and worked in Wisconsin, and—after 1935—in Arizona at Taliesin West, where the apprentices usually moved for the winter. In 1937 a popular magazine wrote of the apprenticeship program that "the creation of the Fellowship is as important to Mr. Wright and Mrs. Wright as the creation of buildings. For here they are designing an entire way of life."[3] Prospective apprentices wrote letters to Wright to explain their reasons for wanting to study with the master, and they sent checks to cover tuition, about $1,000 for each applicant. No portfolio or any other demonstration of skills was required. For most of the Fellowship's history, there was no formal curriculum. The first fellows, with no commissions to work on, quarried limestone, felled trees, and sawed lumber to build the studio and other buildings. "Yet," as the *Milwaukee Journal* noted in its announcement of the opening of the Fellowship in 1933, "the idea is not really 'back to nature,' 'back to the middle ages,' 'back to handicraft,' nor back at all. It is full steam ahead."[4] In fact, during the years of the Fellowship, Wright produced some of his most forward-thinking designs and drafted some of the buildings that became an important part of his legacy, from the S. C. Johnson Wax Building in Racine, Wisconsin, to Fallingwater in Pennsylvania, to the Guggenheim Museum in New York City.

Working with early apprentices, Wright built his famous model of Broadacre City, his answer to the world's problems of urban congestion, the idea for which he had first presented in his book *The Disappearing City* in 1932. The model was a twelve-foot-square representation of a four-mile swath of a new kind of plan for living in which each family would be given a one-acre plot on which to build. Public transit and apartment buildings were present but not prioritized, with the single-family home dominating in residential architecture and the automobile being the main mode of transportation. Broadacre City proposed widespread changes in infrastructure, with buried wires limiting the need for poles and main arterial roads guiding most of the traffic. This model pushed Wright into the international discussion of city planning that would solidify his reputation as one of the nation's most important public intellectuals. It was this plan that caught the attention of David and Priscilla Henken in New York.

Inspired by Wright's bold thinking, young men and women from across the country—and even from around the world—wrote to the architect in Spring Green and asked to come to Taliesin. Some of the fellows came for a few months; some, like the Henkens, came for one or two years. Others maintained a lifelong relationship with the Fellowship, spending their entire careers working for Wright or with the Fellowship even after the great architect's death in 1959. The more famous of these—Gene Masselink, Cornelia Brierly, Edgar Tafel, Curtis Besinger—had long careers and remained associated with Taliesin for the rest of their lives. At first, the fellows were not allowed their own commissions, and they worked strictly on Wright's projects. This changed over time, though, as most architects left the Fellowship and went into practice on their own. Drawings were often officially signed by the group as Taliesin Associated Architects. Now an accredited program, the Frank Lloyd Wright School of Architecture continues to host architectural students who travel between Wisconsin and Arizona just as their predecessors have done since the 1930s.

At first, the Wrights hired cooks and construction hands to do the work on the estate. Soon, however, financial constraints and a desire to make Taliesin more of a communal farm conspired to turn the fellows into laborers as well as architectural apprentices. For the Fellowship, one of the most important of the buildings at Taliesin was the Hillside School, built by Wright in 1902 to accommodate the coeducational school founded by his maternal aunts. As noted by the *Wisconsin State Journal* in 1928, Wright announced plans to reopen Hillside School "as an academy of Allied Arts."[5] Wright turned the classrooms and gymnasium into the dining room and the theater for the Fellowship, and a 1930s addition provided the studio space. Throughout the decades that Wright lived and worked at Taliesin, he constantly improved the building, as did the fellows, who did everything from reconstruction projects and roof repairs to interior decorating. When the Fellowship started moving to Arizona every winter, the fellows also built their own structures and studios at what became Taliesin West. The Fellowship included both men and women architects as well as several spouses who, like Priscilla, were not themselves trained engineers or architects but participated in most activities of the Fellowship while in residence. Taliesin was an architecture school, but it was also a home to as many as fifty young men and women at a time. The fellows lived on-site and took on daily tasks such as tying up grape vines, harvesting vegetables, and touring visitors around the site in addition to architectural drafting. Because of David's skills in lighting and electrical work, he did much of the wiring and rewiring of the buildings, while Priscilla's expertise led her to help edit Wright's autobiography. The fellows went on field trips to local tourist attractions, drank beer at the local taverns, and picnicked often on the vast acreage of Taliesin. They learned to play instruments and sang in the choir. They fell in and out of love with one another. They worked in the fields, in the kitchen, and in the drafting studio. Sometimes they donned formal dress or costumes for parties; often they engaged in lengthy political debates. They interacted with Wright's extended family, including his children from his first marriage, some of whom visited frequently, his sisters and their families, and other local Lloyd Jones relatives. Taliesin also hosted a steady stream of visitors who came to view the estate and to dine and talk with the architect.

The Taliesin Fellowship was received suspiciously by many; newspapers and magazines reported the activities at the farm to be exotic and somewhat strange. One journal noted in 1937 that the place "may seem to be a little Utopia, a Shangri-la," and described the unusual focus on "music and talk" as well as picnics at which "folks loll about.... Sprawled picturesquely over the rocks, some in shorts, some in corduroys, the women in brilliant reds, yellows, blues ... they make an idyllic picture, altogether."[6] Not all observers were so taken with the scene. Beginning during World War II, the FBI focused on Wright's antiwar stance and sympathies with Russia and Germany, and investigated whether Wright was unduly influencing his disciples to have anti-American views. Ten years later, FBI director J. Edgar Hoover was still worried about Wright and the Fellowship, writing to the Bureau field office in Milwaukee that Wright needed to be watched, given that his "school contained no classrooms" and "appeared to be a religious cult." Hoover mentioned rumors that "the foundation held dances to the moon, told the students how to think and that if a student did not attend certain meetings which had nothing to do with the study of architecture, the student would be dismissed from the school." He also reported that his informant "had heard there were homosexuals attending the school."[7] Newspaper reports throughout the 1940s and 1950s made reference to Wright's "communist" views and his nontraditional learning environment. But the young architects and engineers kept coming.

Never one to be overly concerned with public opinion, Wright made the Taliesin Fellowship the crowning achievement in a crowded portfolio of successes. He resurrected his stalled career, established himself as a force in the architecture community well into his eighties, and put to the test his own dreams of the benefits of cultured living, filled with music, film, and literature, in a rural setting. As the *Wisconsin State Journal* reported, "Other modern architectural schools have been located in cities: but this one is in the country, and not by accident.... The leader is convinced that the sunless concentration of the big city is already doomed."[8] Wright offered up his studio in rural Wisconsin, to make some money while training the next generation in what he considered to be a true American architecture.

From his urban apartment building in New York City, David Henken wrote to Frank Lloyd Wright in July of 1942, citing his "belief in the brotherhood of man, in the cooperative commonwealth as a means for achieving it" as the main motivation leading him to Taliesin. He noted that, as a student of mechanical engineering he had "refused to lend my training to the machinery of war," perhaps as an appeal to

Wright's antiwar stance. "In this day of destruction," Henken wrote, "it does not seem to me out of place to think of building for the good life."[9] He promised he was ready for the hard work of the apprenticeship and asked Wright to accept not only him but also his wife at Taliesin. In his next letter, Henken inquired about "clothing necessities" for the Wisconsin venture. [10] Wright wrote back: "You are probably the right sort of human material for Taliesin," and he accepted Priscilla and David for the price of one apprenticeship. The Henkens' arrival date of October 1 was established, and clothing recommendations were made: "Bring with you warm outdoor sport and work clothing. . . . Your good clothes will serve for the occasions when the Fellowship 'dresses up' Saturday and Sunday evenings. . . . Strictly formal clothes are not essential."[11] And so the Henkens' adventure began.

---

1. "A Broad-Acre Project" by Priscilla J. Henken, *Town and Country Planning* (June 1954).
2. "Wright to Reopen Hillside School," *Wisconsin State Journal*, November 8, 1928.
3. "Master-Builder: Concerning Frank Lloyd Wright, Stormy Petrel of Architecture," *Coronet*, December 1937, 175.
4. "Frank Lloyd Wright Called Great Artist," *Milwaukee Journal*, April 9, 1933.

5. "When Hillside School Flourished," *Wisconsin State Journal*, November 18, 1928.
6. "Master-Builder," 179.
7. John Edgar Hoover, Director, Federal Bureau of Investigation, to Mr. W. D. Hathaway, Director, Investigation Service, Veterans Administration, April 1, 1954. Included in the FBI file on Frank Lloyd Wright, 25-133757-1.
8. "Frank Lloyd Wright Called Great Artist."

9. H065 B03, letter from David T. Henken in New York City to Frank Lloyd Wright at Taliesin, Spring Green, Wisconsin, July 17, 1942.
10. H065 C02, letter from David T. Henken in New York City to Frank Lloyd Wright at Taliesin, Spring Green, Wisconsin, August 11, 1942.
11. H065 C10, letter from Frank Lloyd Wright at Taliesin, Spring Green, Wisconsin, to David T. Henken in New York City, August 14, 1942. © Frank Lloyd Wright Foundation.

PRISCILLA (LEFT FOREGROUND) STANDING IN FRONT OF THE TALIESIN APPRENTICE QUARTERS, October 1942.

July 17, 1942

My dear Mr. Wright:

I am writing to ask that I may come to Taliesin and work with you. This is no sudden whim that has come to me. My belief in the brotherhood of man, in the cooperative commonwealth as a means for achieving it, —in other words my desire for the good life—has been growing in me steadily through my five years at college and my six years of post-collegiate employment. I have thought long and calmly, and I stand ready to offer myself as an apprentice.

In this day of destruction, it does not seem to me out of place to think of building for the good life. My course of action from college through the present has been set in just that direction. As a graduate mechanical engineer, I refused to lend my training to the machinery of war. In the field of industrial design, I worked particularly with sheet materials, developing new forms through inventions in flexion. This had its practical application in the design for mass production of packages and displays made stronger and lighter by these new methods. I am working now in the research and development laboratories of a company which specializes in architectural and theatrical lighting.

I do not expect that this body of experience wholly prepares me for the work I must do with you. I need your leadership and your guidance. Given these, I feel that I can grow and make my contribution. Perhaps you will want to know that my wife understands and concurs thoroughly with my plans.

After making provision for her, there is very little I can offer you in a monetary way now. By my labors during and after my apprenticeship, I hope amply to repay you.

I await your response eagerly,

Yours very truly,
David T. Henken

July 30, 1942

My dear David Henken:

You are probably the right sort of human material for Taliesin—but, like you, we lack financial means to afford you and your wife. If you could make your provision for her by incorporating her with you in the Fellowship for the year for a single tuition fee we would consider that and it might be possible to take you both.

We are sending some information concerning our Fellowship work—

Sincerely yours,
Frank Lloyd Wright

NOTE TO READERS

This diary, originally handwritten in two volumes, has been annotated with an eye to providing historical context for the reader, especially with respect to less well-known references. This includes brief biographical information on most of the people who are mentioned, with the exception of many of the Henkens' extended family members and friends in New York. These notes can be found below the diary text. We have silently corrected some spelling errors—slips of the pen or of the ear—but otherwise Priscilla's writing is untouched.

To provide a fuller picture of life at Taliesin, a series of topical essays follows the diary—supplemented by a comprehensive inventory of the films screened and Priscilla's reading list.

TALIESIN DIARY

OCTOBER 1, 1942

Our first view of Taliesin in daylight after a 6:50 rising. Beautiful view of sloping hills from our guest room. A carved wooden figure in the attitude of prayer outside our bathroom window. Fluffy white feathers on the stairs as we went up to breakfast, escorted by Davy Davison. Feathers are peacocks'—white, gray, iridescent. There are two little pea chicks—there were five, but they died as a result of being stuck to a newly tarred roof. Met the Fellowship at breakfast—we're 22 with the Wright family. Ruth and Eleanor showed us around. Picked up our luggage at the station. Met Mr. Wright—wonderful, warm personality. "A man is no good without his wife." "You must find your own work to do here. No one will give it to you." Olgivanna, his wife, studied at the Gurjieff Institute in France—for development of human being. There Katherine Mansfield died in her arms. Must find out more about it. Into work clothes after lunch. Dug up parsnips in the vegetable garden—with Ruth. It's fun turning over the rich brown earth, and using a spading fork. Her enthusiasm frightens me, tho. She bit into a parsnip with the wet earth clinging to it—and liked it. I brushed mine off gently before attempting to follow suit. David hauled gravel from Mazomanie. Picked 6 bushels of apples with Ruth and Marcus. At tea, Mr. Wright told David to sit next to me, and I said he had to because I was the only

---

Allen Lape "Davy" Davison (1913–1974) joined the Fellowship in 1938 and remained until his death in 1974. He was married to another fellow, Kay Schneider Cuneo, in 1941, and they had two children, Tal and Celeste. He was both an illustrator and construction supervisor for the Fellowship. After Wright's death in 1959, Davison served on the staff of the Frank Lloyd Wright Foundation.

Ruth Ten Brink, wife of fellow Howard Ten Brink.

Eleanore K. Petersen (1916–2003) joined the Fellowship in 1941, after graduating from Cooper Union in New York, and left about two months after Priscilla and David arrived. A native of New Jersey, she spent fifty years in private practice from 1952 to 2002. She was the first woman architect in New Jersey to open her own office and in 1985 became the first woman president of the New Jersey chapter of the American Institute of Architects. She was named an AIA Fellow in 1991. Her work is archived at the International Archive of Women in Architecture at Virginia Tech.

Olgivanna Lazovich Milanoff Wright (1898–1985) was Wright's third wife; they married in 1928. She had a daughter, Svetlana, from a previous marriage, and a daughter, Iovanna, with Wright. Olgivanna was born in Cetinje, Montenegro, and was a student at the G. I. Gurdjieff Institute for the Harmonious Development of Man, a school run by the philosopher and spiritual leader. Gurdjieff's teachings provided much of the underlying philosophy for the Taliesin Fellowship. While at the Institute, Olgivanna met Katherine Mansfield (1888–1923), a New Zealand author, who had moved to Europe and turned to Gurdjieff to help cure her of tuberculosis.

Marcus Weston (b. 1915) was born and raised in Spring Green, Wisconsin, the son of William Weston, the primary carpenter who built the original Taliesin as well as its subsequent incarnations. He joined the Fellowship in 1938 and was there until January 1943, when he was transferred to a federal facility in Sandstone, Minnesota, as a CO (conscientious objector) during the war. He returned to Wisconsin in 1946 and practiced architecture in various offices until his retirement.

familiar thing he had seen all day. FLW told David that he had ridden with a CO (Howard Ten Brink). David said, "So has Howard." Immediate approval of his anti war stand. Visited Hillside after tea to see the drafting and weaving rooms and the Theatre—just like the pictures with the reflex seating, big stone fireplaces, with Welsh motto, one with quotation from Gray's Elegy, two giant Shivas, two grand pianos, a Scott radio, a Capehart phonograph. Unpacking after dinner difficult till we get our own room. There are T'ang dynasty statues, Ming vases, carved teakwood, lacquered screens, Buddhas, and Shivas—just like it says!

OCTOBER 2, 1942

Getting up in the morning is an ordeal—it's icy. Spent all day making apple butters with Eleanor. Charming, intelligent—born in Passaic, lived in N.Y.C. seven years. Ken and Johnny in the kitchen were sweet and well informed. David plowed two rows of potatoes, picked several bushels, and took pictures. Watched the Ten Brinks making a comforter. Slice apples into water and salt to keep from turning black. Just boil and boil with 1 part cider to 2 parts apples, add cinnamon, allspice, sugar—result: apple butter—did 10 gallons.

Howard Ten Brink (1915–2000) joined the Fellowship in June 1942 and remained until the late summer of 1943. He was a conscientious objector during World War II and served at a work camp. In the late 1940s he was part of a partnership in founding a building company, the Wolverine Real Estate Company, in California. He was active in peace and justice organizations throughout his life.

Hillside Home School opened in 1887 as a progressive, coeducational school run by Frank Lloyd Wright's maternal aunts, "Aunt Jen" and "Aunt Nell," Jane and Ellen Lloyd Jones. Wright designed the main building in 1902; after major renovations it became part of the Taliesin Fellowship complex in 1933. The walls of the Hillside Home School featured quotations that Wright engraved as tributes to his maternal relatives. *Y Gwir yn Erbyn y Byd*, translated from the Welsh as "Truth Against the World," was the motto of the Lloyd Jones family. "**Gray's Elegy**" refers to English poet Thomas Gray's (1716–1777) masterwork, "Elegy Written in a Country Churchyard," published in 1750. Wright included the stanza, "Oft did the harvest to their sickle yeild [sic],/ Their furrow oft the stubborn glebe has broke!" as a tribute to his grandmother, Mary Lloyd Jones (1808–1870), who had been scheduled to recite the poem on the day of her death (from Maginel Wright Barney, *The Valley of the God-Almighty Joneses*).

A **Scott radio** was an upscale radio of the period, advertised as "The Stradivarius of Radio Receivers." Similarly, the Capehart phonograph was a high-end record player, featuring a mechanism that turned the record over.

Kenneth "Kenn" Burton Lockhart (1916–1994) joined the Fellowship in 1939. After the Wright's death in 1959, he worked for the Frank Lloyd Wright Foundation, Taliesin Associated Architects, and the Frank Lloyd Wright School of Architecture. He specified the materials for Wright's projects and was a Fellow of the Construction Specifications Institute. The Phoenix Chapter of CSI has honored his memory with the Kenn Lockhart CSI Scholarship Foundation.

John "Johnny" deKoven Hill (1920–1996) joined the Fellowship directly from high school in June 1938 and became one of Wright's most trusted collaborators. He remained until 1953, when Wright recommended him to Elizabeth Gordon in New York, who was recruiting an architectural editor for *House Beautiful* magazine. He stayed for ten years, becoming the publication's editorial director. He returned to the Fellowship to become the secretary for the Frank Lloyd Wright Foundation and collaborated on projects at the Fellowship in the late 1960s and 1970s. He was honorary chairman of the foundation when he died.

OCTOBER 3 SAT.

Helped Eleanor, Henning and Tom clean up the theatre. Special guests* meant no picnic but afternoon at the theatre. *Mr. Parker of Madison's Capital Times—editor. Lunch served in the theatre—saw the Forgotten Village and A Russian Fairy Tale. Wonderful to see a movie with your back to a roaring log fire. Latter picture stumped us until FLW began explaining it to Mrs. Barney, his sister, an artist and illustrator—and we eavesdropped. A clever allegory. The night was black and full of stars—the air's so clear we saw constellations we had only seen in the Planetarium before. Reminded me of Truro and Provincetown. Received a letter from Burton in answer to my thank you note by air mail—a circumlocutory fondness evinced.

OCTOBER 4 SUNDAY

My birthday—the only one I ever spent away from friends or family. FLW was at breakfast—discussion on the rebelliousness of youth—David joined. Marya Lilien, teacher connected with Chicago Opera, Polish refugee, joined us. David and I took a three hour walk, took pictures, gathered apples. Dinner at 7:00 in the Wrights' living room. We, as newcomers, had whiskey when the rest had wine. The Herbert Jacobs were there. FLW—"You don't know the Jacobs, but they live in a world famous house." David discussed Mumford with FLW, formerly a close friend. Resents M's printing personal letter of his in Daily Worker, and falling out on war issue. Embarrassed when all the Wrights, guests, family, and Fellowship sang,

---

Henning Watterson joined the Fellowship in 1941. Watterson was a master weaver who brought his own looms to Taliesin for weaving the various curtains, rugs, and other textiles.

Thomas Weigle joined the Fellowship in 1934.

The *Capital Times* was Madison's progressive newspaper, founded by William T. Evjue (1882–1970) in 1917 because the *Wisconsin State Journal* had dropped support for Robert "Fighting Bob" La Follette's progressive politics. In the 1940s, **Cedric Parker** (1907–1978) was the managing editor of, and a reporter for, the *Capital Times*, covering crime and political corruption.

Burton Pollin (1916–2009), a friend of Priscilla's who became a professor of English at City University of New York and a leading authority on Edgar Allan Poe.

Marya Lilien (1901–1998), a native of Poland, joined the Fellowship in 1937. She later founded the interior architecture program at the School of the Art Institute of Chicago and taught the history of architecture at Columbia College in Chicago.

Wright designed two houses for Herbert and Katherine Jacobs. The "**world famous house**" is the first of the two, built in 1936–37 in Madison, Wisconsin. It was a prototype of the "Usonian" house, which Wright conceived of as a group of relatively small, affordable dwellings for the American middle class. The house's characteristic Usonian elements include a concrete slab floor incorporating radiant heating, abundant windows, an open carport, and flat roofs with broad overhangs providing summer shade and winter sun and creating visual continuity between the interior and exterior.

Lewis Mumford (1895–1990) was an historian and literary critic who wrote extensively about architecture and urbanism. He was architecture critic for the *New Yorker* from 1931 to 1963. Wright and Mumford had been corresponding since Wright's days with Louis Sullivan in the 1910s. Their relationship soured during World War II because of Wright's opposition to the war. They made up briefly, only to fall out again in 1953 after Mumford published a scathing review in the *New Yorker* of an exhibition of Wright's work.

"Happy Birthday, dear Priscilla, happy birthday to you." Concert—Gene Masselink sang, chorus directed by Curtis Besinger, trio—Johnny Hill (piano), Ruth (cello), Svetlana (violin); recorder ensembles; Iovanna (harp). Received phoned in telegrams from the Jussims (Happy Birthday, darling. May we spend the next one together) and from the Henkens (Happy Birthday, and a wonderful year).

OCTOBER 5 MONDAY

More peeling and preserving of apples. They leave a black stain on your hands removable only by lemon. Burton sent me a beautiful compact via air mail—from Argentina—wonderful smooth brown alligator lined with white suede—"Many happy returns—or just one—sooner?" David laid more gravel beds and paved 25 yards of road. Tom started teaching me the recorder after supper. Chic-ngai Chow taught David Chinese; I taught Chic-ngai English. After tea, Curtis, David, and I climbed a hill on Wes Peters' property, and talked. FLW read from Reality, a British news weekly at tea—honest, straight thinking publication, but FLW underrates the honesty of similar American ones. Olgivanna in long garden dress, floppy hat, and

---

Eugene Masselink (1910–1962) joined the Fellowship in 1933 and was affiliated with the Frank Lloyd Wright Foundation (as a member of the board and as its secretary) until his death. Trained as a painter, he designed and printed many Taliesin-related publications and created abstract works for numerous Wright projects. Gene increasingly took on administrative tasks in the 1930s, after the paid staff left, signing correspondence as "Secretary to Mr. Wright." Among other things, Masselink answered the telephone, took Wright's dictation of correspondence, dealt with the bills and the creditors, ordered supplies, and figured out the living arrangements for the apprentices.

Except for his three years of national service between 1943 and 1946, **Curtis Wray Besinger** (1914–1999) was a Taliesin fellow from 1939 to 1955. He had earned a bachelor of science degree in architecture from Kansas University in 1936 and returned to teach there after leaving the Fellowship. While teaching, he was affiliated with Fred Benedict's architectural practice in Aspen, Colorado. He retired in 1984. His memoir, *Working with Mr. Wright: What It Was Like,* was published in 1995.

Svetlana Hinzenberg Wright (1917–1946), the daughter of Olgivanna Lazovich Milanoff and her first husband, Vlademar Hinzenberg—was adopted by Wright and married Wes Peters, a fellow, in 1935. After two years on their own, they returned to Taliesin, where they had two children, Daniel and Brandoch. Trained as a musician, Svetlana helped shape the musical life at the Fellowship. She and Daniel died in a car accident in 1946.

Iovanna Wright (b. 1925), was the younger daughter of Frank Lloyd Wright and Olgivanna Wright.

Chic-ngai Chow joined the Fellowship in 1941.

William Wesley "Wes" Peters (1912–1991) began his Taliesin Fellowship in 1932 as a founding member. He married Olgivanna Wright's daughter Svetlana Hinzenberg in 1935. From 1970 to 1973 Peters was married to Svetlana Alliluyeva, Joseph Stalin's daughter, with whom he had a daughter, Olga. Throughout his career, Peters worked as an architect and engineer alongside Wright. Peters's **property**, named Aldebaran, was one of several farms purchased by apprentices as part of Wright's goal of creating Broadacre City right there in Wisconsin.

Twip, tremendous collie—looking just like a calendar picture on the hill above the tea terrace. Birthday card from Julia.

OCTOBER 6 TUES.
Peeled apples again. Cut watermelon rinds for pickling. Knife went through middle of my thumb nail and underneath. Messy—I nearly fainted twice. Eleanor was my first aid girl. The second time, FLW saw me turn green (a shade he afterwards said contrasted nicely with my hair), led me to the hill garden, and spread a Chinese rug for me. Keeping my wits about me, because it's warmer that way, I said, "When I write my autobiography, I'll say FLW spread a carpet for me." David is still graveling and sodding, and even FLW helped with the hoeing. Olgi. baked some "bulka" for tea which we had on the office terrace—view of the winding stream and gentle pounding of the dam. FLW wants Henning to teach me weaving—he wants the rug completed.

OCTOBER 7 WED.
More canning apples—I shall soon hate them. Digging parsnips in the garden. Ted went in to Madison; so I subbed for him in tea preparation. FLW did not appear—glad even tho the set up was attractive. My spirits were dampened by having glass pitcher full of boiling water burst on me. I think I invite trouble. Gene notified us our room was ready. Moved boxes and luggage, and sat in the mess. Put up the antimony and Chinese figures first—this must be home. Stone fireplace that looks beautiful but deflects the heat. Pine branch and bittersweet over canopy the bed. Two good Japanese prints. David hauled more gravel and laid more sod. He sits in at chorus.

The dog's name, **Twip**, was a contraction of the mountain called Toroweap Point, or Tuweep mountain, now part of Grand Canyon National Park, which is near Taliesin West in Arizona.

Julia Jussim, Priscilla's younger sister, the Jussims' second daughter, was nineteen at the time of the diary. Julia married George S. Brody and became a librarian after earning degrees from Hunter College and Columbia University. She retired from the New York Public Library as Associate Director for Central Library Services and Chief of the Mid-Manhattan Library.

Theodore "Ted" Dixon Bower (1922-2009) was part of the Taliesin Fellowship from 1941-1948, after which he worked on several of Wright's projects, including the Usonian houses in Mount Pleasant, New York. In the 1950s, Bower worked with architect Le Corbusier on the plans for the city of Chandigarh, India, and later opened his own architectural practice in Seattle.

PRISCILLA WITH A WHITE PEACOCK FEATHER IN HER HAIR, October 1942.

OCTOBER 8 THURS.

Began weaving on rug at Hillside. Navajo stitch. Colors are blue, green, beige, brown. Will be 400 square feet when completed. Intricate design of Wright's made in 1935. Four sections—red, blue, brown, green. I'm working on the blue. Trundles, pedals, loom, warp, swift (for spools of wool). Canning in the afternoon. Time off to complete room. David built shelves and I put everything away—and out came our appropriate cloisonnés. Sad letter from Clarice, and over and under exposed Kodachromes arrived.

OCTOBER 9 FRI.

Weaving—loose stitch getting tighter. Canning in afternoon. Folk dancing at Hillside in evening. Dances taught by Howard and Ruth; Johnny at grand piano. Presided over by two giant Shivas. Lots of fun. Henning's a wonderful dancer. Thought of Burton and the folk dances we didn't do at Cambridge because of "bicycle seat." Mom sent strudel—gave some to Ken and Eleanor, a plate full to the Wrights, and the rest served at supper. What tribute to the strudel! A steer broke its leg and David had to lift it onto the truck to be sent to the butcher. He's still sick because it looked so helpless and pathetic. FLW's reputation here is low as far as creditors are concerned—has to trade far from the locality. Wes Peters manages instead. David made cider—hated the flies and bees. Everybody thinks this is a free love dive—I mean the Spring Greeners. Completed Krishnalal Shridharani's My India, My America.

OCT. 10 SAT.

Weaving in the morning. Picnic in the afternoon—truck artistically draped with Chinese, Indian, and sheepskin rugs, giant pumpkins, bushels of food, benches, and architects. Roast weinies and coffee at a birch grove 30 miles from here. Lots of fun

---

The rug Priscilla worked on while at Taliesin was designed by Wright and organized by master weaver and apprentice Henning Waterson. Curtis Besinger remembered the rug in his book, *Working with Mr. Wright: What It Was Like* (1995): "The yarn for it was purchased from the Navajo Indians [near Taliesin West in Arizona]. It came in large loose hanks of naturally white and black yarn with some brown mixed in it. These were used for the white-and-black areas. The yarns had to be dyed for the other areas of color. . . . The rug, to be about twenty-five feet square, was designed to be made in strips that could be woven on a four-foot loom and then sewn together. Unfortunately, the assembled rug did not lie flat on the floor as desired. Mr. Wright then decided to use the long strips as drapes and hung them at the sides of the tall windows in the living room and the theater at Hillside." The weaving project that Priscilla and many other fellows worked on during the winter of 1942–43 hung as curtains in the Assembly Hall and the Theater until most of the panels were destroyed by fire in 1952.

but the return trip was freezing. We stopped at a filling station, and 2 men coming out of the bar, stared in amazement:

> They: What the Hell!
>
> Us: Bet you think you're seeing things.
>
> They: God, that awful stuff Charley serves us!

Saw the Male Animal at the theater. FLW loved it, especially the picture of the American college trustee. Folk dancing afterwards. F insists on calling me Patricia. Strange. Welcome letters from Mom and Henkens.

OCT 11 SUNDAY

David's birthday—and no gift. Walked to Hillside—browsed and collected rotting old plates of Wright's, and a German edition of one of his books. Read. Amused to discover La Rouge et Noir and La Chartre de Parme left in our room after Burton had searched all over for them in the city. Concert. Spoke to Miss Edwards, (worked for Spanish Republicans, knows Robeson intimately)—thought this place feudal. FLW read from Ilka Chase's Past Imperfect. He said Hearst was the most sinister man he had ever met.

OCT. 12 MONDAY

Jared's birthday—sent him a hand made card. Weaving; canning. Served tea because Kay had forgotten to assign someone. Birthday card to David from Julia. Charming letter from Nat. David is an exhausted kitchen helper with Kay as cook—he hates it. Such fuss in serving the Wrights. Nightly lessons with Chic-ngai—long talks.

OCT. 13 TUES.

Weaving. Canning. Serving lunch and supper and washing supper pots and Wright dishes. David is already worn out as K.P. Panicked them at tea by answering

---

Paul Robeson (1898–1976) was a concert singer who became known for his political views and who helped raise money for the Spanish Republicans in the late 1930s.

Jared Jussim, Priscilla's brother, is the youngest of the four siblings; he was seven years old at the time the diary was written. Jared became a lawyer after earning degrees from City College of New York and Harvard Law School, and was Executive Vice President, Intellectual Property Department and Deputy General Counsel, at Sony Pictures.

Cornelia "Kay" Schneider (1918–1996) joined the Fellowship in 1935 and served as Mrs. Wright's secretary until her death in 1985. She also worked for both the Frank Lloyd Wright School of Architecture and Taliesin Architects. After a brief marriage to a fellow, Larry Cuneo (1939–1940), she married Davy Davison, another fellow, in 1941. They had two children, Tal and Celeste. She married twice more, both times to men from the Fellowship: Stephen Oyakawa, with whom she had a son, and then John Rattenbury.

TALIESIN FELLOWS GATHERING WOOD FOR A PICNIC BONFIRE (FROM LEFT: RUTH TEN BRINK, CURTIS BESINGER, DAVY DAVISON, AND KENN LOCKHART), October 1942.

PRISCILLA (RIGHT, FOREGROUND) SITTING ON THE LAWN OUTSIDE THE HILLSIDE DINING ROOM, October 1942.

Wright's "What is a quince?" with "Something in Canada that has to do with Dr. Dafoe." Grant Wood patched fields—Bellied and bosomed hills. Schreiber clouds, pink tinted. Trembling into your clothes in the morning, peeling them off in layers toward noon, knife edge iciness of sheets at night.

OCT. 14 WED.
Ran out of natural thread in weaving. Dyed it. Mordant keeps dye in—sodium sulphate and acetic acid in heated basin of water. Add a little brown dye. Soak till dye disappears. Remove wool. Add more dye, and so on until you achieve your color. Hang up to dry. Theory of light in color instead of pigment in color—same as David uses in lighting. Primaries are red, green, and blue violet instead of red, yellow, and blue. Rearranged shelves in root cellar—chutney, all sorts of jams and jellies, pickles, vinegars, ciders, fruits, vegetables, fruit juices, catsups. Long, dreary day for David. Delightful letters from Burton and Judeth.

OCT. 15 THURS.
More weaving; more canning. Chic-ngai left for Ann Arbor to visit the Chinese fraternities and his brother and Wright homes. Hans hates chorus because of the Catholic hymns. Lack of democracy in Fellowship. Howard classified 4E (CO)—went for physical. Marcus's case still being examined by State Board. Letter from George Brewster. Eleanor and Ken are that way about each other; Henning divorced his wife to Herbert, whom she didn't marry after all. Had a design for living for a while. She left Henning a business and Herbert a farm. Kay married photographer here, Cuneo; left for a year; left him; returned on her knees; married Davy a few months before the baby was born. Eleanor and Henning are my dirt distributors.

Dr. Allan R. Dafoe (1883–1943) was a Canadian doctor best known for delivering and later becoming joint guardian of the Dionne quintuplets (the "quints"), the first quintuplets to survive infancy, who were born in 1934.

Grant Wood (1891–1942) was an artist known for his paintings of farms and small-town life.

Georges L. Schreiber (1904–1977), a Belgian artist, moved to America and traveled the country in the 1930s as a painter.

Judeth Henken is David's sister; she later married Odif Podell.

Hans Koch (d. 1947) joined the Fellowship in 1934. Originally from Germany, Koch was a master craftsman who came to Taliesin from New York City where he and his wife, Anna Reidel, had been active in the Modern School movement and other progressive causes.

George Brewster, a friend and colleague of David's at Display Finishing Co. and at Richard E. Paige, Inc.

Design for living is a reference to the three-way relationship featured in the Noel Coward play *Design for Living*, which premiered on Broadway and as a Hollywood film in 1933.

Photographer **Lawrence J. Cuneo** joined the Fellowship in 1938.

OCT. 16 FRI.

Muriel's birthday—sent her a card and received a delightful letter from her. She writes well. More weaving and canning. Gene's party in the evening—wine, crepe suzettes, fruit salad, popcorn. Folk dancing, dull games. Announcement of famous paintings as theme for Halloween party. Annoyed by Mrs. W's insistence on knowing who would throw the next party. Gene's room is charming and friendly. FLW so human—he picked all his favorite fruits out of the salad bowl.

OCT. 17 SAT.

Weaving—Henning is pleased with my progress in skill and speed. Read. Movies—Mozart—quite informative.

OCT. 18 SUN.

Guided tours to two teachers from the University of Minnesota, a curator of a museum, and Miss Vogel, a weaver from Cranbrook. They annoyed me by trying to find out everything about me, and by calling Eleanor a duck and a dear child. About Cranbrook: Saarinen is a Mannerheim fascist from Finland; his wife was dismissed because of inefficiency (he created the designs and her weavers executed them); Carl Milles, the sculptor (we have his Jonah and the Whale here) is warm, human, and like Wright. Breakfast table discussion on the war. FLW said Jews were mistaken in giving impression they had started the war, but David was a remarkable exception. He (David) spoke courageously and fluently. FLW read from Reality—that started it. Concert in the evening—rather dull—I still need an evening gown. We both helped Ken in the kitchen. David is so happy this is his last day as K.P.

MON. OCT. 19

Weaving. Canned 5 gallons of apple sauce. Rode around locale in Miss Vogel's car.

Muriel Jussim, Priscilla's younger sister, the Jussims' third daughter, was thirteen years old at the time of the diary. She graduated from Hunter College and married Rolf Landauer.

The **Cranbrook** Academy of Art, in Bloomfield Hills, Michigan, was established in 1932 and figured prominently in the development of American modernism in the mid-twentieth century. Eliel Saarinen (1873–1950), a Finnish-born architect who immigrated to the United States in 1923, designed the Cranbrook campus—including a museum and preparatory schools for boys and girls—and served as the first director of the art academy. "Mannerheim fascist" refers to Carl G. E. Mannerheim, the leader of Finland's military at the time, who maintained a relationship with Nazi Germany. Saarinen's wife, **Loja Saarinen** (1879–1968), was director of the academy's weaving department until 1942. Eliel later practiced architecture with his son Eero Saarinen (1910–1961), who became a renowned architect in his own right. **Carl Milles** (1875–1955), a Swede by birth, was the sculptor in residence at Cranbrook. His fountain Jonah and the Whale is still on view at Taliesin.

PRISCILLA ON A TRACTOR, October 1942.

Stopped at the Wright Lloyd Jones Unity Chapel. Ten Brinks and David brought in rugs from Hillside, then visited and talked endlessly.

TUES. OCT. 20

Weaving. Peeling apples and making apple butter. Wright's story of Woollcott's visit—he put his hand on the coffee pot handle at 8, didn't remove it till 12, talking all the time, and when lunch was served, complained that the Fellowship ate too much. After tea, regaled Ken, Jack, and Curtis with the explanation of Middle English, and thus emboldened went in to FLW and told him that I had been thinking about it for some time but didn't dare ask him because my youth would make it seem like impertinence, but could I proof read his Autobiography. So wonderful of me to offer, delighted to have me do it, he doesn't know who is better qualified. After supper, Svetlana heard me blow on the recorders—I think I'll choose alto; and then Henning traipsed after me for candy and to hear me blow some more. The tones I get! But they say even the stupid can learn the recorder. Our 4 other packages arrived by freight today. We're finally settled—or almost. David built more shelves and intends to build still more. Everyone here is so artistic they notice the color of my hair in sunlight, patterns shadows make, lines, colors. Ted, carrying Wright's principle of carrying the outdoors into the house strews dead leaves on his floor. Organic architecture means that the building is in agreement with the natural surroundings, the personality of the owner, the times. Read Bauhaus and Raymond Hood's Modern Architecture, and Moderne Plastike. Ruth treads where

The **Unity Chapel**, in Spring Green, was built in 1886 as a private church for the Lloyd Jones family (Richard and Mary Lloyd Jones were Wright's maternal grandparents). The Rev. Jenkin Lloyd Jones, a Unitarian minister and Wright's uncle, oversaw construction of the project, which was designed by Chicago architect Joseph Silsbee (1848–1913) with the young Wright serving as draftsman.

Alexander Woollcott (1887–1943) was a critic and writer for the *New Yorker* magazine and an original member of the Algonquin Round Table, a group of prominent writers and critics. During the Depression, he was also a radio commentator. A proponent of normalizing relations with the Soviet Union, Woollcott traveled there in the 1930s. The Wrights considered Woollcott a good friend. *Woollcott's Second Reader*, an anthology of short stories and novels published in 1937, was widely circulated at Taliesin, and Priscilla read from it liberally.

John H. "Jack" Howe (1913–1997) joined the Fellowship in 1932, immediately after high school, and remained through 1964, with the exception of his years at the Sandstone federal prison in Minnesota where he was a conscientious objector. A talented architectural renderer, he ran the drafting room at Taliesin for some twenty-five years and was part of Taliesin Associated Architects. Before opening his own office in Minnesota, he joined the office of another former fellow, Aaron Green. He retired in 1992. His papers are at the University of Minnesota's Northwest Architectural Archives.

Wright's five-volume ***Frank Lloyd Wright: An Autobiography*** was first published in 1932, the same year that the Taliesin Fellowship was formally established, and was extensively reworked over the next ten years and republished. The book covered five broad themes: family, fellowship, work, freedom, and form.

angels fear to—she's making abstractions for Xmas. Wright began them at the turn of the century for wall decorations; they reached their height in Paris with Picasso; deteriorated in the crazy twenties under the name of modern art; and are now beautifully coming into their own. Even FLW sits down to do them fearfully. Letter from Blanche. Visits from Ted, Johnny, Henning for art books—Halloween is bothering them—and us.

WED. OCT. 21

My eyes are bleary. I proof read 73 pages of the Autobiography. The style is intricate, involved, frequently turbid; alternation of long and short sentences, Run-ons and non-sentences, and mispunctuation. But it's the style as the man speaks. Olgi's hand is in the mentioning of apprentice's names—not strange, therefore, that Kay's and Davy's wedding should get such a rousing report. Interesting being on the inside of the inside. Breakfast was late because the boiler broke, but even the extra time wasn't enough for all David's repairs. The day is gray, foreboding, snow in the distance. How disappointing not to be able to go to Arizona—especially as it gets colder here—because of gasoline, rubber, and money shortage. You can warm your toes at the fire—an iridescent molten glow—beautiful, but I'd prefer radiant heating. John Steuart Curry was invited to the Halloween party, but he probably won't come. Davy tells an amusing story of the Fellowship's overnight stay at the Benton home in Kansas City, on the way to camp. All the boys, including the short, square, black-mustached Thomas Benton had imbibed freely. While he swung in wide arcs from a swing with 25-foot long ropes, the boys stood on the porch singing to Kansas City till the wee hours Palestrina, Bach, spirituals, and folk songs. Then he and his sons entertained them with chamber music composed of harmonicas and recorders. Which reminds me, I've tried playing Svet's recorder. I keep on blowing C, but it sounds different all the time, just like adding columns in arithmetic. The weaving

---

Abstraction was an avant-garde art movement of the early twentieth century. Wright's abstractions were designs derived—and abstracted—from nature. His *September Abstractions, The Desert* (1925-26), for example, featured the familiar blue, yellow, red, and green geometric shapes that he also used in a wide range of contexts such as stained-glass windows, ceramics, glass, metalwork, and textiles. Wright often abstracted the natural scene—mountains, trees, scenic views of all sorts—into the lines of his buildings.

Taliesin West in **Arizona** was built by Wright and his apprentices in 1938 as a winter home for the Fellowship.

Usually the Fellowship made the cross-country trip to Arizona for the winter. However, they did not go in 1942 because of wartime rubber and fuel rationing.

Wright personally knew many of the artists of his time. **John Steuart Curry** (1897-1946) was an American painter from Kansas. He, Grant Wood, who had recently died, and **Thomas Hart Benton** (1889-1975) were the "Regionalist Triumvirate," a group of well-known Midwestern artists in this period. While working in Madison in the late 1930s, Curry visited Wright at Taliesin.

is progressing splendidly and it felt good not to do apples. In the week's activities, next to my name it says Apples. Nothing more. So completely have I become misidentified. And Gene keeps calling me Patricia. Finished Vol. I of Stendhal's The Red and The Black. David nailed shingles today, and worked in the draughting room for the first time. The Board is still quibbling with me about my checks. Letter from Judy—all sorts of money complications. Today is Marcus's last day or he can be jailed for not appearing at the Induction Board. He's too sweet to be hurt. I've finally been able to describe the peacock's cry—a cross between a Bronx razz and a kazoo.

OCT. 22 THURS.

Weaving progresses nimbly, as does the proof-reading. I'm pleased with changes I've made. Will he be? Tea in the studio today revolved around bringing up children, with special emphasis on Lloyd, the eldest, and Iovanna, the youngest. Reread Millay's Fatal Interview with its poignant dedication to Elinor Wylie. Received a letter from Judy and wrote to Gellart et al and Bonawit et al. David likes my style. Had a long post-prandial talk with Marcus about l'affaire CO. Nothing exciting today but pleasant. That tree on the crest of the hill has a black and voluptuous beauty outlined against the morning mist and the afternoon's cloudless sunshine. FLW teased David about frying off some of his grease in Hell—why does such a remark annoy me more than David? Ordered the recorder today.

OCT. 23 FRIDAY

I am beginning to look positively shapeless—excess poundage and excess clothing. When I'm fully dressed for the brisk, cheek-tingling walk to Hillside, my arms are fully 6 inches away from my body. It was so cold in the weaving room, I wore gloves first, and then we moved the loom in front of the fireplace in the dancing room— Truth Against the World /|\. Fingers so numb that when I re-ratcheted, I didn't feel the scratch on my thumb till I saw it bleed. Proofreading continues interesting, and I'm pleased that FLW, in 75 pages of corrections, rejected only one—and acknowledged the conscientiousness at Svet's party. This was a great success with grand food, the Wrights being particularly charming, folk dancing, and drawing

---

Dorothy Bonawit (d. 1970), a senior colleague of Priscilla's in the New York public schools and a mentor to her, worked as a high school principal in the 1950s and 1960s. P.S./I.S. 49 Queens is now known as the Dorothy Bonawit Kole School.

Priscilla drew here the three-pronged symbol /|\ that Wright used to signify his family motto, "**Truth Against the World**." Known as the symbol of *awen*, inspiration, this and the motto were not ancient but were developed by Welsh poet and antiquarian Iolo Morganwg in the early nineteenth century as part of his dissemination of Welsh culture.

charades. Kenn invited us and Eleanor to his room first for some good popular records and wild grape wine, and came to our room afterwards bearing the wine— and, a little loneliness perhaps? Mom sent a letter plus my evening clothes, which I even tried on backward for the effect it would create. Am I going arty too? Leaves falling sound like footsteps—or rain drops. At our 2 hour long tea, FLW mentioned Clarence Darrow—spoke of their great friendship and mutual respect—also their visits to Hawaii, Porto Rica, and the Phillipines and American aggression—outright cruelty—there.

SATURDAY OCT. 24
Raked leaves, swept stairs, cleaned Hillside this morning. Some useless work. David was on duty with and had to stoke the boiler and burn leaves. Read, served, wrote letters. Received charming letters from Bessie Henken and Muriel. Served and washed dishes after the movie Artkino—A Musical Story. FLW kept on greeting me as if he had just noticed me.

SUNDAY OCT. 25
David didn't go to breakfast this morning and FLW asked him afterwards whether he had overeaten. Ken and Eleanor came in to visit till 1:00. Talked about everything, especially the future of us in relation to the Fellowship. Went to Hillside, I to learn how to project (an intricate business), and David to learn to show visitors around. Concert in the evening. The bright moonlight seemed to give the road the appearance of fresh snow. Went up to Kenn's room afterwards to discuss his and Eleanor's future and ours. Marcus said he had been controlling it all evening, but he wanted to tell me how lovely I looked.

MONDAY OCT. 26
Received my loyalty oath from the Bd. of Ed. and had it notarized; a letter from

---

Clarence Darrow (1857–1938) was a lawyer who in 1915 defended Wright and Miriam Noel against charges that they had violated the Mann Act by crossing state lines as an unmarried couple. He persuaded the federal authorities to drop the case. Darrow is best known for his role in the Scopes trial (1925), in which he defended high school biology teacher John Scopes, who was accused of violating a Tennessee law that made the teaching of evolution illegal.

American aggression: The Spanish-American War in 1898 had repercussions throughout the island territories, leading to decades of revolts and unrest. In 1942, Hawaii was annexed by the United States as a territory; Puerto Rico—commonly spelled as "Porto" in this period—was a U.S. colony; the Philippines was a commonwealth of the United States.

Beginning in 1934, New York public school teachers had to sign a **loyalty oath** pledging support for the State of New York and the U.S. Constitution. This requirement of employment was revoked in the U.S. Supreme Court case Keyishian v. Board of Regents in 1967.

Mom; one from the Rubins; a card from Murray who's stationed in Rochester, Minnesota; and a letter from Nat who called me an oasis and said of my letter: "It sounds precisely like you, and there is no one here who sounds like that, nor will there be." Moved the bench, wool, and swifts over from Hillside, and tried to gather chard and lettuce, but they were frozen, and so were we. Temperature 20. David's insulating the boiler, and well he may. Oh, my checks arrived too. A little weaving, a little proofreading, lots of freezing—so passed the afternoon. Helped David with tea. Special concoction by Mrs. Wright in honor of the Masselinks. Washed laundry. Supper with Wrights, again as special honor. Party—Folk dancing, popcorn, charades—Gene's room. Partners were John Hill and Marcus. Marcus (reminded of it by reading the Autobiography) is the son of Bill Weston, carpenter, who was nearly killed during the "massacre." Their son and brother was, however. Party lasted till 11, with a few nasty ones (charades) aimed at the schoolteachers, (g— d— their petty jealousies) Ruth and me. Heard a good story about Arch Oboler and Wright. They both went up one of Oboler's hills to see the sunset and the view (sites of shooting How Green Was My Valley and Wuthering Heights). Oboler is dramatic, sentimental, and FLW put his arm around him and said, "whenever you look at this view, Arch, I'll be with you." "I know, Frank, I know you will." ("But I didn't feel it, I didn't feel it.") That evening Charles Laughton met Oboler at a party. "You know I just had dinner with FLW. He told me he likes to play up to his clients, so he put his arm around you and said "___." And you said, "___." (See above.) But I didn't feel it, I didn't feel it. So there we both were, hammier than ever." Henning has been going out of his way to tell me I look Dopey, and to separate David and me lest we form a clique. Why must some people see the world in their own image?

TUESDAY OCTOBER 27
Interrupted my weaving this morning to visit a cheese factory. Wisconsin is studded

---

Murray Rubin, Priscilla's cousin, served in the U.S. Army during World War II and was godfather to Priscilla and David's son, Jonathan. Rubin retired from AT&T.

In August 1914, Mamah Borthwick was at lunch at Taliesin with her two children and some men working on the property when Julian Carlton, a recently hired domestic worker, locked all the windows and all but one door, set fire to the house, and attacked with an axe those trying to escape, murdering seven people. The **massacre** brought both local and nationwide attention to Wright's already scandalous relationship with Borthwick, since at the time both were married to others. Wright rebuilt Taliesin at the same location.

Arch Oboler (1907–1987) was an early radio performer and playwright who also produced and directed television programs and movies. His estate in Malibu, California, was designed by Wright and built in stages during the 1940s. The complex is notable for its walls of irregular stone—a rarity in Wright's work.

Charles Laughton (1899–1962) was a Hollywood actor, producer, and director. Like many other Hollywood stars, he knew Wright personally and was a frequent visitor at Taliesin West.

with these small private enterprises. Proofread—paralleled corrections on carbon with those on master sheet. Helped David serve tea—the Wrights like the variety and arrangement. Good. Letter from Judy full of bills and IFC news. Not so good. David still isn't eating—not since last Sat. night. I hope he gets over his sick-to-stomach-ness soon. Ironed the laundry. Kenn whispers a lot to me of Eleanor and marriage; also of South Dakota where he lived, and the honest picture presented of it in Giants in the Earth. David has just fixed the fireplace so it gives heat. Typical of FLW's humor is this passage from his book, describing his love of music and musical criticism—the love of an amateur. "Such are the joys of the amateur and far from innocent they are. I am sure Franklin Roosevelt gets much the same reaction where his command of the Army and Navy is concerned." Answered Nat, Murray, and Judy. Judy speaks of how beautiful our room must be, to which I reply: What we have written is true, and yet not completely. It's true that the walls are Cherokee red, but white plaster shows thru; true that we have shelves and desk, but I can remember some Finnish furniture that had an infinitely finer finish; true that we have a flax rug, but what footprints!; everything true and yet not true. The Wrights consider us their children, but they're not our parents. We live here but it's not home. Faces are familiar and friendly, but not loved. Discovered that FLW considers Jack Howe one of the finest draftsman he ever had—loved drawing so much he'd sometimes work till midnight.

WEDNESDAY, OCT. 28

Completed my section of the rug. Have to wait for Henning to be relieved of KP before I can cut and sew it. Proofreading rest of day with the exception of time out to help David with tea. Went into Spring Green in the evening with Curtis, Marcus, and Johnny to buy crepe paper. Worked on costume till 10:30—what a lot of bother. David and I will represent Renoir's "La Loge." Heard an amusing anecdote. When Erich Mendelsohn (German architect who built the new houses in Palestine) visited

---

Cherokee red was one of Wright's signature colors. He used it extensively to paint metal features and walls, among other things, especially in domestic interiors. In 1955 he collaborated with paint company Martin-Senour to produce the "Taliesin Palette," which included Cherokee Red.

For the famous painting-themed Halloween costume party, Priscilla and David were dressed as a couple at the theater, the man looking through binoculars at the stage, in Pierre-Auguste Renoir's **La Loge** (The Theatre Box), 1874, a masterwork of impressionism.

Erich Mendelsohn (1887–1953) was a German Jewish architect best known for his design of the Einstein Tower (1919–21) in Potsdam, an icon of the Expressionist movement, and his later, more streamlined designs for the Schocken department stores in several German cities. After fleeing the Nazis in 1933, he settled in London, going on to design noteworthy buildings in both Great Britain and Palestine. He immigrated to the United States in 1941 and continued to practice architecture while teaching at the University of California, Berkeley.

Taliesin, he used to work in the draughting room and demanded music all the time. "Music makes me work." Wright answered him, "That's the difference between you and me, Eric. My work makes music." Today's part of the autobiography tells of his love for Zona Gale, and his visits to Rio de Janeiro, England, Tokyo, and Moscow. When he's at work—either at the writing desk or drawing table—he looks more like those severe pictures of him and less like the crinkle eyed wit we know at tea.

THURSDAY, OCT. 29

Proofread in my room practically all day. Cosy and comfortable—able to walk outside with just a sweater. Everyone's so busy plucking geese, chickens, and turkeys, I had to help with the house ironing. I told FLW that his writing was unconventional. He asked, "Do you mean ungrammatical? I at least want to be intelligible." Mrs. Wright helped David out at tea today by making delicious cinnamon buns. Walked and gossiped with Eleanor after tea. FLW, giving a lecture at Madison, was congratulated by a woman, "I liked your lecture very much." "Thank you." "Don't you remember me?" "No." "I'm Catherine." (His first wife—6 children) Would the beast that wants discourse of reason have mourned longer? I read Erich Mendelsohn's German volume on American architecture (more plates than text). In today's section FLW met Eliel Saarinen who asked him how he liked his plans for the new church. "When I saw them I said what a great architect—I am." My unglamorous red woolens arrived today, not to mention David's grays. Thus have we become Sears Roebuck farmers. And dare I forget the letter from Burton? How much further the war seems to us than it does him. We really are in exile here. Helped sew David's costume on Ruth's sewing machine— another machine I'm beginning the mastery of. Finished the 3rd volume of the Autobiography—Work—very impressive.

FRIDAY, OCT. 30

Proofread from 8 a.m. till 10 p.m. Rainy warmth today. Everyone busy for Halloween. Think I've got a politician's job. Davy: "You check only for typographical errors, don't you?" Yes—and for intelligibility. Shock, consternation—presumption. Mr.

Zona Gale (1874–1938) was a playwright and the first woman to win the Pulitzer Prize for drama. In his *Autobiography*, Wright wrote: "My people all knew Zona. My mother and my aunts much admired her... She was always glad to see us, asking me to come, although she said she valued her Regency at the University of Wisconsin too much ever to be seen with me in public. . . . But you couldn't quarrel with Zona. She was too complete and lovely in herself. She was like something exquisitely carved out of ivory."

the beast that wants: from Shakespeare's *Hamlet*.

The "**new church**" is most likely the First Christian Church (1940–42) in Columbus, Indiana.

Wright read the last part aloud to me as he corrected. We both laughed at the tangle caused by 5 subordinate clauses with no main clause. Suggested that his last sentence was weak and negative—he crossed it off; repetition of 'stalwart Wes' like homeric epithet—omitted; 'lousy' good cussing but not in keeping with mood—altered that. Asked forgiveness for daring to criticize. "I've been absorbing suggestions and criticism all my life—and they've always helped." David's still working on his intricate cardboard abstractions—all the boys would be more profitably employed at the drawing board.

SATURDAY, OCT. 31

Heard that Lloyd Lewis read the MS. after he arrived last night. If it's good with his train and work fatigue, it's good. Met him this morning—said he's been nagging Frank for the last 4 years to write it. Urged him to talk it first, so it would be no effort to write. Rode around the countryside this morning with Eleanor waiting for Mrs. Williams. Sunshine turned the dull browns of the trees to copper and magenta. Marvelous valley nestled in hills. Letters from Mom and George. What wit, clear thinking, and style he has! Helped Kay with the hors d'oeuvres. David worked on his double costume—bearded gentleman in full dress for La Loge, and cardboard abstractions for color. I wore my tulle wedding dress trimmed with vertical strips of blue crepe paper, glassy pendulous earrings and necklace borrowed from Kay, flowers at bosom and in my hair, hair curled and dripping over my forehead ala Mme Récamier. "Elegant." "Éclatante." "You looked as if you belonged in a box." FLW—"Quite a picture you and David made." Helped turn lights & kept on getting electric shocks because I held one hand on the metal box. Dining room was beyond all description beautiful with lanterns, pumpkins, witches, balloons, juniper, pine, geese on spits, mince pie, costumes, etc. Mr. and Mrs. Wright wore magnificent Montenegrin costumes. They danced popular numbers together beautifully. Iovanna and Kay—bustle affairs. Davy as Matisse's "Lady with the Plumes" was so seductive that Jack who had 3 dances with me, wanted to cut in to dance with her (him), and did. I always knew Art was superior to Nature. Kenn as Van Gogh's

---

Lloyd Lewis (1891–1949) was a friend of Wright's and a writer, historian, and journalist who served as editor of the *Chicago Daily News.* Wright designed a house for him in Libertyville, Illinois, completed in 1941.

Éclatante: French for "brilliant" or "glittering."

costumes: Other fellows dressed to match the following paintings: *The Plumed Hat* (1919), by Henri Matisse;

a trumpet boy attributed to Vincent Van Gogh; a pastel-clad girl from a Marie Laurencin work; God from William Blake's *Ancient of Days* (1794); the Egyptian Pharaoh Tutankhamun; figures from one of Rembrandt's most famous paintings, *Night Watch* (1642), and as Grant Wood's *Daughters of the American Revolution* (1932), a dour painting featuring three conservatively dressed older women.

The Boy Trumpeter. Eleanor as Marie Laurencin's Girl in Pink. Curtis as an Indian in amazingly clever costume and rhythmic war dance. Johnny as Tut-en-khamen (probably wrong spelling)—wonderful body—got into stylized position & slid across on skates. Howard & Ruth as the Anglers. Svet as the fourth Mary in a backdrop with the other three painted on. The chorus as Rembrandt's Night Watch with heads sticking through. Jack as Van Gogh's Boy in Yellow Jacket. Henning & Ted as Japanese prints. Tom as Whistler's Mother. Marcus as God in "Creation"—creating the world with a giant compass. Three of the choir boys as Grant Wood's Daughters of the American Revolution. Gene & Wes—M.C.'s—art critic & Mr. Whistler. Me in exhibition folk dancing with Curtis as my partner—a French woman on the slightly expensive harlot side square dancing with a Navajo Indian! Such is Taliesin! A wonderful evening in spite of all misgivings and perhaps slightly because of some wonderful gin in the punch. Mrs. Williams looked at us, shocked, as if we were all punch-drunk—which we were—or slightly crazy—which we may be. Finishing 4th volume of the Autobiography while waiting for David to finish washing the dishes.

The landscape changes as the sea changes.

SUNDAY NOV. 1

Breakfast table repercussions about our costumes. FLW: "It was a stroke of genius." Last night, Lloyd Lewis applauded, bowed—ingenious. Everybody wants to know David's principles of folding—mathematical formulas, etc. He told them all he was Prof. Tenfelsdrake of the University of Weiss-nicht-wo, an illustration by Jean-Marie Sans Raison for Carlyle's Sartor Resartus.

As for me, everyone told me how beautiful I looked. Mrs. Wright said she wished I could always be dressed like that— very French curls, earrings, feminine, graceful movements. We looked just like the picture. How long did we practice the pose? etc.

Lloyd Lewis's wife is Catholic. She & the children went to Church during breakfast. FLW commented on the hold of the Holy Roman Empire—neither Holy, Roman, nor Empire. Lloyd—"You can't stand anybody's worshipping any gods but yours, Frank."

Society column people here: 2 Mrs. Bloodgoods—Madison, Milwaukee; Norah Berry—Chicago.

Svet brought Brandoch in. Mrs. W —"Come to your relation." Mr. W—"Why don't you say Grandmother, & be done?"

Brandoch Peters (b. 1941), the son of Svetlana (Olgivanna's daughter) and Wes Peters.

FRANK LLOYD WRIGHT SEATED AT HIS DRAFTING TABLE WITH TED BOWER,
undated (1942–43).

GROUP OF TALIESIN FELLOWS AROUND FRANK LLOYD WRIGHT AT A DRAFTING TABLE,
undated (1942–43).

Saw "The Reluctant Dragon," a tour thru the Disney Studios with Robert Benchley—amusing and informative. Braved sleet to make it.

Met John Christophason, C.O., Quaker, engineer, who met Alice and Irwin Stark at the work camps. On tour of inspection—amazed at our sloppiness and unfulfilled potentialities.

Cozy fireside chat with Eleanor and Kenn. Fried liver sandwiches and <u>our</u> iced champagne.

Concert dull—everyone tired. Mr. W. read from his Autobiography. Glad that David resents "the Ever Womanly" section as much as I do. "She can't wait to get a shovelfull of coals for a little Hell of her own." As if this were Paradise—or he doesn't have his own little Hell. "She can turn any Fellowship into a nursery." "No ideals." "Those who come with the least have the servant mind, refuse to do menial tasks, are the first trouble makers." Not true—not fair. Tributes to Lindbergh, Henry Ford, John Haynes Holmes. What bedmates! And what dignitaries worthy of tribute! Occasionally he soars to poetry but not as frequently as in his youthful days when he was 63, and wrote the first four volumes.

MONDAY, NOV. 2

Light flurries of snow—yet warm enough for just a jacket. Wearing very un glamorous but very warm red woolens—in direct reversal of the FLW principles, I'm sacrificing the esthetic for the comfortable.

FLW's attitude toward money—that the world owes the artist a living—the world being small farmers, shopkeepers, etc. is very reminiscent of Shaw's artist in "The Doctor's Dilemma." As "intellectuals," we sympathize with the artist; as people who have earned our daily bread by the sweat of the brow, we sympathize

---

Friends of the Henkens, the Starks lived in New York City: **Irwin Stark** (1913–1994) was an English teacher at the time; he later became a professor at City College and an author of such novels as *A Room in Hell,* about a corrupt U.S. senator. **Alice Stark** became an English professor at New York University.

In the "**Ever Womanly**" section of *An Autobiography,* Wright discussed—and was resentful of, in some respects—the presence of women in the Fellowship: "The Woman always wins. This, the Eternal Feminine, is a Fellowship problem of no mean dimensions: the one we have not yet solved and may never solve as long as we hold to our coeducational ideal." In a section of *An Autobiography* entitled: "To The American Eagle" ("You know who I mean"), Wright praised pilot **Charles Lindbergh** (1902–1974): "you not only think straight

but you dare speak straight." In the same section, Wright called industrialist **Henry Ford** (1863–1947) a "true American," and Unitarian minister **John Haynes Holmes** (1879–1964) a "courageous hero." All three men stood against the war, but had different politics, making them strange bedfellows: Lindberg and Ford voiced anti-Semitic opinions while Holmes helped found the National Association for the Advancement of Colored People (NAACP) and the American Civil Liberties Union (ACLU).

The Doctor's Dilemma is a play written by George Bernard Shaw (1856–1950) and first staged in 1906. The protagonist has only enough tuberculosis cure for one patient, and must choose between an honorable man and a scoundrel, an artist who thinks his genius excuses his taking advantage of others.

with the shopkeepers. There will be some people who won't like this aspect of the Autobiography; especially the local townspeople who know best exactly what he means.

Re-warped the loom today. And now we're ready for a new section. How nimble my fingers are becoming!

First real lesson on the recorder—CDE, EDC, DEC, and variations thereof. If David complains, I'll remind him of sundry sacrifices I've made on his behalf.

Read Constance Rourke's biography of Charles Sheeler, which she aptly subtitles "Artist in the American Tradition." As usual with her, an appreciative study.

Redecorated the room with pine & juniper. Little Chinese jade green lady against wine-dark plate near pines on shelf—illuminated from below. Very effective.

Witty, urbane gossipy letter from Miss Bonawit—commends me for my courage. I have none. Or is it courage to face what you fear? Also good haul from Julia, Ada, Frances Salzman. So my letters are sheer poetry, and are being read in chains. Truly, a prophet is with greater honor outside his own country.

Bad news after supper—I'm to be cook next week. Mrs. Wright: "Anyone who can do so many other things well, can cook well—and with a little creative temperament. . ." Wonderful, but I was in tears afterwards—the criticisms can be either vicious or damning with faint praise. Kenn came in to give me some advice, information, and cheer. But no cheer in my heart. Oh well. . .

TUESDAY, NOV. 3

Election Day—and we're not even absentee voters! But we went down to Wyoming County—and voted Socialist. No questions asked. No registration necessary. Funny, isn't it?

Helped Kay in the kitchen—made Bitki and potato patties. Both successful. But how I dread it. Kay and Mrs. W. whined to Mr. Wright to move out two walls of the kitchen for more working space. Marcus agreed with Mr. W. that it was unnecessary, and they jumped on him that he always wants the easiest way out. Feline felicity supreme.

Received letters today from Murray and Honey. I wonder if week-end arrangements will be possible for him. —or unwise.

Recorder—get the notes but not the timing.

Chic-ngai left today. He spoke to Saarinen about a Cranbrook scholarship, possible no earlier than eight weeks from now. Returned from Detroit today and spoke to

---

Wyoming County: Actually the town of Wyoming, in Iowa County, Wisconsin.

FLW, who stormed at him without waiting for explanation. All Chic-ngai wanted was advice on how or where he could get the most time for working out his ideas. FLW sent Gene after Chic-ngai to tell him to leave this very afternoon. So he's all alone in Spring Green till tomorrow, probably as heavy-lidded as he is heavy-hearted.

Financial ethics here are dormant, if at all alive. Eleanor was once asked to pass a bad check for lumber; and after months of hiding in the desert every time collectors were imminent, the bill was finally paid.

FLW once drove his car and wrecked it so badly that repairs cost $1500. He asked Rowan & Jerry to pick it up on their return from a visit to California—and to ask Rowan's father for the money. Rowan Sr. refused; Wright wrote him: "If this is all the Fellowship means to you, both children can leave immediately." They did, when things became more unpleasant—as with Chic-ngai. Temper? Temperament? Or God?

New epithets: Eleanor called me a brave little soldier; Chic-ngai told David to thank me for "the education."

Served and washed dishes today. The kitchen has few charms to soothe this savage breast—it even spoils my appetite.

WEDNESDAY, NOV. 4

Add more stories to what is getting to sound more like an exposé than a diary. Gordon Lee, fine draftsman, owned a dog of which he was very fond. When its barking became too annoying, Mrs. W. asked him to shoot the dog, whereupon he told her to shoot Twip. Upshot—immediate dismissal.

Once at tea, when the three happy sisters were shopping in Madison, FLW told the Fellowship that work is more important for a man than woman. She serves a very useful purpose, but after that, one has to keep on yes-ing her just to keep peace. Passion with poetry?—only for publication.

Made pumpkin pudding in the kitchen today. Learned that custards and puddings should be kept in a pan of boiling water to prevent boiling within and subsequent formation of whey.

Germaine "Jerry" Schneider Maiden, the daughter of Wright's gardener, joined the Fellowship in 1934. She married another fellow, Rowan Maiden (1913–1957), who had joined the Fellowship in 1939. Maiden came to Taliesin from the University of California. A CO during the war, he later became an architect in California, best known for his Nepenthe Restaurant on the Big Sur coast.

few charms to soothe: a reference to William Congreve, The Mourning Bride.

Charles Gordon Lee (1918–1966) joined the Fellowship in 1941. He served in the Air Force and later opened an architectural practice in Denver, Colorado, where he designed several schools as well as the Rocky Mountain National Park Administration Building, in affiliation with Taliesin Associated Architects.

Two recorder pieces—Ticker Tape and South Wind. Sounds silly to me, too. Practiced with Marcus.

Letter from Adrienne Reeve. School really seems to be an ordeal this term, with students more serious (extra-curricular), and paradoxically more careless (curricular) than ever.

Laundered rugs today. David and I play with the washing machine and mangle as if they were strange and wonderful. They are. David is still working on boilers down below. We get more and more like that cartoon of slaving over the hot stove while you work in a nice cool sewer. But all experience is an arch where through gleams that untraveled world . . . . What worlds I'm traveling to!

Obsessions with aristocracy appear frequently—today, especially, at tea. Mrs. W. was once told that she resembles Empress Elizabeth of Austria—since looked her up and discovered her to be not only beautiful but a "wonderful person." Said her own grandfather was a Duke, but it was a title of achievement, and therefore not hereditary. Third mention so far of their acquaintance with the Earl of Sandwich, and some Italian counts. Come to think of it, anyone would like to mention casually scions of such ancient lineage.

Everyone was so full from our Viennese coffee at "tea" that my dear little pudding went unheeded. But there's always tomorrow. I have arrived at the perfect motto for a cook of my caliber: I have done that which I should not have done; I have left undone that which I should have done; and there is no health in me.

New instructions from FLW say that I should proofread with one hand, and learn to cook with the other.

THURSDAY, NOV. 5

Made Italian Spaghetti and pumpkin tarts with my own little hands. And people wanted seconds!

Fifth re-reading is a little tiresome, but Tom's officiousness amused me when he detected my neglect of neice.

Letters from Esther Grossmark and Muriel.

Svet was 16 and Wes 19 when they met. Married one year later with complete parental disapproval. Svet taught music in Chicago; he opened his office. Then they returned, welcomed as prodigal children improved by their contact with "the world."

A **mangle** is a machine that uses rollers for ironing large pieces like linen.

gleams that untraveled world: A quotation from Alfred Lord Tennyson's poem "Ulysses," 1833.

Wes's father drove the Ku Klux Klan out of Indiana practically single handed.

Johnny had his C.O. interview aided by David's pamphlets.

At tea, FLW added typing, now that Eleanor left for N.Y., to my proofreading and cooking. Mrs. Wright was annoyed when I returned his "mess of papers" to him at tea—as he asked me to. "Tea is not the time for it," etc. My face revealed my anger, and he very placatingly asked me to put them on the piano—out of the way.

Marcus and I played duets of scales on our recorders, with Henning in to show how it should be done. Then we all 'washed' with Kenn in the Kitchen. Add new worries: The Christmas Box.

FLW met Ogden Nash, his inseparable friend Bob Benchley, and Dorothy Parker, at tea once. Described Nash as a tall, pink faced cherub.

FLW a very good friend of Carl Sandburg's whom he teased once while he was playing the piano by saying that if he had not become an architect, he would have become a musician, & further shocked him by saying that knowing how the creative mind works, he probably would have been a second Beethoven.

FLW conducted the trio—cello, piano, and violin, and I was privileged to hear him play the piano alone today because I sneaked in early to tea.

FRIDAY, NOV. 6

Svet ran away from home even before she was married choosing the anonymity of Susan Wylie. Olgivanna, trying to help her, used to send her packages marked "from Susan Wylie's mother." She really does have moments of rare understanding.

FLW is in a hurry to see his MS off. He wants to take it to the N.Y. publishers and possibly arrange a lecture tour at $350 a lecture—altho he hates it. But money is a necessary evil.

At tea today, Mrs. W. presented us with Baba, a Russian bread. Ruth, intending to compliment her, said it was just like sponge cake, only not so sweet. Mrs. W. gasped, sighed, and said, "How dare you? It is out of such ignorance you speak.

Wes's father: Frederick R. Peters (d. 1935) was a longtime editor of the *Evansville Press,* a prominent newspaper in Evansville, Indiana. The first newspaper editor in his state to condemn the Ku Klux Klan, he was a vocal critic of the group and its political supporters.

The Christmas Box was an annual Fellowship tradition. One apprentice created the box itself, building it differently each year. Into the box went original drawings and creations from all the fellows, spouses, and even the children living at Taliesin. The box was then presented to Wright for Christmas.

Wright, who by this period had been famous for many decades, had met many luminaries of the twentieth century. Here he referred to poet **Ogden Nash** (1902–1971); **Robert Benchley** (1889–1945), a humorist who wrote for *Vanity Fair,* the *New Yorker,* and other publications; **Dorothy Parker** (1893–1967), a poet, critic, and satirist; and **Carl Sandburg** (1878–1967), a writer and Pulitzer Prize–winning poet. Sandburg was also a socialist activist in Wisconsin.

Sponge cake takes ten minutes to bake. This is yeast-risen dough, twice-risen." Mr. Wright who saw how Ruth blushed & apologized, placated them both by saying, "Don't you realize this bread is blessed by centuries of tradition? When you eat it, you eat ikons, and monks, baptized babies, the whole Greek Orthodox Church!" Mrs. Wright was offended, altho he patted her on the head and chucked her under the chin. And then she got up and walked away, and refused to tell him where she was going. Ten minutes later, when he was absorbed in reading <u>Reality</u> to us, she peremptorily called him to take a walk. He backed out of the room slowly, but out he went.

Bob May, a former apprentice, sent 5 pounds of wonderful candy, signed "Yours as ever, Bob May." Mrs. W. added "if ever." Kenn whispered "From now on, if you want to send anything, and also want to avoid being torn to pieces, just write 'Guess who?'"

Add sense experiences: Kenn killed 5 chickens for me to roast on Sunday— watched them being plucked, red necks dripping on white feathers. The golden folds of ribbon sorghum makes.

Mrs. W. asked me to teach Iovanna typing—but, alas, I'm only a 2 finger typist. Nevertheless, my speed in doing 16 pages in addition to planning next week's menus, hemming my new evening skirt, practicing, and making New England cracker pudding, amazes even me.

Letter from Goldie who is "envious" of me. Do we really write so glowingly or are our shells too confining elsewhere?

Connected with the Homestead rammed earth houses, interesting to note how FLW came to design them. The Central State Cooperatives owned the Circle Pines Camp, & then wanted to build homes. By scraping pockets at weekly meetings they gathered $12,000 for 120 acres. A Ph.D. in the group asked Wright to be the architect, to which he replied with the story of the Chinese Ambassador in Washington, an eligible bachelor much sought after by the dowagers. Whenever one of them seemed imminently successful, he'd ward her off by 3 questions:

Robert Carroll May (1914–2000) joined the Fellowship in 1939. After serving in the Navy during the war, he practiced architecture in Hartford, Connecticut for several decades, later moving on to architectural firms in New York and Pennsylvania.

The Cooperative **Homesteads** (1941–42) were designed for a group of Detroit-area autoworkers, teachers, and others who had formed a housing cooperative in the late 1930s and subsequently purchased a large tract of land on which to build. Wright viewed the project as an ideal prototype for a low-cost, low-density housing development incorporating communal farming. It also provided an opportunity to experiment with rammed-earth construction, an update of traditional south-western adobe brick techniques, in which Wright had developed a strong interest. Internal conflicts among the cooperative members, coupled with the induction of many members into the military after the beginning of the war, kept the project from proceeding.

How old are you? How much money do you have? How did you get it? The coöp representative answered "3 years" to the first question, & "no money" to the second. Nevertheless for a nominal fee, Wright took on the job—and the plans for the houses are fascinating. The earth is rammed in wood blocks which are then removed, & the finished wall has the appearance of concrete.

SATURDAY, NOV. 7

Baked bread—10 loaves—it came out good, but slightly crusty. Also made mocha icing, caramel gelatin, and gravy. Planned my menus several days in advance—but what a big cooking day tomorrow is!

The weather was sad glad like growing old in early Spring.

Movie was "Louise" with Grace Moore, which evoked a flood of reminiscences on the part of Wright for Parisian bohemianism. His son, John, & his wife were there. Mrs. Wright had left early, refusing to sit near the children of the first marriage, & with her back to them, carried on an animated conversation with Johnny & me. FLW placated her by rubbing her shoulders, tossing her hair, fondling her neck— old husband tricks in company. No help. As for Paris, FLW met Gertrude Stein there. Spoke of her influence on Picasso & the other "moderns," strange because she was the most unattractive, uninteresting, & dull person he had ever spoken to. At a lecture she gave, she wore a man's jacket, an ankle-length skirt cut like men's trousers, and he strongly suspects a wig to cover—yes, he really thinks she was bald. Told the derivation of name Alice B. Toklas—Gertie wanted to do all the talking, so she said: "Alice, be talkless."

John built an awful house for his new wife—divorce recent—called Shangri-la.

Mrs. Wright was furious at Carl Sandburg. When he was here at a time of great crisis for the Wrights, he deliberately paced up & down in front of them, & spoke in as deliberate a drawl: "When I worked on my 'Lincoln,' I learned one thing when I had to make a decision. Right or wrong, make a decision." Wes despises Sandburg, because he's a millionaire many times over & poses as a "common man." As a

---

Wright's children from his first marriage were often visitors at Taliesin off and on through the decades as the relationships waned and improved. His six children were: Frank Lloyd Wright Jr. (1890–1978); **John Lloyd Wright** (1892–1972), who often worked with his father and was the inventor, in 1918, of the toy Lincoln Logs; Catherine Wright Baxter (1894–1979), the mother of Anne Baxter (1923–1985), an actress who was cast in *All About Eve* (1950) and *The Ten Commandments* (1956) and appeared regularly on television through the 1970s; David Wright (1895–1997); Frances Wright (1898–1959); and Robert Llewellyn Wright (1903–1986), a Washington, D.C.-based lawyer for whom Wright designed a home in Bethesda, Maryland.

Gertrude Stein (1874–1946), American poet and art collector, acquired works of Picasso and other modern artists. She lived in Paris most of her life with her partner, Alice B. Toklas (1877–1967), with whom she hosted a popular salon. Whether or not Wright had meant this as a joke, Alice B. Toklas was indeed her given name.

matter of fact, FLW teases him for this too, once dressing him up in corduroy baggy trousers gathered at the ankle, artist's cape, velveteen beret; both of them were snapped, and Sandburg has been trying to get the picture ever since, fearing that if it's published, it will destroy his "man of the people" reputation he's been building up for years.

Because of some family squabble, FLW hadn't seen his daughter Catherine in 15 years, tho he admitted that John & Lloyd are nothing—she's his favorite. Catherine's daughter, Ann Baxter, has the lead in "The Pied Piper" & the "Magnificent Ambersons."

It was FLW who suggested that Steichen switched from painting to photography.

FLW also mentioned Lloyd's desire, a hangover from university days to visit Maxim's in Paris. Everything was gay when the music played—and went dead when the music stopped. After a respectable young English engineer quietly threw up all over Lloyd's new tuxedo, the party broke up—chastened. But FLW himself was not disappointed—he had expected it.

The peacocks were amusing today. One would stand in front of his tail as if it were a back-drop; when he turned around, & kicked his legs slightly, he looked like the rear view of a can-can.

My dreams these nights are painful, fatiguing series of mixing batters, stirring stews, chopping meats, pounding pumpkins.

Letter from Chic-ngai who feels as if he's left a cloister for the world. Full of this world's anguish—and tears—and gratitude to us. Perhaps it is a good thing for the enlargement of his concepts.

Kenn dropped in after theatre for cosy chat, bringing his own wine. Strange reversals of hospitality we have here!

Hans is going to the desert to fix up the camp—very much alone, with no chance of our going, altho David has hinted very strongly that he wants to go too. I should have stayed in N.Y. in that case—tho that's another story.

Jack, my kitchen help, has been practicing being sweet to me. With us, it requires practice—no innate ability. He hopes I'll make some good Jewish meals because he likes that type of cooking. Hope springing out of ignorance of my culinary ability.

Gene asked me to squeeze proof-reading into my cooking next week. A simple matter of a 36 hour day.

Edward Steichen (1879-1973) was a photographer who became a museum curator of photography. Steichen curated *The Family of Man* at the Museum of Modern Art in New York in 1955, perhaps the most important photography show of the twentieth century.

SUNDAY, NOV. 8

Well, today certainly was a success. Marcus & I were in the kitchen—with help from Kenn. Emerged the tenderest roast beef I've ever eaten, with oven browned potatoes, carrots, lettuce with Taliesin dressing, 4 squash pies, good hot coffee.

Everyone complimented me, to say nothing of second & third helpings. When I came into the room, they all applauded. Of course, I modestly, but honestly, said that the meal ought to be good because I had been cooking it for the past 5 nights. Mr. Wright said I was a girl of all-round talents—cooking, proofreading, etc. From a genius—that's a feather in my cap!

I pointed out 2 places for Mr. Wright to fill in—where he says he'll discuss something later—and forgets to. Now I'm to match main & carbons, & proofread as quickly as possible; in fact, quicker. He wants to go to N.Y. even this week.

Marcus & I drove down to Spring Green after the concert—to get a letter on the evening's train—11:20. Told me about the many unfulfilled promises to his father for back pay, father's loyalty thru the 1914 crisis up till 1940. Now some un-understood resentment, with little hopes of reconciliation.

The excitement & the flattery have given me my first splitting headache in months. I know I was made for mediocrity.

MONDAY, NOV. 9

A dreary numbness pains my sense.

As tho of cooking I had done.

Lunch ménu: rutabagas, fluffy mashed potatoes on the half shell, Swiss steak with bay leaves.

Supper: blintzes, cooked vegetable salad with Taliesin dressing, split pea soup, rice pudding.

Mrs. Wright came in to tell me that the meal was wonderful, & that she & Mr. Wright have agreed that I'm an artist. When I told her that I was very pleased, she said, "Oh you don't know how pleased we are!"

Taliesin Dressing, from the Taliesin Cookbook, assembled over the years by the fellows (currently held by The Frank Lloyd Wright Foundation):
3 c. Mazola oil
3 c. vinegar
1 T sugar
6 cloves garlic mashed
Salt to taste
Juice of 3 lemons

A dreary numbness: A reference to John Keats ". . .a drowsy numbness pains/ My sense, as though of hemlock I had drunk," from *Ode to a Nightingale*, 1819.

The Wrights have left for Chicago for a few days.

Marcus told me he doesn't want to move over from Hillside, because he expects to be arrested any day as a C.O., and he knows how his stuff will dribble away here—whereas at Hillside, his father can collect everything.

Announcement of Bessie Passow's marriage—and card from Steinleins. Proofreading tonight.

Discovering the use of kitchen tools is a delight—even if I chip off bits of skin in the process.

David copied drawings of the Burlingham house in El Paso, Texas, one of the most revolutionary houses ever designed, looking as if it were molded—to be included in the MS.

TUESDAY, NOV. 10

Menus: Lunch—English Beef Stew, onions, carrots, cole slaw, home-made mayonnaise. Supper—macaroni & cheese, stewed tomatoes, Viennese tarts. Five hits—no miss—second portions, "best beef stew ever tasted," "not stew perhaps—but another preparation?", etc.

It was fun making my own mayonnaise—and good mayonnaise too. Having had a chance to rest today, wasn't too tired to dance around in the kitchen with David, either.

Still matching carbons with main sheets. Several of his corrections are improvements in style which I thought of, but didn't dare suggest.

A very Nat-like letter from Nat. It seems strange that he should still go to Coronet, see all those movies, hate Chelsea, go to Union dances with Burt—and I'm not part of it. I don't miss not being part of that life, strangely enough. And yet is parting a little bit like death? Missed for a time and the wound closes up and heals, leaving perhaps a slight scar, but no ache?

David's still working on drawings for the Forum. I'm pleased that his hand grown steady on the hoe or hammer will grow just as steady again on the pen and compass.

Wright's final design for the Lloyd and Hilda **Burlingham House** in El Paso, Texas, dating to the early 1940s, was dubbed the "Pottery House" because it was to be made of adobe and was curved in plan, suggesting the shape of a flowerpot. The Burlinghams subsequently left El Paso without building the house. In 1982, a real estate developer purchased the rights to the design and built a modified version of it in Santa Fe, New Mexico, under the supervision of Charles Montooth from Taliesin Associated Architects.

Architectural Forum was a major journal published from 1892 to 1974. The January 1938 issue of the magazine was devoted entirely to Wright's work, and thus symbolized the rehabilitation of the architect's career following years of personal scandals and professional disappointments. An apparently planned 1942 piece on Wright never materialized, perhaps because of limited editions of the journal during the war.

Mary Ellen Chase, a teacher at the Hillside Home School founded by Wright's Aunts Nell and Jane, portrays them very sympathetically in "A Goodly Fellowship." Incidentally, this was probably the first co-educational home school in the country.

Marcus came in to duet the recorder with me; Kenn came in to chat—I think Marcus finds us comfortable, and Kenn finds us necessary in his loneliness for Eleanor.

WEDNESDAY, NOV. 11

Ironic! Today is Armistice Day and the U.S. Marshal came to take Marcus away because he's a conscientious objector to this war. At tea time, he looked out the door and said, "I think my time has come. Two men are looking for Gene." Five minutes later Gene came in and beckoned to him. Marcus knew by my face I was worried, and said, "You don't worry, Priscilla. You just go to tea & look pretty." It seems this marshal knows his way around already for obvious reasons, and told Curtis he hoped he wouldn't have to come here again, to which Curtis answered that he was afraid he would. When Mr. Wright arrives tomorrow, he'll probably bail him out until his trial.

Menus today: Lunch—Bitki (40 big balls of it—16 people to eat—and the pan was scraped clean), rutabagas sweetened with sorghum, brown rice. Supper—potato cheese puff, buttered corn, stewed tomatoes, whipped frothy jello with whipped cream. Kay—'Priscilla sure has imagination.' Henning— 'Yummie.' Ted—'Splendid!' Svet—'What a wonderful supper!' And so many second helpings. Even I'll begin to think I'm good.

Letters from Burton, Mom, Dave Wertman; gift of evening blouse from Judy. A day, therefore, of mitigated pleasures.

Pleasant chat with Johnny. I amused Curtis who corrected me on my misuse of bring and take (careless error, not error of ignorance) when I told him, "And now that you know me fallibly human, am I not doubly dear?"

It's so cold I can scarcely tremble over to my proofreading. Alas that steamheated apartments precluded David's ever learning to build a fire properly, and my learning to tend it.

My recorder lies mute.

I am tired.

THURSDAY, NOV. 12

Evjue, editor of Madison's Capital Times, in friendship to the Wrights, raised $2500 bail for Marcus. Marcus was back with us today awaiting trial on Saturday. He and Kenn chatted with me in the room after supper—Kenn about his gift box for Eleanor.

David is working on the plans of the Burlingham house for the Architectural Forum—this is one of the most ingenious and original of Wright's recent ideas—it looks as if it were molded of plastic. Of course, he's still working on the roof.

Ménus today—Lunch: roast chicken, roast turnips and onions, potatoes; Supper—chicken soup, frozen vegetable salad, squash, beets, pumpkin pie with whipped cream. Mr. Wright told me after supper, "Well, it doesn't take long to make a good cook out of a clever girl." All very well, but I didn't enjoy plucking pin feathers, stewing giblets, dressing the raw insides, and trussing chickens. And that new veal that was stored in the cooler today! (Butchered by Howard & Graves) I'm on my way to becoming a vegetarian—only it's such a bother in a place like this.

Curtis has had quite a correspondence with Lewis Mumford about Wright recently. It will be interesting to read the letters.

Wes returned from delivering Hans to Libertyville today. Says he brought back a Cherokee red tuxedo. It's funny, whether it's true or not.

Letters from Honey, Burton, Helen. Typed answer to Burton.

Ted's father was a professor of medicine in Temple U., Phila. When he resigned, quite a scandal ensued. Reason unknown. But now he's on the State Board of Examiners. The fault was more probably with the University than with Dr. Bower.

Marcus returned at about 11 after a visit to Spring Green to get a recipe for a cake for tea—and chatted with us till after midnight giving all the gory details of his stay in jail. The U.S. marshal was just as nervous reading Marcus's warrant as Marcus was listening to it, and all along on the trip he told him of sad stories of C.O.'s in the last war who are pariahs to this day. The jail was very noisy—9 men, 3 of whom were evading their sentences by joining the army; one who stole guns from the government and sold them to civilians (not as accomplished as Morgan who re sold them to the government); and other oddments of petty criminals. Marcus's crime, of course, was non appearance for induction, to which he pleaded not guilty,

---

Ben Graves once worked as a farm manager at Taliesin and later raised cattle on land near Taliesin with Wes Peters. Graves was a neighbor of Wright's along with his wife Lucille Graves and their children: Robert Boynton, Benjamin Ross, and Elizabeth.

Curtis Besinger wrote about this **correspondence** in his memoir: "Mr. Wright and Lewis Mumford came to a shattering difference of opinion with regard to the war. . . . But a full-page ad appeared in the New York Times in which Mumford accused Mr. Wright of being an American quisling (Vidkun Quisling was a pro-Nazi Norwegian who had betrayed his own country by aiding an invading enemy.) . . . I wrote Mumford to protest his accusation. I hadn't expected a response, but much to my surprise we exchanged two letters. Neither of us changed our positions."

re-sold them to the government: This refers to a legend about industrialist J. P. Morgan (1837–1913), alleging that he financed a scheme (the Hall Carbine Affair) during the Civil War in which he bought defective guns from the government and sold them back as nondefective at an exorbitantly higher cost.

because he had notified the local board that he would not appear, and the reasons therefor. He refused to sign any documents whatsoever, on the advice of a friend of his, Anna May Davies, Socialist party candidate for attorney general and secretary of the Fellowship of Reconciliation. At 2, he was surprised by a visit from Mrs. Wright, followed by Gene and Mr. Wright, bearing Evjue's precious $2500. All of them were fingerprinted, and Mr. Wright boasted to some waiting prisoners that a jail was familiar to him. Mrs. W.—"Yes, we visited one, once." Mr.—"No, we were prisoners. Don't you remember?" Mrs., hopelessly, "Oh. . . yes, I remember, dear."

FRIDAY, NOV. 13

Marcus went to Madison to go over his papers with his lawyer for tomorrow's trial.

Letters from Prof. Bischof, Sylvia Brody, and George Brewster. Three of the most charming and witty it has been my privilege to read. A good haul.

Ménus: Lunch—Chicken a la King, brown rice, parsnips. Supper—tomato rice soup, scalloped potatoes, carrots, cheese, cocoa cup cakes. Meals still good, tho Mr. Wright noted that I looked almost as if I were worn to a frazzle, and Mrs. Wright was upset that the soup was made of beef instead of chicken stock, which she can't digest. Special meals for them of steaks, peach floating island, green beans, baked potatoes. It's still hard for me to remember the fine points of her diet.

At tea, Mr. Wr. read an article by a former Gurdjieff pupil, an acquaintance of Mrs. W., on music and the revival of the recorder, interjecting his own comments liberally, to the intense amusement of the fellowship, & the more intense annoyance of the wife. Later he played a little hand organ that you hold on your lap, grind with one hand, and play with the other. Then he played the piano as part of the trio with Johnny and Ruth.

Folk dancing in the evening over at Hillside with a notable shortage of women.

Marcus's hearing delayed till December 15.

SATURDAY, NOV. 14

Wes's Achilles heel is cocoanut cream pie. So we urged him to prepare enough ingredients to make it. Result: the most delicious pie I've ever eaten, and from

---

Anna Mae Campbell Davis (1896–1991) was a lawyer with a specialty in conscientious objector cases, labor, and civil liberties law. She was also a prominent socialist who ran for office several times. She was active in the Fellowship of Reconciliation (FOR), an organization that started in Europe in 1914 and worked internationally for peaceful solutions to world problems.

The **recorder** was popular in medieval music but had fallen out of favor for serious musicians until a resurgence in Germany and the United States in the early twentieth century. Olgivanna Wright was part of a larger movement to reestablish the recorder's place in musical performance.

the comments—well, these people just haven't eaten any pie till now. Ménu: Lunch—Fellowship—brown bread, baked beans, cole slaw. (Additional—I made mayonnaise and ten loaves of bread.) Wrights—T Bone Swiss steak, baked potato, lettuce. Supper—Fellowship—sauerbraten, mashed potatoes, gravy, squash, oh yes, cocoanut cream pie. Wrights—roast chicken, asparagus, etc. Wonderful salad dressing for the lettuce. Again Mr. Wright told me I was a true artist, had a sense of the aesthetic, "here we either make them or break them" (with the obvious implication that I had been made). Henning believes the flattery will turn my head. Of course, the evening started wrong—I was late because Jack purposely was, so as to keep the Wrights waiting because they always kept him waiting, & he forgot to heat the plates. But Kenn has been so invaluable, I would have been lost without him—at least, I would have broken down & wept.

Movie Sascha Guitry's Nine Bachelors which was very amusing. Mr. Wr. thought it was ingenious, but repetitious as I did, too. It would have been better if concentrated on one or several episodes instead of so widely diffused. Mrs. Wr. thought it was a ghastly, grotesque nightmare. She would.

For me, the nightmare of kitchen is over for three weeks. Hallelujah!

David starts boiler duty tomorrow.

Letters from Judy & Muriel. Upset by Judy's scolding us for not writing. I'll have to get after that man of mine—I scarcely had time to breathe.

Mr. Wright asked David if he weren't pleasantly surprised by his wife—"good for such a little thing, isn't she?" In the afternoon, he thought I must have prepared the steaks so wonderfully by some method I must have learned at home. Mrs. Wright thought I hadn't. I knew I hadn't. I told him it would be very pleasant to "rest" Sunday, collating carbons & main copy, wielding a pen in my hand instead of a cleaver. Wr.—"But think how happy we all were while you were wielding the cleaver."

SUNDAY, NOV. 15

Sixth (I think) proofreading and collating from breakfast till supper, Wes helping to check on factual aspects. Amusing note: Wright refers to Kansas City, Missouri, where the rivers run poured concrete (reference to their graft, their clerk-architects, their cultural backwardness). Curtis tells me not only is it good figurative language, but true. A creek in K.C. actually runs on a bed made of poured concrete. Kenn tells me Lloyd Lewis is a Lincoln expert, author of "Myths after Lincoln." When Kenn

---

In the 1930s the Army Corps of Engineers attempted to control flooding of Brush Creek in Kansas City by paving the creek with **concrete**. It became a major scandal, since the concrete came from Thomas Pendergast, a notorious political boss.

stayed there in Libertyville, he was introduced by Lewis as the greatest authority he knows on the Des Plaines River, which runs past Lewis's house. (Pronounced Děsplanes).

Visitor is Aaron Green, former fellowship member, now supervising the building of the Cooperative Homestead while awaiting his army commission. The Wrights are furious at the renunciation of his C.O. stand.

The Wrights are leaving for N.Y. tomorrow bearing the MS. and plans for the Architectural Forum.

Marcus's name appeared in Evjue's Saturday paper, & a radio talk on C.O.'s was prominent in today's Madison program. Not just pure coincidence.

David began his firing-boilers duty today.

I gave Kenn a box of nuts with the note—"Thanks, Kenn, but for whom I would have wept. (No white sugar.)" He seemed as surprised as he was touched.

Violent war-anti-capitalism-c.o.-discussion at concert. Both Mr. and Mrs. very vociferous. Grand finale when Mrs. W. scolded Curtis & Marcus for recommending "that grotesque, filthy, obscene" picture last night. She's convinced that all the men & all the women were Sascha Guitry. The music was good, Iovanna as usual protesting that both she & the harp were tired; Curtis annoyed because the chorus forgot its lines; Johnny & Curtis doing a good job of a Brahms duet; Svet, Tom, Johnny & Ruth a Glück sonata, & Mr. Wright keeping time with his foot & leading with his hand. Afterwards, Fred Benedick, a former apprentice, now on ski patrol, showed us the most magnificent Kodachrome shots of Mt. Rainier & Mt. Baker, & the general Oregon-Washington region. On seeing the glaciers & peaks 10,000 feet high, Mr. Wr. said 12,500 was high enough for him. He reached that height—Longs Peak at sunrise, & "promptly leaned over the rim & vomited like a sick dog."

MONDAY, NOVEMBER 16

Back to weaving again today—with the looms moved over to Midway. Slow, yawning process, and not much accomplished, partly because I had to keep on making spools, and partly because I worked with 18 threads.

Aaron Green (1917–2001), a fellow from 1940 to 1943, served in the army during World War II and later moved to California, where he opened an architectural practice, Aaron G. Green Associates, Inc. Green worked with Wright on more than forty projects over the years.

Frederic Benedict (1914–1995), earned his bachelor's and master's degrees in landscape architecture from the University of Wisconsin. Wright invited Benedict to serve as head gardener at Taliesin in 1938 and he was a fellow until 1941. He was drafted into the 10th Mountain Division of the U.S. Army. After the war, he settled in Aspen, Colorado, and eventually designed more than two hundred buildings in the area, primarily modern residences. He was instrumental in the transformation of Aspen from a former mining town to an internationally known ski resort.

Ornithology department: The peacocks poke their beaks around at a little oil sac under their tails, & then oil their feathers with their beaks. Like good parkas, this makes them water and wind resistant. And the little brown hens run around with feathers down to their chicken ankles, looking like so many Scarletts wearing pantalettes—very reminiscent of how they might be dressed at Longchamps. Roasters have 3 inch claws at the backs of their feet, which when sharpened, make them good fighting cocks. Even in the daily pursuit of their affairs, this makes them pretty dangerous when mad.

The Wrights left at 6:30 this morning. All is calm. All is bright. But I hope business-ly speaking, the affair is a successful one.

Practiced the recorder—I still don't close the holes properly. But—courage!

Pre supper chat here with Kenn, who asked Mrs. Wright permission to remove Eleanor's second unwanted bed & replace it with a desk of his own manufactured as a surprise for her return. Post supper chat with Marcus who is busy wording his statement to his lawyer.

Finished reading Wright's Sulgrave Manor Board Lectures on Organic Architecture—Architecture for a Democracy.

Pop-corn & toasted marshmallow & Cuba libra Party for Fred in the studio. Henning's absence (because of a quarrel with Svet—how obvious we are in our affections!) was noticed.

The day was balmy and windy, with a mild spring shower in the evening. Rare & portentous weather.

Tom is a pompous child—and annoying. He told me today that people who like "Information Please" are mentally decrepit. (My words.) I, of course, answered that if his intolerance did not represent immaturity, it would certainly be mental decrepitude. He, Jack, & Henning just rouse me to verbal blows. Davy always looks as if he just outgrew his suits—strange because they're tailor-made. Iovanna is a little girl becoming aware of her femininity—studied curling on couches, ballerina twirling in wide skirts when we folk-dance. Gene always speaks hurriedly & nervously as if he were doing ten things at once, & only nine were getting done. Ruth's enthusiasm burst her into the room this evening to go sketching—I think I'll just be a desk artist for a while.

In 1939, Wright gave a series of lectures at the invitation of the **Sulgrave Manor Board** in London, later collectively published under the title *An Organic Architecture:* *The Architecture of Democracy.* Sulgrave Manor, in Northamptonshire, was the ancestral home of George Washington's family.

TUESDAY, NOV. 17

The morning was very pleasantly spent in setting up Mrs. Wright's loom in the studio. Sun poured in, & we had a nice time exploring the lavish opulence of the rooms—plates, Chinese hats, Montenegren costumes, liqueur candies, statues, urns, vases, prints, screens. But gloom settled over me in the afternoon. Henning—the most detrimental element in the Fellowship. He & Svet continued their quarrel before me, cornered. He told her he was disgusted with himself; that she had only come in asking for a shuttle to start a conversation; that she was flirting with him—or he with her; that he wouldn't go over with her to Midway—that she could ask other boys who thought she was lovely—like Ted or Gene. But evidently they made up in the course of the day. He, trying to get some venom out of his system deliberately misworded a joking remark of mine that we ought to pay people to come to our fête, as a deliberate distaste for these old faces, & a desire for new ones, so that Gene & Curtis were shocked & felt that was "a bad attitude." He also hinted strongly that David's & my marriage would go on the rocks—eager desire to see us in his image. Said he understood why children got nothing out of school if the teachers were all as young as I.

Sketched in Kay's room with Kay & Ruth after tea. The first time I've tried anything of that sort since High School—poor stuff, but good for loosening my fingers.

Letter from Ethel Gersten envying us our courage—it seems to me I'll need this dubious quality more & more.

Long chats with Kenn—thank God for a wholesome attitude, even if he's known as neurotic. At least one can trust him, whereas Henning has neither discretion nor loyalty, & one secretly hopes he will perish by his own type of sword.

Finished Ilka Chase's "Past Imperfect"—witty, urbane, amusing, and a much more healthy personality than her Sylvia Fowler characterization.

The dogs howl in symphony with the sounding of the tocsin—To Weep (named after mountain in Arizona so beautiful it makes you want to weep), and Bluzco (?)—one in bass baritone, one in contralto.

Howard's job is to turn lights on in the chicken coop very early to make them resume daylight activities. Can he fool all the chickens all the time?

Novelist and actress **Ilka Chase** (1900–1973) played the role of Sylvia Fowler in the Broadway production of Clare Booth Luce's comedy *The Women*, 1936. Fowler's character spread rumors about the infidelity of her friend's husband.

WEDNESDAY, NOV. 18

A warm, brisk, clear day for this time of year and my first trip to Madison, "the big town." The fact that I wore a hat evoked more comment than my best pie. Jack looked as if he had never seen a hat; Henning looked as if he had never seen me.

First, I settled my postal savings certificate business—identification, finger prints, and all. Dashed off two cards—one to the Henkens, one to the Jussims. (Mail from Mom who I suspect is very ill—and Irving Weingarten).

Then a visit to the State Capitol with its elaborate marble, gilt work, & wide staircases looking just like Boston or Washington, except that this perches a goddess of liberty on its dome instead of an Indian. Visited the G.A.R. Memorial Hall & Museum for relics of Civil & Spanish-American Wars. Learned that we are now using the tenth American flag, several of the first employing the pine tree as a symbol. And I was delighted by the homey touch of incorrect grammar—"this had laid there for years"—and by the friendliness with you who lean on showcases. One card read: "This is a piece of the high board fence around Camp Randall. Say, Comrade, did you ever climb it? If so, what for?"

The Supreme Court & Senate & Assembly Chambers yielded two items: 1) Murals of Greeks in legislation, of medieval English in legislation, of Indians in legislation, of Benjamin Franklin & the Independence fathers—all with the exception of Franklin looking as if they were posed by one model who had been resting on a long staff for years. 2) An encounter with a Supreme Court Judge who bumped into me as I exited, & who laughingly asked me for a license. I apologized & promised to stick out my left hand next time, & blow my horn hard.

Lunch with Svet & Iovanna at Wright's favorite eating place—the counter of Woolworth's. Then on to helping Iovanna shop for a dress—crabby, head-achy, dull, & speaking always as if she were reciting lines she had memorized, but which had no direct relationship with her listener. I'm afraid she's one of those geniuses who won't forsake her Lloyd-Wright appendage so that she can be successful on her own merits. One can talk to Svet—and she understands. Iovanna thinks Civil Service is connected with the Red Cross.

On to the University of Wisconsin. Students at work in the library still look the same—some hunched over books on their laps; some with the base of their spines touching the front edge of the seat; some with neat little columns; some with big, messy, much-shuffled notebooks. All this I saw with an airplane view from

---

The Grand Army of the Republic (GAR) **Memorial Hall** held Wisconsin's Civil War relics, including many battle flags, in the state capitol building.

the visitors' balcony. Then several exhibits in the State Historical Museum—the pioneer printer, the pioneer kitchen & drugstore, furniture, paintings, toys, ceramics, pre-historic cliff-dweller Indian pottery & Indian stuff; and a Zona Gale Collection. (She's from Portage, Wisconsin.) During a 3/4 of an hour wait for Svet I had time to notice that coed college girls are lucky—they can hold hands when coming out of class, & they can chat for hours on the street corner pretending they're deeply involved in Stendhal or Bergson. I was amused to hear one boy loudly declaiming to a pretty bit of fluff beside him: ". . . or I will turn your bones over for sepulture." Where had I heard it? Ah, yes—"she would make him some flaccid potatoes fried in oleomargarine." The Webster Second-International Dictionary pronouncing paragraphs that we all boned up on for our orals.

Madison lies snuggled in amongst four lakes—two of which I walked along the edge of—Mendota and Monona—clear, placid, and ideal for a college town rapidly becoming a soldier town.

I know now what frost is. When we left, a sparkling gray film covered all the hills & valleys—it was frozen dew, later melted by the noonday heat.

I felt very blue this evening—clever little quip by Gene about not recognizing me without a hat, etc. Pretty soon the bow shots of vicious gossip will be directed at us. Or perhaps I'm being kind—they may already have begun.

Wrote a long letter to Miss Bonawit—she'll probably think I'm glowing with enthusiasm.

Mousie is sitting on my lap, purring gently. This, too, I would not have believed two months ago.

I'm not nostalgic—just plain home-sick.

THURSDAY, NOV. 19

Warm drizzling walk to Midway—Midway is now the weaving penal colony to which Henning consigned me because he couldn't stand anyone around today—a real quarrel. But time passed quickly alone—more quickly than in company. Am I becoming an introvert?

Completed canning 3 gallons of pumpkins begun by Ruth. Cleaned halls and bathrooms. Kenn wanted me to go to Hillside with him to get foliage for Eleanor's room. We got just beyond the bridge above the dam when the bantam stalled. We

Wright was an automobile enthusiast who owned several different models—among them a Mercedes, a Jaguar, and a Lincoln Continental. The Fellowship had several **Bantam Roadsters**, a small car manufactured from about 1937 to 1941, often painted Cherokee red. The cars were used both to drive around Spring Green and as part of the annual caravan to Arizona.

pushed it back uphill part of the way—& it stalled. We pushed it down & it stalled. Kenn told me to drive, while he pushed it. I drove—approaching the dam straight from the right—approaching the creek straight from the left. But it didn't help. However, now I'm intent on learning to drive.

I spoke to Curtis after tea explaining Henning's remark, and Curtis told me to "tell Henning off," and not to worry about him because he likes to cause trouble between people. And how! Even Curtis knew that Henning expects an imminent break up between David and me.

Sketched with Ruth & Kay after tea. We drew each other. Kay's rendering of me in blue, orange, & yellow belongs on a True Confessions cover. Ruth's of Kay shows improvement. Mine of Ruth was mistaken either for a man, or an aloof, sophisticated female, neither of which Ruth is.

Accumulated fatigue sends me to bed at 8:30. (Kenn and Marcus visited yesterday till 11:30.)

FRIDAY, NOV. 20

The sun rises after breakfast these mornings.

Cries we thought were the mating calls of deer last night proved to be Jack yelping because a rat had gotten into bed with him—a rat so large no cat would cope with it.

Everyone all agog about our hunting season opening soon. People return with tales of deer, foxes, ferrets, and possum. Howard practically has his scalping knife in his belt by now.

Wove one line at Midway when Kay phoned me to go to Dodgeville with her & Tal—a gray dismal drizzly day—but the valleys & hills, & the sand-barred Wisconsin flowing between clumps of trees are perpetually beautiful. Dodgeville has a population of 2,000 and is therefore the center for this area of all rationing boards. Its population is mainly Cornish, for this is an old mining town, the lead mine running right beneath Main Street clear across. The town Hall is dated 1859.

Kenn tells me that annual jumping frog contests are still held in Calaveras (accent on ver) County, California, with such unpromising frog experts as Kay Kyser occasionally officiating as judge.

The Wrights have returned. The Forum issue will appear February 1; the autobiography March 1. Kay was closeted with Mrs. Wright immediately, telling

---

True Confessions was a women's magazine featuring inspirational stories of love, tragedy, and romance. Each issue featured a painting of a young woman on the cover, often in a sultry pose.

James Kern "Kay" Kyser (1905–1985) was a radio personality and big band leader who had a popular radio show from 1938 to 1949 called Kay Kyser's Kollege of Musical Knowledge.

her that she "took them sketching every day, & the strange thing is they have no inferiority complex." Goddam—that must mean "they" should feel inferior—but don't. Life is so constituted that there is always an opportunity for someone at some time to cultivate snobbery.

Read Bemelmans' Hotel Splendide—and realized some of his sketches appeared in the New Yorker.

David is teaching me drafting after tea. Street intersections, visible & invisible lines, dividers, swastikas, hexagons, etc. It's fun—and stranger than all else—David suspects me of intelligence.

Played duets with Marcus—and long talk afterwards—in which he told me he hoped if I went back to teaching it would be only for a short time, so that I could stay at the Fellowship always. In the meantime, Kenn & David chatted their dear little hearts out. Kenn was all dressed up, ready to meet Eleanor at the station—if she comes.

The plasterers came—and this room looks as messy as our living room did on some fateful days in September, 1942.

Mr. Wright gave us permission to invite Murray some weekend. David was the one who dared ask, not I.

FLW read an article about moving the Capitol from Washington to some geographical center west of the Missouri River—the boys will probably spend all winter drafting plans for the new Capital—they could do worse.

Week end guest is Prof. Frederick J. Schevill, of the History Department, University of Chicago. It was he who helped incorporate Wright in his bad days of 1927–28, paying at least $12,500 of his own. He is very glowingly portrayed in the Autobiography.

SATURDAY, NOV. 21

Drafted—using compasses and ink for about 4 hours. Practiced recorder. Read Rex Stout's Fer de Lance, a Nero Wolfe mystery.

Letter from Judy—worrying about our hard work. David is smudgy, grimy, & tired from boiler duty.

The **swastika**, a shape with straight lines, was useful for students learning drafting techniques. An ancient symbol found in Sanskrit and eastern cultures, it also appeared in many Native American designs. Although it was adopted by the Nazis as their party symbol in 1920, it was not shunned by the general public until after the war.

Ferdinand Schevill (1868–1954), a scholar of European history, was a long-time professor at the University of Chicago. Wright called him "my best friend" in *An Autobiography*.

Add another visitor—Noguchi—Japanese sculptor, whom Mr. Wright wanted here as a Master Artist.

'The Stars Look Down' was just as good the second time over, and I squirmed & trembled just as if I didn't know what the end was. Mrs. Wr. thought it was true, realistic, but ghastly—the best acted and directed picture she had ever seen, but she hated it. Surprising this shying away from ugly realities. Mr. Wright was deeply impressed by it but felt the cloud-banked conclusion with hope for the future was no solution. We concurred.

Marcus & I rescued David from his boiler duties, & we all walked up past Wes's farm on the frozen road under a brilliant high moon, with the largest ring around it I've ever seen, a herald, farmers say, of icy weather. And David jumped out of bed every two hours to tend boilers!

SUNDAY, NOV. 22
Wonderful breakfast table conversation on Organic Architecture. Mr. Wright boasted that "the principle" seeks men; men don't find the principle. It found Laotze, and Jesus, and himself—the principle that the reality of the cup was not in its form, but in the space within; the reality of a house is not in its form, but in the dwelling space within. The rôle of the artist is to create this outer form as suitable to the character of the man for whom it is intended, and the time and place for which it was intended. Thus he classes Jesus not as a carpenter, but as an architect. Dr. Schevill said that Jesus used the simile of the lilies of the field only to point a moral. Wes felt Jesus was so conscious of beauty that he didn't have to point it out for its own sake. In a tangential track, Noguchi explained that the Japanese are fighting "foreign goods and gods," the encroachment of Western Capitalism so they can return to their own way of living. It was generally felt, however, that in the attempt to destroy another way of life, they would simultaneously destroy their own. Mr. Wright teased his wife a lot because her comments, in the effort to evoke details, blotted out his bird's-eye view.

Kay showed her picture of me—"fiery hair" and eyebrow line were recognizable. I was reminded of Luigi Pirandello's "Right You Are If You Think You Are."

Jack caulked up our windows against winter blasts.

Isamu Noguchi (1904–1988), a Japanese American artist, furniture designer, and landscape designer, voluntarily took up residence during World War II at the Colorado River Relocation Center at Poston, Arizona, sharing art with the Japanese Americans interned there and proposing designs for recreation areas.

Right You Are If You Think You Are: A reference to Italian playwright Luigi Pirandello's play *Così è (se vi pare)* (1917), with the theme of conflicting versions of the truth.

Family relationships here are interesting. Wes's sister, under the name of Margaret Peters, formerly circulation manager, is now editor (George Dillon was drafted) of 'Poetry: A Magazine of Verse,' founded by Harriet Monroe. Her husband is Haiakawa, Japanese-American, author of a book on Semantics, "The English Language" a recent Book-of-the-Month Club choice. Marcus has known Mr. Wright as far back as he can remember. The Westons & the Wrights went to the Arizona Camp, Ocatilla, together in 1928. Svet and Marcus went to school together, and used to play together as children.

Last night, Howard said something very typical. When we discussed Cronin's picture, we also mentioned "The Citadel," which I described as a study in the possibilities of socialized medicine. Howard said, "Yes, that's why we went to see it. It was all about cooperative medicine."

Noguchi is asking Mr. Wright's advice in building a camp for 100,000 Japanese on the West Coast. He himself is permitted abroad only with a pass, and he's now on his way to Washington, to the Department of Interior. He went to camp voluntarily, to help his people.

Traced the plans for a Kansas City Bank today. Slow but sure progress—as on my recorder.

In a long nostalgic conversation for our "Sunday Evening," Wright reminisced his way through 4 volumes of his Autobiography, and part of the fifth. He spoke of Chicago as having the best park system in the U.S. because it recognized its lake front—with the help of Dankmar Adler & Montgomery Ward. Bridges across the railroad were built, half by the city, & half by the railroad. Therefore most bridges are half Doric, and half wooden trestles. FLW also told of his grandfather who came here because everything was "free"—and within 6 months, he was tried by his church for heresy.

Read "Poems for Every Mood," an anthology compiled by Harriet Monroe.

Margedant Peters (1915–1998) was an editor of poetry and horticulture journals. She met her husband, S. I. Hayakawa (1906–1992), in the English Department at the University of Wisconsin. Hayakawa served as a United States senator from California from 1977 to 1983.

Dankmar Adler (1844–1900), a German American architect who rose to prominence in post-fire Chicago, hired Louis Sullivan in 1880, and the two became business partners in 1883. Wright worked for the firm from 1888 to 1893.

Aaron Montgomery Ward (1843–1913) was the founder of the first mail-order department store, Montgomery Ward and Company. He became a vocal defender of Grant Park and Chicago's lakefront, even suing the city to remove buildings it had constructed in the park.

MONDAY, NOV. 23

Clear bright cold walking to and weaving at Midway so that I had to stop every now & then to exercise. Warmed up, but oh, that Charlie Horse!

Canned 3 gallons of pumpkins this afternoon, and pressed David's shirts, a job I've always thought was worth the 12¢ you paid the Chinese laundry. Well, I'll be a qualified worker in many fields before this year is up.

The females were pushed gently—not too gently—into the chorus today for Palestrina's Ave Maria. Of course, I've always been relegated to the aisle of pariahs—the monotones & listeners, but no one would hear a word of it. False modesty. False? No! At first I had a complete mental block. My mouth opened, but no bird sang. I couldn't even peep—a nightmare reaction. Well, I warned them.

Mrs. Wright and Dr. Schevill went on a tour of inspection today—much washing behind the ears. At least my floral arrangements were satisfactory.

Letters from Anna Kubick & Alice Shaw—typical.

Long talk with Johnny (poetry & word derivations), with Kenn (hot music), with Marcus (people, and loneliness, and women). Not quite the gamut, but a good evening's work because words drawl their way along here.

Mr. Wright asked David to lend him money so that he could pay $1000 for the last installments on the car & the harp. David explained that he didn't get money from his parents, but worked for everything he paid into this. Mr. Wright reminded him of the favor he was doing him in regards to me, & David is signing a note for $450, the rest of his tuition fee due in January. The same old struggle about whether the world owes Wright a living. He knows it does! But are the apprentices the world? They certainly give as much or more than they take.

TUESDAY, NOV. 24

Eleanor returned today, all bubbling with energy & enthusiasm, & a desire to learn as much & as quickly as possible, so that she can return to real work and ideas in or near New York by the second week in January. Mr Wright asked her for money, too. For the harp of that imperious little Iovanna, who called Henning rude & stupid because he suggested that she use an alarm clock instead of asking him to wake her at 6:00. Eleanor refused to sign a bad note again.

Too bright and clear a day to waste on canning squash as I did.

I wonder what will become of such attendant satellites, imitators even of mannerisms to say nothing of opinions, as Davy and Kay, for example (tho there are others), without Mr. Wright.

Continued tracing farm house attached to the Bear Run Kaufman House—if it's good it may be squashed down to 1/6 life size and appear in the Architectural Forum.

Tom & I still disagree violently about anything and everything, especially "cesspool" New York. The wonderful ignorance of immaturity, the blind intolerance of idolatry.

Mrs. Wright scolded all Sunday recorder players, especially Marcus, about not practicing enough so that they are an embarrassment to her, while Henning played with "such sensitivity & Heavenly sweetness." Jack told Svet to tell her mother, "We have work to do; we can't take off all day to practice." Henning did, today. Naughty, naughty, Snooks. Marcus has decided to give up the recorder, and play only cowboy songs on his guitar; however, he did play some duets with me.

Kenn, Eleanor, David, & I walked to the Bridge under this starry, moonlit sky, with clouds piled on top of each other, like higher mountain ridges. I paid off my bet to Kenn about David's eating a beef heart, with a beer, and the rest of us had "black cows" (rootbeer with ice cream). It would have been altogether pleasant, if Eleanor weren't worried about the note she's being coerced into signing for Mr. Wright, and if she hadn't lost a twenty dollar bill. Tom's been asked for money, too—which he'll probably borrow.

Prompt, charming, newsy letter from Miss Bonawit—the theater, bright lights, school, etc. I have decided that if Burton had joined the army, or died, or something, she would have told me—so there must be other reasons for his not writing.

David is exhausted. Mr. Wright sits under a draughty window, with air, & not fire coming from the fireplace, and wonders why he's cold. Temperature reading for the room is 73°. We're always sure we can do the same thing better—I'm waiting for the next boiler man to take charge.

I have a sneaking suspicion that an army of Wright creditors could write an amazing sub rosa biography.

Wrote to Mom, Rose Halpern, the Orloves.

WEDNESDAY, NOV. 25

Weaving, and canning 3 more gallons of squash and pumpkins. Surprising how I'm learning to maneuver those tremendous butcher knives of which I've always had such deathly fear. Noted that on our property alone—not Wes's—we had 23 cows, 2 calves, 18 piglets, and flocks of geese. A clear, warm day for this time of year.

The **Bear Run Kaufman House** was Fallingwater, Wright's landmark house for Edgar and Liliane Kaufmann at their weekend retreat outside Bear Run, Pennsylvania. Kaufmann, a department store owner from Pittsburgh, often commissioned Wright to design buildings during slow times for the architect: perhaps the farmhouse, never built, was an example of that largesse.

KENN LOCKHART WEARING MOTORCYCLE GEAR, undated (1942–43).

CHORUS REHEARSAL, undated (1942–43).

EVENING MUSICAL PERFORMANCE (FROM LEFT: SVETLANA PETERS, OLGIVANNA WRIGHT, RUTH TEN BRINK, AND DEL [UNKNOWN]), undated (1942–43).

As the trees become barer, the stretch of landscape from our windows becomes wider, yielding hills, sand bars, and the winding Wisconsin.

At chorus, Kay, Svet, and Ruth, "regretted" that colds prevented their attending, which left as pitiful a sight as you ever saw, Eleanor & me, two old crutches, with nothing to support. No gratia plena to you, Ave Maria.

David and Marcus busily wired our two rooms for permanent electricity. David insulated our closets, and cut linoleum to size for the coffee table.

Svet's pleased with my recorder progress. Still tracing the Kaufman house.

FLW read again from "Reality" at tea with potent contradictions from Dearly Beloved Husband. Good though.

Played Coronet quiz games with Kenn and Marcus. Marcus even brought in his own arm chair for greater comfort.

THURSDAY, NOV. 26

A white Thanksgiving. Cows walking in single file along the creek and up to the red barn—a beautiful pattern against the snow and dark clumps of trees. The red barn & placidly grazing cows seem to be symbols of the Wisconsin countryside.

Mrs. Wright, in an article on Katherine Mansfield, who died at the Gurdjieff Institute, reveals more about Olgivanna & Gurdjieff than about Katherine. This excerpt, quoted from "The Bookman," seems to indicate what I have always suspected, that the feminine influence on Taliesin is patterned after the Gurdjieff Institute for the Harmonious Development of the Human Being, of blessed memory. "Possibilities of developing knowledge & achievement are much greater than those already achieved. Reaching it by way of ordinary life: in the gardens, in the kitchen, doing housekeeping, farming until the day's work to keep up the Institute was done." Mrs. Wr. herself, appeared with the dance group to give demonstrations at Carnegie—before she met Mr. Wright. I should like to know exactly—and not couched in vague generalizations—what it was that they and she did in order to temper neuroticism to normalcy, and what brought her there in the first place.

Read "Frank Lloyd Wright on Architecture," selected writings from 1894 to 1940, edited by Frederick Gutheim. Most interested in the ideas on the nature of materials. Recognized several selections, particularly on the Soviet Union to appear in the new fifth volume.

Big Thanksgiving dinner by Kenn—turkey, mashed potatoes, dressing, gravy,

---

Gratia plena, Latin for "full of grace," part of the Hail
Mary prayer, which became the lyrics to Schubert's
"Ave Maria."

carrots, cranberries, pickles, lettuce, wine, mince and pumpkin pies, coffee. David was too busy cleaning ashes & stoking boilers to attend. Iovanna brightly suggested that he had probably thrown himself into the furnace with a "there, will that satisfy you?" Hence followed two hours of psychological analyses of former apprentices. Tedious and disgusting. Howard expressed it well by saying that what he has to be thankful for is that he's not a former apprentice. I felt like Margels Gillmore in "The Women"—"I'd hate to be the first to leave this party." I was quite upset by this, tho a brisk walk with Marcus to Hillside was refreshing.

Saw "Peg of Old Drury" again—still very charming, & light buffet supper in the theater. David in the meantime completely insulated the closet, our cold storage space.

Read Robinson's "Man Against the Sky" and "Children of the Night." Robinson suits my vanitas vanitatum mood at the moment.

Letters from the N.Y. Central R.R. about my ticket and from Murray.

I feel weary, stale, flat, and unprofitable.

Marcus was publicly tried at dinner for giving up his recorder. We'll probably lay bets as to who wins. I have scarcely heard an original thought here—everything seems traceable directly or indirectly to books written by FLW, or dogmatic statements made by him at tea or breakfast, or in the studio. Fortunately, he protects most people from his wife's tongue, seeing in them human faults, frequently his own. But no one dares speak up for anyone officially disliked—he must hide his affection or loyalty, like a light under a bushel.

FRIDAY, NOVEMBER 27

Canned 5 more gallons of pumpkins to the rhythm of Beethoven's Ninth. Chorus. Recorder.

Letters from Judy, Chic-ngai, and the telephone girl in David's place. Chic-ngai seems to have gotten some job, but doesn't say what. I wonder if anybody quite understands our letters.

Read a weird book, Carson McCullers' "Reflections in a Golden Eye." It's been going the rounds here.

FLW read from Nehru's "Glimpses of World History" at tea.

Served & washed dishes. When Jack got a little uppity, I shot off a few witticisms of my own. Marcus thought I was "kind of cute" at supper and "held my own." I can, when driven to it.

---

vanitas vanitatum: Latin, from Ecclesiastes 1:2, meaning "vanity of vanities."

weary, stale: from Shakespeare's Hamlet.

David made little cabinets in the book cases, and we have a new uninstalled radiator. I'm anxious to get at painting and cleaning up this mess.

Completed plan of the Kaufman lodge. Jack definitely says he'll use it for the Architectural Forum.

SATURDAY, NOV. 28

Add clichés: Ruth was surprised that I said ai for eye and not oeye since I'm a New Yorker. Do they all think New York is vulgar, [un]cultured, boorish? We are evidently not the only provincials in these broad United States.

Walked thru about 9 inches of snow to Midway. The light tufts of snow on strawberry patches, between the rows of corn, on the upper side of branches, leaving the underside black, on the hill slopes with etched patches of woods—like so many extraordinary Christmas cards. One of our fires exploded slightly landing in sparks on the loom with a smell of burnt chicken feathers—really singed wool.

Chatty letter from Mom, and a letter from Bert Slanhoff who writes with the same breeziness with which he speaks. Julia sent her graduation picture, which looks just like her when she's all dressed up, but slightly supercilious.* Sent $15 anniversary gift to Mom & Dad. *(Marcus wonders how soon she'll visit us.)

Practiced high A on recorder till my throat feels like the end of a "socialized recitation."

Kay asked me to do her a favor and change cooking weeks with her so that she can be with Mrs. Wright constantly next week when her dressmaker comes in from Madison. So I begin being kitchen drudge again tomorrow.

Tea in Gene's room—still holding my own with Jack & Ted. Supper, Japanese prints in the studio. Mr. Wright gathered us all around him under one big lamp, & around one big drawing table and showed us about a thousand Japanese prints & New Year's cards—the works of Hanorabu, Chumpho, Shunko, Shunman, Utanaro, Hiroshigi, Yeishii, Ari, Biencho, Hokasi, and Yonakushi. Fascinating, but very long discussion. Informative.

SUNDAY, NOV. 29

Cooked all day with a last minute's rush, & not even time to sit down. Mrs. Wr. felt too nauseous for roast chicken, so I boiled it for her. When it was completely boiled, she sent word that she felt better & wanted it roasted. So, presto, chango, a boiled chicken became a roasted chicken. Ménu: Sauerbraten, potato dumplings (beautiful before they hit the boiling water, & then they all fainted. Mr Wright, however,

---

Bert Slanhoff, a friend and colleague of David's at Display Finishing Co. He served in World War II.

DAVID HENKEN, undated (1942–43).

thought they were excellent, & got a separate dish of extras), carrots, peas, & parsley, excellent sour cream gravy, and apple pie with corn flake crumb crust (honey for Wrights as sweetening, cinnamon, sugar, nutmeg for us—"delicious," "wonderful," "some more of that excellent pie"). Mr. Wr. said I was a genius. I'm not, but a good pie must be a bee line to a man's heart—especially if sweetened with honey. So all's still well.

Mr. Wright asked afterwards what we would like him to do with us—walk, talk, read—because we had entertained him. (I, too, sang Ave Maria in chorus. Curtis wore a look of patient resignation, with a slight flicker of amusement.) Ted suggested that he read from Rabelais, the description of the building & personnel of Pantagruel's Abbaye. Amusing at first, but it wore on tediously toward eleven.

MONDAY, NOV. 30
It's been snowing steadily for three days now—light, gentle drifts.

Lunch—chicken paprika, mashed potatoes, rutabagas, garlic pickles, and cornstarch blanc mange with blackberry syrup for the Wrights. Mrs. Wr. sent in her compliments, & Mr. Wr. came in to say it was a very tasty meal. "You can't tell me you're an amateur." "Well, if taken in its original sense as meaning one who does things for the love of it, yes." "You can't tell me you don't love it, or you wouldn't do it as well." I consulted Mrs. Wr. about her diet & preferences, & again she praised me for my potatoes & pie, & because I looked so pretty, and delicate last night. Ruth put it almost as succinctly with, "My, I bet your waist line's not more than 24 inches." "22" I told her.

Norman Hill, former cook here, now working at Merrimac on the housing projects connected with the defense plants there, visited us, puttered around in the kitchen, and bought two treats supreme, oranges for breakfast, & ice cream for tea.

Johnny is good kitchen help. But supper was a semi-tragedy. The gas in both drums ran out at 6 with supper to be served at 6:30. Of course, it was late—6:45, with no squash. But fortunately I had enough—vegetable soup, brown bread, tomatoes, corn, & rothe gruetze with whipped cream. The Wrights added baked tomato & egg, & spinach.

I'm tired but looking forward to oyster stew at Marcus's house tomorrow night.

David's tracing again for the Forum—but this room looks worse than 37-47 in its hey-day.

Long, quiet, pleasant chat in Marcus's room till 11:00.

TUESDAY, DEC. 1

6° today, and it felt it. Lunch—veal paprika, boiled potatoes, rutabagas. Supper—oyster stew at Marcus's. Baked bread after lunch, & then helped Marcus fix dressing, cake, etc., etc., at his house. Johnny & I went over earlier. A very pleasant evening, including the boys sitting around the table restraining burps & singing. I helped Mrs. Weston comb her hair—almost blind, & a broken arm is mending. Fell asleep during charades—partial desire in order to avoid the malice of "sticking" someone. Mrs. Wright liked my muffins very much & wanted the recipe. Both she & Mr. Wr. suspect I've brought along a little private hoard of treasures.

David's made cabinets in the bookcases. A sweet & erudite letter from Burton, & one from Rose.

WEDNESDAY, DEC. 2

Letter from Mom, thanking us for our anniversary wishes but refusing to accept the money gift. Letter from Murray, and typically charming one from Nat.

Johnny & I, practically crawling from fatigue like reptiles, prepared for lunch: Veal stew (Mrs. Wr. thought it was delicious), hashed brown potatoes. for supper: spaghetti with butter & olive oil sauce; tomato soup; pickled beets, gold cupcakes.

Kenn's busy persuading Eleanor to remain here, so our only visitor was Marcus—sweet as usual. I dread to think of his trial on Dec. 15.

THURSDAY, DEC. 3

Another letter from Mom, with an anniversary letter from Dad to her enclosed. So sweet it brought the tears to my eyes.

Lunch was very simple today to allow time & room for Iovanna's birthday party supper held in the theater. Lunch: Baked beans, Brown bread, sauerkraut. For the Wrights: Rice gruel, sauteed chicken livers, spinach, squash, Rothe Gruetze. Supper: Roast chicken, superb dressing & gravy (and enough other people seconded me), potatoes, carrots, birthday cake made by Mrs. Wright. Mr. Wr. told me I proved the worth of the amateur over the professional.

Iovanna was serenaded by Marcus in a Mexican Sunday hat, to the accompaniment of his own guitar. He looked shy & sweet, & surprised us very much by his courage in singing at all. Later, Kay treated David & me, Kenn & Eleanor,

76

Marcus & Vlasta (the dressmaker) to beers at Stuffy's Tavern, while Marcus went pleasantly through his repertoire. It was so pleasant, I thought of New York with no longing. Afterwards, we went into Kay's room for some of the wine left over from the party. She acted cuddly with Marcus—all sorts of hoary gags about the best man at her wedding, his being dangerous, etc., & then she started on David, burning a hole in his jacket with her cigarette. After wondering out loud about a dozen times whether David was jealous or not, she passed out like a light.

David went skiing before supper. He seems to like it, & I can hardly wait to be free to join him.

The icicles are brilliantly beautiful in all lights, pendant crystalline abstractions.

FRIDAY, DEC. 4
Ice-skating has been added to skiing for Taliesin sport—but still not for me.

A charming & unexpected card from Burton, & a letter from Judeth.

Lunch: Chicken Paprika, rutabagas, potato balls in cornflake balls, baked, sweet pickles. The Wrights added green beans, & apples specially baked by Johnny.

Supper: Chicken soup, macaroni, cheese, tomato, Baked cauliflower, fruit jello with whipped cream. Wrights—spinach timbale, squash. People still ask for seconds, & not from sheer hunger, so perhaps I've not shot my bolt yet. However, I was so tired that I had what Henning would have termed an "emotional upset." Marcus came in later to pop some corn for us, and we had a pleasant chatty evening, but still up too late.

I had a slight hangover this morning, & Kay such a big one, that she changed her cooking week with Kenn. He's furious, but she's getting away with murder.

SATURDAY, DEC. 5
Letter from Julia—all's still well as can be.

Lunch: corn fritters (5 & 6 helpings for some people), stewed tomatoes, & squash. Wrights: Chicken soup with chicken & vermicelli, Peas, Baked potato,

---

Stuffy Vale, a former cheese-factory owner, ran a tavern frequented by apprentices in the 1940s. The tavern was walking distance from Taliesin, and Wright objected both because the building blocked the view of the river and because it was a distraction for the fellows. Wes Peters told the rest of the story in Edgar Tafel's book, *Frank Lloyd Wright: Recollections from Those Who Knew Him*: "After the war, Mr. Wright bought the Tavern when Stuffy wanted to retire, much to the consternation of its patrons. We transferred the papers right there in Spring Green, at the bank. We filed the actual deed in Dodgeville. We were having a picnic over there, and Mr. Wright said 'Well, I've decided we'll have a big bonfire. We'll go burn down the tavern.' The tavern was already empty. Everybody sort of protested to Mr. Wright that it would be better to try to sell its materials. But it probably wasn't all that valuable. Mr. Wright had us go down there with the picnic and burn the tavern down—something you wouldn't be allowed to do nowadays."

DAVID IN WINTER, 1942.

stewed tomatoes, & baked custard with caramel syrup. Supper: Roast veal & roast sauerbraten. (Mrs. Wright, having discussed my menu with me full well, asked if I could also roast a chicken for her.) That meant the wood stove, with its uneven heat, had to be kept going too, burning the fluted edges of all my pies. Mashed potatoes, carrots, lettuce, Taliesin dressing, Pumpkin pie.

Supper in the living room, & slides of Taliesin Mid-West & West, Winter & Summer, At Work & Play, in the Studio. Johnny & I served coffee, cheese & crackers until Lee Stevens, guest of Mr. Wright's, appeared. Marcus helped me do the dishes afterwards. Johnny is in for breakfast again, although he asked Gene & Henning to take over. He was very hurt by their refusal.

SUNDAY, DEC. 6

Lee Stevens, our guest, is an efficiency expert in Washington. Here are some of his ideas: Russians are paid for their ability to produce; therefore the top bosses are paid about ten times as much as the workers under them; & in some cases, higher than Americans in similar positions. Wilkie is personal ambassador of Roosevelt's, because Roosevelt is in a position whereby he can't criticize Churchill publicly. The country is in the control of about 20 men—the conservative Southern Democratic senators. England is the best armed fortress in the world—she has so many of our soldiers & so much of our ammunition. Wilkie in speaking to Stalin, said that he had raised the literacy quotient from 10 to 80%, higher, therefore, than that of the U.S. and that the people might some day be so educated that they would run Stalin out. To this, Stalin replied that even if they did that, he would be satisfied that they were educated.

Went visiting at Marcus's home today—popping corn, reading magazines, talking—a real Sunday-afternoon-at-home spirit.

The dam has frozen into a gleaming cascade purpled by the setting sun. Clumps of birch, maple, oak, pine, & juniper stand out in dark patches against blue snow.

C. Leigh Stevens (d.1962) was a businessman, efficiency expert, and industrialist. The house Wright designed for him was the centerpiece of a working farm named Auldbrass—Wright's reinterpretation of the nineteenth-century name Old Brass—which was built on land assembled from several historic plantations. The property included barns, stables, chicken runs, two cottages, and offices for the owner. Construction of the complex, located between Charleston, South Carolina, and Savannah, Georgia, began in 1938, and Wright continued to work on the project until his death in 1959.

The primary residence and key outbuildings share a hexagonal module and distinctive tilted exterior walls. Hollywood producer Joel Silver bought the property in 1986 and has commissioned the restoration of existing buildings and the construction of structures planned by Wright but previously unexecuted.

Wendell Wilkie (1892–1944) ran against Franklin D. Roosevelt in 1940 and then served in his administration, traveling, in 1942, to the Soviet Union and to China as part of a "one world" tour promoting internationalism.

Sang Ave Maria in the choir again tonight. David & Curtis did dishes. David seems to have discussed me with Johnny, & told Johnny that it was his idea to come here—not mine, & that, although he hated the words, I was a "good soldier." Johnny told him that I had entered into so many things so thoroughly and conscientiously that I was really making a success of myself here. Kenn told me that I had been very highly praised, and if a failure (I said that neither my cottage cheese nor milk had soured), the most successful failure in years. Marcus, in answer to my remark that I had tried to be as friendly as possible, told me I had succeeded wonderfully well with him, & gave me a picture of him. A nice note on which to end a tiring week!

MONDAY, DECEMBER 7

The anniversary of the bombing of Pearl Harbor. A year of war, a peace snuggles into these hills, & it is with a sharp jolt that we discover that the conscientious objectors here are objectors to war!

Letter from Dave Wertman, saying he works 52 hours a week & overtime pay discontinued, which means $25 a week to him.

Relayed compliment from Mrs. Wright. She told Johnny that she was surprised by my conscientiousness, and ability, and by the high order of excellence for all the meals during the week. Johnny told David that I didn't have Kenn's strength or knacks about the kitchen, but that I was just as efficient, and that this was one of the easiest weeks he's spent in the kitchen.

Wrote 6 letters, slept, played the recorder, began tracing plans for the Leigh Stevens House, Yemassee, South Carolina, read John Glogg's "Industrial Art Explained."

Marcus is terribly concerned—wishes he had been abandoned by the Fellowship, wants to get the jail sentence over with, etc., etc.

David has been doing wiring in the house, the little dining room, & the bathrooms.

Evening visits from Kenn, Ruth, & Howard. All the girls, except Eleanor are busy sewing dresses for the Tsarina & the princesses. How soon will they get me?

TUESDAY, DECEMBER 8

Weaving at Midway morning and afternoon—set up loom to make table linen for the Wright's Christmas box. Misty morning walk thru knee-deep snow drifts and hoar frost glistening on trees. We roasted weinies in the wood stove and ate 3 apiece—all while weaving. Stepped into the barn, and all the cows turned toward the light & open door with the precision of the Rockettes.

Because Eleanor has an abscessed tooth, David is doing kitchen duty for the week, and wiring at the same time.

Letter from the Tabors, and George Price's "It's Smart To Be People," a Christmas gift from George Brewster. What fun it will be looking thru it!

Funny coincidence: Mrs. Gadsby, heroine of the foundling asylum picture, "Blossoms In the Dust," is one of Mr. Wright's clients—one of the most exotic houses he's ever planned. In his autobiography, he uses the words, "there are no illegitimate children, there are only illegitimate parents." Those are the very words which she uses in the movies as the key to her attitude.

Everyone's labor here is cheap—but that of the King and Queen. Mrs. Williams is paid 25¢ an hour. The seamstress, working 9–10 hours a day, was paid $6 a day—she even worked Sunday. Hers was the sort of professional skill that should have received from $75 to $100 for a 5-day week. The same tactics they use on the chicken farmers & small storekeepers here. Credit and credit, with no cash to back it up, but wild hopes that they may beg or borrow some—and very few debts paid. "The world owes me a living, heigh-ho."

Continued tracing after tea. Almost impossible to see plans printed in rosy ink on pink paper and re-lined like a palimpsest.

David burned the inside of his right hand grabbing a hot pan—suffered painfully. I pinch-hit for him as kitchen help.

Ted, Curtis, Johnny, Marcus, Wes, & Kenn have leaned over our shoulders and laughed hilariously at "It's Smart To Be People."

Read Carl Sandburg's Fairy Tales, "Rootabaga Country." Mr. Wright praised them so highly in his Autobiography that I read them—and they're just as charming as he said they'd be.

Long talk with Marcus in his room till about 12:00—about everything—race prejudice, anti-semitism, gangsterism, personalities, work, direction, etc., etc.

WEDNESDAY, DEC. 9

Set up loom at Midway; mangled Fellowship linen.

Kenn, Marcus, David all shouting at each [other] for Marcus to give up his I-don't-care attitude as regards his hearing. I wrote down the points for him to remember—especially the difference between succumbing and passive resistance.

Florence and Sol Tabor, longtime family friends and political allies of Priscilla and David. David designed a house for them in Briarcliff Manor, New York, in 1959.

Mrs. Gadsby was actually Edna Gladney (1886–1961), an advocate for children's rights and well-being who successfully lobbied the State of Texas to stop using the word *illegitimate* on birth certificates of children of unmarried parents. She was portrayed by Greer Garson in the 1941 movie *Blossoms in the Dust*. Wright designed several unbuilt houses in Fort Worth for Gladney during the 1920s.

Session lasted till 1:00 A.M. with me—feminine influence—to have the last words. Attachments are becoming obvious.

THURSDAY, DEC. 10
Mangled Fellowship linen. Traced.

Marcus went to see his lawyer. Tom left for the army.

Eleanor, face swollen to disfigurement, is still having her abscessed tooth drained.

Marcus home at 9. Knocked at his door—he was in bed, tears trickling down his nose. I tried to comfort him as I could without asking questions, altho he did say he had gone thru a terrible experience, & would be here when I returned—evidently a postponement. He wanted to speak to no one but me.

FRIDAY, DEC. 11
Marcus came in this morning to tell me what he couldn't last night. His lawyer could fix it so that he'd be sent to C.O. camp—whisked away in a day or two—but uncertain as to whether classification would be C.O. or criminal. Went to District Attorney Holmes, & there in the midst of the questioning, he fainted. This threw a new light on the case—physical exams, etc. Is he in good enough condition to go to a C.O. camp? More delays until January. He feels as if every postponement is an admission of guilt.

Asked Mrs. Wright's permission to clean up Tom's room for Murray's arrival.

Mrs. Wright discovered today—tho why not sooner with Kay around, I don't know—that Eleanor was being taken care of by Kenn in his room. She stormed up after supper—told her her conduct was disgusting and morally revolting; what would people think if they knew she had a male nurse; that she was a burden to the Fellowship and had always been; that she should have taken Mrs. Wr. into her confidence where she was, or that her room was too cold; etc.; etc.; etc. Eleanor returned pretty nearly in kind. Eleanor decided to leave tomorrow tho we tried to dissuade her. Kenn told us that he more than anyone else would like her to stay, and yet he wouldn't want her to after facing that nastiness & pettiness.

Whispers floated thru the studio when I worked there afterwards on my tracing.

At 11:30 Kenn and Marcus drove us down to the bridge to meet the bus. We sat there with freezing toes until Murray arrived. I suspect that Marcus is being much more than merely gallant—even when he keeps my toes warm. Quite pleasant to see Murray, tho we dumped him almost immediately into bed after his 7 1/2 hour ride.

SATURDAY, DEC. 12
We let Murray sleep till about 9:30. Then Kenn made special breakfast for him— and we walked over to Hillside where I gave him a guided—and perhaps slightly

misguided tour of the place, the plans, Broadacre City. How much better I understand them now. The temperature was about 10–16 below zero, and as we ploughed knee-deep thru snow, I felt that my nose—the only really exposed portion of my anatomy were coming off. Everyone was quite friendly to him at lunch. Afterwards, I traced for a good part of the afternoon, while he and David (off from kitchen duty for a few hours) wired the music stand.

Supper with the Wrights in the dining room was a most pleasant affair—and the nuances were particularly amusing. Mr. Wr. spoke of the movie and said "pick-chah." "Isn't that the way they say it in N.Y.?" I said that I didn't have the typical N.Y. accent, whereupon Davy haw-hawed. So I smiled, and said I had forgotten but Davy had overheard me say toity-tree boids was sittin on a koib boipin and choipin. Mr. Wr. laughed, asked me to say thirty-first. I obliged, correctly, and he said that was right. Johnny added pointedly to Davy, "Of course, she had to think first." Discussion of Emma Gadsby, and Mr. Wr. told us that "there are no illegitimate children. There are only illegitimate parents" which appears in his Autobiography, was attributed to her in the picture, whereas it is originally his, with no credit given him. I was the only one who remembered the sentence. Then he spoke quite fondly of his granddaughter, Ann Baxter, who acted magnificently in "The Magnificent Ambersons"—a good, sincere actress (19 years old), but not glamorous. He's amused that Hollywood is paying $25,000 for a glamorizing press agent campaign. Mrs. Wr. felt that she was cold, and non-emotional, and immediately changed the center of interest to <u>her</u> grandchild, Brandoch (11 months old), and his future as a sensitive artist. Well, she is a fourth wife, and must hold her own against previous loves & previous attachments.

Movie in the studio—"University of Life"—a cinematic biography of Maxim Gorki sent by Artkino and based on Gorki's "My Universities." A deeply moving, human, warmly emotional picture.

Eleanor's dentist told her she was too sick to travel—so she's leaving tomorrow.

A cornerstone of Wright's architectural ideology, **Broadacre City** was a model for suburban development that he conceived in the depths of the Great Depression and continued to explore until his death in 1959. First published in his book *The Disappearing City* (1932), Broadacre City was to be a community of some 1,400 families covering four square miles. The concept reflected Wright's mistrust of cities—buildings were to be widely dispersed, entailing a dependence on private automobiles (or flying versions thereof, in Wright's imagination). Although residents would live in different types of dwellings, each family was to have its own acre of land. An exhibition about this proposal, including a large-scale model of the entire planned community, was presented at New York's Rockefeller Center in 1935.

fourth wife: Olgivanna was actually Wright's third wife, but this calculation likely includes his long-term relationship with Mamah Borthwick.

SUNDAY, DEC. 13

Pleasant breakfast discussion on the superiority of drawings over models, because in models we can't scale ourselves down to fit, whereas drawings allow greater play of imagination.

Discussion with Curtis on Ulysses. Watched Eleanor pack. Walked down the road.

Marcus, Kenn, & I took Eleanor & Murray to the station. Murray seemed truly impressed by the natural beauty of the place, by the greatness of Wright, and by the marvelous experience this is for us.

I pitied Kenn his painful farewell, but envied him his manliness in doing nothing dramatic (altho he is intensely emotional), and accepting his loss with outward grace. Mrs. Wright tried to probe him (why must pseudo psychoanalysts be so painful?) and asked him how he felt. He shrugged his shoulders, and said, "That's life." Then he felt remorse because he was not telling the truth—he was really suffering greatly. We thought it was just as well, because he doesn't want their public commiseration, nor does he want them to think his work will be affected. He and David are making plans to routinize their education—a plan a week, submitted to Mr. Wright for approval, etc. I hope they can carry it out. Eleanor said she came with high hopes, & is leaving with high hopes—which is as it should be.

Amusing post prandial conversation on shop lifting & window shopping with Mr. Wright taking the cake for being most expert in both. For the former, he said all he does is have them send it C.O.D. —it's so much easier. For the latter, he gave an example. At an art dealer's in Chicago, he saw two giant bronze Chinese dogs to fit in perfectly at the entrance with reflecting pools of water. He bargained them down from $6000 to $1500, the shipping charges from China. He told the man we would keep it for a year, have the satisfaction of their beauty, and then if we didn't have the money, we'd return them. It was a deal. But the partners stepped in, and asked for $1000 down payment. FLW wired back, "Sorry, can't accept. This was not in the spirit of the deal." Then he added, "So I was spared worrying about where we'd get the money, and he spent about the best 2 1/2 hours in his life.

Concert not so good, as the group thins out. When the choir sings, they get no joy out of audience reaction—usually because there's no audience, except for Mr. Wright.

Ted recited a beautiful love poem of Byron's, and Marcus whispered he would mean it all for me, after FLW said that it was the right kind of poem for the right kind of woman. Entangling alliances? And where was David all this time? Sorting the 1911 German edition of Wright's plans for Christmas gifts.

MONDAY, DEC. 14

Wove morning and afternoon on Wright's table linen. Murasaki (violet of Japanese prints), beautifully greyed by the gold. Traced in the afternoon—after tea—I wish the Leigh Stevens house weren't such an important plan.

David sent off my valises, & Chic-ngai's & Eleanor's trunks. I'm carrying wine for Mr. Wright's sister & sister-in-law, & lists of instructions on what to bring back.

Ice-skating is in season—even Mrs. Wr. is learning—tho she says Mr. Wr. skates as if there were a Strauss waltz in his head.

Had a hunch Kay would get me to serve before I left. I served, tho David did about 2/3 of the dishes.

Kenn & Marcus dropped in to chat in the evening.

TUESDAY, DEC. 15

Marcus drove David & me down to the station, snow falling quietly all the way. Because of all the abracadabra about my ticket, I made the Chicago train in one minute. Strangely enough, it is with great reluctance that I go.

Henning is buying a 120 acre farm up the valley near Wes's. FLW is going to a lot of trouble about the deeds. Some of the money is coming from his mother, who's making a settlement on him—as his wife did. He even gets money from his mother-in-law. He tells this story to illustrate how clever he is, but it is revelatory. When he got back from the Phoenix hospital, he couldn't pay the bill. So he wrote to his mother in law (his separation had already gone thru) saying that he'd received word from the hospital that she had paid the bill, and that she was too kind; he was very grateful, etc., etc. She was too embarrassed to contradict him—and paid the bill.

Window shopping in Goldblatt's & The Fair in Chicago. Strange how you remember the way around. Its slums & backwash are as ugly as New York's—"well-planned & potentially most beautiful city in the country" tho it may be.

Raced thru heavily falling snow in Illinois, Indiana, & Ohio. How much more real than map names South Bend & Elkhart seem now that I've seen children trudging home from school in them—snow delightfully whipping cold faces & well-wrapped bodies. Staccato rhythm of small towns—Wausau or Butler or Mazomanie or Cross Plains or Black Earth—distinguished by one main brightly lit thorofare at right angles to the tracks with a movie house named Crossway, and a restaurant squarely facing the station, with a neon sign as big as the store itself—EAT. Dusky arrival into Toledo. Pretty good sleeping all night considering it was coach travel.

WEDNESDAY, DEC. 16

City stark, gray, & cold.

Delivered Taliesin wine to Mrs. Barney & her daughter, Mrs. Gilham. Mrs. B. was disappointed that it wasn't gooseberry catsup. Then to Mrs. Lazovich, warmly Russian, who was most grateful, and invited me to tea next week.

Visited Daddy up at the place, and he helped me with my luggage. Everyone delighted to see me—have you ever heard of the effect created by Lazarus? Played the recorder for the children. Visited the Henkens in the evening with Julia. I flowed in a steady stream of conversation for hours. Bessie H. seemed overworked and consequently irritable. She kept on interrupting to say she was not interested in anything or anyone else, only David. When I happened to mention the 1914 massacre, she said FLW was probably crazy, and all David seemed to get out of it was to be a farmer, and that I must write him to come home immediately.

THURSDAY, DEC. 17

Got my fur coat out of storage.

Pictures to develop at Fotoshop.

Waacs by the dozen dis-grace our fair city. I hate to see women so completely manful in a man's world.

December Miss Subway is a Barnard College Freshman.

Johnny Belinda is being done by the Jewish Theater, starring Miss Jean Platt. (née Jennie Platnik?)

Hitler size posters of U.S.O.—Labor We Produce; Railroads—We Deliver; Defense Stamps, Etc.

Visited AJHS. All the teachers were glad to see me but greeted me with a nos morituri smile. They're badly in need of teachers, & I was welcomed gladly. But, of course, I told them it's a nice place to visit, but I wouldn't like to work. I told Miss Bonawit that my dependency didn't count, because I could get a job easily enough.

---

up at the place: Priscilla refers here to her father's millinery factory.

Approximately 150,000 women served in the Women's Army Auxiliary Corps (**WAAC**) during World War II, doing everything from rigging parachutes to analyzing aerial photographs to crimping sheet metal in support of the war effort.

The **Miss Subways** contest ran from 1941 to 1977 and has since been revived as Ms. Subways. December 1942 winner Marguerite McAuliffe "aims to be a doctor as

good as her dad" according to the poster presented on the subway during the month of her reign.

The United Service Organizations (**USO**) posters built domestic support for the troops overseas.

AJHS: Andrew Jackson High School, in the Cambria Heights neighborhood of Queens, New York, opened in 1937. This is the high school where Priscilla taught before she joined the Fellowship.

nos morituri: Latin for "we who are about to die."

"You certainly can. Don't you go to the draft board, & say I kicked you out." When I told her Miss Munn had phoned frequently, & she had said that she was the first person I was to get in touch with when I returned permanently, D.B. laughed "That's what she thinks. Sic transit gloria Munn."

Had dinner with Burton at his home. Stony was the silence that greeted his enthusiastic & frequent exclamations: Oh, mother, isn't it the most wonderful luck that she could come? Doesn't she look radiant? Aren't you happy she's here? And he served me 3 wines, one for each course!

Burton, & Leo, & Irv Cohen, & a couple of thousand others, I suppose, have sent letters in reply to a request for teachers of experience with H.S. knowledge of math & physics to learn meteorology at Grand Rapids, Michigan, beginning Jan. 4, at $140 a month, & then to teach it as second lieutenants.

George Brody has been transferred to parts unknown. Sylvia Brody is on maternity leave.

Long talk with the folks in the evening—Daddy came home earlier & was terribly hurt that I wasn't there.

Dinner invitation at D.B.'s for the 29th.

FRIDAY, DEC. 18
Easeful, lolling day, writing, reading, odds & ends.

Helen Steinlein phoned—dinner appointment for Monday.

Supper at the Henkens—Nat & Burt came up later—pleasant evening. Nat summarized my appearance of good health (I suppose) by "How could David let you go?"

Wright's name appeared in AP and UP press—as "under fire for obstructing war activities at his private school in Spring Green, Wisconsin." Journalistic language can be wonderfully misleading.

SATURDAY, DEC. 19
Visited Mrs. Melamed who was on the verge of tears all the time. Said the Dr. had to have uniforms specially cut to cover his pupik.

Spent some time with Mom & the kids.

Sic transit gloria Munn: From the Latin, *sic transit gloria mundi* (thus passes the glory of the world).

George Brody was dating Priscilla's sister Julia during the time of the diary and later married her. He served in the U.S. Army in World War II and later worked as a certified public accountant.

pupik: Yiddish for "belly button."

Had cocktails with Burton at 4:00 at the inn where I had my first cocktail—the road to perdition. Then harp and piano recital—Grandjany and Jones—at the Library. He showed me a N.Y. Times clipping—all this FBI business started as a result of the trial of Marcus Earl Weston, 27, who was given time to think it over until Jan. 12. I'm so worried I'd like to run back.

Dinner with Judy, the Saias, & Whites. Cross-examination about Taliesin. Clarice said she had never heard me speak so lengthily before—but nobody asked me. After all, I've lectured in the classroom.

SUNDAY, DEC. 20

Leisurely breakfast with the Jussims.

Museum with Nat—John Barrymore in Beau Brummel, & an excellent exhibit of comparative 20th century portraits—2 pieces of sculpture by Naguchi made me feel quite at home. Then we dined in a charming French restaurant—the Champlain—and up to Burt's for liquor and a Bloch concerto. Nat said it was the best Sunday he had spent since we left, and Burt was friendly and flattering. Even Gladys was cordial.

MONDAY, DEC. 21

N.Y. papers boast this the coldest 21st in 71 years.

Lunch by Mom for Sonia, Goldie, Celia, & Fannie.

Supper at the Steinleins.

Saw Lucia di Lammermoor at the Metropolitan with Lily Pons, Jan Peerce, and Warren Leonard. Very beautiful piece. Judy took me because Murray couldn't go— he was studying for the music regular.

Letter from David explaining in detail what had happened. Judge Stone, a Catholic, Legionnaire, one of the greatest forces of reaction in the State, with the usual quota of sons "in the colors," requested Marcus thru his lawyer to come up to see him. He found then that he was on trial. The Capital Times gave him 3 full columns headlined by "Judge Stone asks FBI Investigate Wright." The judge ordered Marcus to leave the Fellowship, go home, think it over, & report on Jan. 10. He will have the choice of army non-combatant service or jail. The AP & UP have requested

While in New York City, Priscilla took advantage of the opportunity to take in cutting-edge culture of all sorts, including music, ballet, theater, and gallery exhibitions. She visited large and small **museums**, attended both classical and popular concerts, plays, musicals, and all sorts of other productions, many during their opening run. She ate at a wide variety of restaurants as well; all of these experiences reflect the differences between New York and her rural Wisconsin experience.

statements from FLW, who wrote an open letter to Stone, released in Sunday's paper, & inviting investigation. The whole thing interrupted a telegram to Joe Stalin advising him on the conduct of the war. Marcus left the Fellowship. David wrote a statement to the papers, reworded in his own style by Marcus, & David also wrote to the War Resisters for legal help enclosing a note from Marcus.

Taliesin with our favorites—Chic-ngai, Eleanor, and Marcus—gone, grows a drearier prospect. Why do the gods play with such little lives? What puny satisfaction it must give them!

TUESDAY, DEC. 22

Took Mom to a Gynecologist's—a lot wrong with her, but no operation necessary. The rest is in the hands of a family practitioner.

Supper at Bessie Henken's—gift of the 2 volume Random House edition of the Greek historians from David, with a very tender note. Handkerchiefs & Tweed—gifts from Bessie.

WEDNESDAY, DEC. 23

Rehearsal of the National Orchestral Association with Leon Barzin conducting. Piano auditions plus Clarence Adler. Played Mendelssohn piano concerto and concerti 15 and 35 by Mozart. Fascinating to see them at work. Barzin took me on the stage, and one of the boys showed me the back view of the orchestra.

Took out pictures from Fotoshop—many quite good.

Sent cigarettes, halvah, & cards to Taliesin.

Exhibit on scientific rubber by Dodge & Chrysler.

Quiet evening at home.

THURSDAY, DEC. 24

Conversation at concert: "Koussevitsky told me that Barzin is America's foremost coming conductor." "Who? Koussevitsky? Oh. . . you mean Serge."

Visited Aunt Nina—thinks she's going crazy—suicidal tendencies.

Visited Nat—long talk—met Burton at AAA Galleries—Kleinholz exhibit—lawyer who first started painting 4 years ago, at the age of 37. Both boys treated me to a light supper.

The Associated American Artists **(AAA) Galleries** specialized in affordable fine art prints. The gallery was an important distributor of "art for the people" in the 1930s and 1940s. Frank Kleinholz (1901–1987) was a modernist painter specializing in urban life in New York. The AAA show in 1942 was his first solo exhibit.

Supper at the Starks. Practical exchange of gifts under the Christmas tree. Alice amused me by introducing me to her landlord as coming from a super-cooperative. Stayed overnight.

FRIDAY, DEC. 25

Visited Bubbie & the Barney Jussims.

Saw Oy is Das a Leben with Mollie Picon & Jacob Kalish, autobiographical musical comedy. Spontaneous, verve, charming—Give My Regards to Broadway in Jewish idiom, & "Jetzh iz die zeit. . . . Far jeden jid" to the dot dot dot dash of Beethoven's 5th. Fraedins were there too to celebrate the Henkens' 28th anniversary. Supper at Farmfoods.

Party with Burton at the Traisters. More proselytizing. An hour walk home in slight drizzle—delightful.

Molly Picon (1898–1992) was a popular and successful actor during an age of thriving Yiddish theater. With her husband and collaborator of fifty years, Yonkel (Jacob) Kalish, she performed all over the world. The play Priscilla saw was *The Joy of Living*.

Far jeden jid: A twist on the Bund freedom song "Now is the Time, Now is the Hour," this is Yiddish for "Now is the Time for each Jew."

While Priscilla was in New York, she and David exchanged several letters. On Christmas Day, David wrote to describe the occasion at Taliesin:

December 25, 1942

Dearest Pris

My 1st Christmas away from you . . .

Last Saturday we saw Woman of the Year—Good in spots—but disappointing. Both pretty much miscast. Xmas eve was a huge dinner based around the Architectural Forum Hams—boy were they delicious—cloved and spiced so well & served in generous helpings of goodly associates—hot mince & pumpkin pies. Ah wilderness be paradise enow. After supper I did dishes my usual luck & we retired to the living room for carols & etc. Curtis did a wonderful job on decorations. Well Iovanna opened her gifts a neat assorted 50 odd & Frank & Olgivanna & Kay opened some of theirs under the tree. Frank's attitude amusing but "John Anna" made me slightly nauseous. Then a most charming Russian film TANYA 3/4 of it was sheer delight the rest bogus patriotic crap. but enjoyable—or rather tolerable. Retired. No reindeer, no mice (since my trapping exploits) & what's more no Santa. Xmas breakfast most delicious pascha cheese & baba & Halvah & eggs & etc. Olgivanna got up on "linka zeit." [Yiddish for "left side of the bed."] Frank in wonderful spirits. Incidentally our guests are Bennie & Shirley Dombar. He was here for seven years & left last year for the defense plant & now he is a staff sergeant in the Army . . . The Xmas box well made by Davy & pretty good contributions some of which were excellent. He liked mine or seemed to "Well presented!" "It looks like you drew before," minor criticisms, of course, too but he amused me by starting off "By God David you're a sensualist! —A Dali of Architecture." At my request he will give specific criticisms & suggestions tomorrow & I intend to keep him well supplied with drawings . . .

Then dinner at 2:00. Delicious dry wine Turkey Duck & Goose cranberries stuffing & fruit pudding soaked in brandy & ignited (gorgeous sight) served with hard sauce, wine sauce or both. בוי, איך האב געפרעסן. [Boy, ikh hob gefressen, Yiddish for "I gorged myself."]

After a dinner chatter in which I held forth on everything—I was in form—we went to the studio where FLW had lain out a series of prints as his gifts to us. We chose in order of seniority & since many weren't here I had wide latitude in choice after choosing one that I thought you would like Kenn & Curtis suggested one that you'd prefer to my choice. After weighing and reweighing—dammit they were right. So now you and I each own one genuine Hiroshige I print. —both going together & would make a beautiful spot in that oriental corner you are planning in our home of homes in that coop venture of the Whites, Saias, Judy & spouse, of course, &

ourselves & all other men of good will. We are now going down to tea after which we will see some more Russian shorts & then to bed. I hope the cheese & butter came in good condition—I sent them Friday afternoon & he promised them Sunday or at latest Monday morning delivery.

Till my "Post Tea comments" I'll discourse on other matters. Your cards were most charming—especially your little comments. Svet, Curtis, Ken & Ten Brinks seemed charmed or amused. I don't know the Wright reaction yet...

As for the Marcus case do not worry. It is beyond repair The only salvage is that after his imprisonment the WRL will work for his parole to a CPS camp. Otherwise he with his ערבער יונגערס [grober yungers, Yiddish for "country," "naïve"] ways is making my life "miserable." When the Judge said "Get off that Wright Plantation & go home & then come back to me Jan 10th. And it's the Army non-combatant or jail." Marcus said or grunted "uh-huh." Since then he feels that the grunt was in the same category as a vow by the brow of the Thou most Holy. He won't put his foot on an inch of Taliesin soil. Won't even write to the Judge & tell him that he has tried separation but that it makes no difference in his opinions. It's no use I don't think it is worth my constant fighting to help these people here. They recognize my ideas & energy—witness Marcus newspaper statement & the Fellowship's radio broadcast (by Evjue) statement—both written by me & FLW sending Marcus to me with the words "See David, he has definite IDEAS . . ."

Tempis Fugit a couple of hours

Well tea at 6:30 was in the living room, fruit cakes nuts goodies galore and I might say ad nauseum. We were so full from dinner that we dispensed with supper. Frank read some jokes from a gift book he received killed himself laughing at each joke so that we couldn't hear them at all. I managed to piece a few together as samples show.

Father: When George Washington was your age, he was working as a surveyor and was making a success of himself.

Son: When he was your age he was President of the United States.

Grandmother to granddaughter: Dear I want you to promise me never to use a certain two words—one is swell and the other lousy.

Grandaughter: Why, of course, I'll promise. What are the words?

And so it went. I told a few. We sang carols then to the movie. The shorts were Russian ballet & folk dances some of which we have seen at the Ballet Festival & since we all liked it so much TANYA again some darn good singable songs. Well now at 12:30 that I've finished explaining the Fourth Dimensions & Einstein to Ken I'll go to bed. My love to my little radiator

From

David

SATURDAY, DEC. 26

Supper with Burt & Nat at Sea Fare in Greenwich Village. Visited George Brewster, adding Judy to the party. Old New Yorkers, music, wonderful food.

SUNDAY, DEC. 27

Visited E.E.B. Absolute lack of understanding of what we're doing, but Mr. Gellert misses me.

Visited Henkens. Wisconsin cheese arrived.

Visit by Rubins & Joe on furlough.

Visited Salzmans with Julia—3 smug teachers & me at my repartee-ist, for retaliation.

MONDAY, DEC. 28

Said good-bye to Abie Greenberg—leaving for army Saturday.

Gave Elsie her record; book to Steinleins; train reservation for Sunday's Pacemaker. Fare up to $40.32. Had a hard job convincing the ticket agent that Spring Green existed.

TUESDAY, DEC. 29

Bought a new evening gown.

Cocktails & dinner at Miss Bonawit's. Beautiful service; intelligent, lively conversation, but vague on her stand on the war. Showed her correspondence with William Rose Benét & Edwin Arlington Robinson.

WEDNESDAY, DEC. 30

Tea with Eleanor at Peg Woffington's. Met Nat, Judy, Luba—Supper altogether at the Eat Shoppe. Eleanor seemed to charm & impress everyone.

Clever, optimistic comedy in the evening—Thornton Wilder's "Skin of Our Teeth" starring Tallulah Bankhead, Frederick March, and Florence Eldridge. Nat & Henkens & Blanche there, too.

Sweet letter from Marcus.

The Emmanu-El Brotherhood (**E.E.B.**), a Jewish social settlement agency in New York City, was very important to the Jussim family. Priscilla's mother had joined it as a child and eventually served as secretary on the board of directors. Priscilla and each of her sisters taught Sunday school there.

Both **William Rose Benét** (1886–1950) and **Edwin Arlington Robinson** (1869–1935) were important American poets.

Skin of Our Teeth had just opened on Broadway in November.

THURSDAY, DEC. 31

Day and evening with Burton—thoughtful & considerate beyond my expectations. Museum exhibit—talked more than we observed; twilight walk thru Central Park; dinner at Chinese restaurant; concert of Philharmonic plus new symphony of Roy Harris's based on American folk songs at Carnegie Hall; cocktails at his house. Happy New Year!

Clever & amusing letter from Kenn.

FRIDAY, JAN. 1

Seemed to infuriate the Saias by not going to their party. How little may we choose for ourselves without offending others. Violent opposition to my statement that I couldn't conceive that my absence or presence could make such a difference to them.

Supper at the Henkens.

Saw "Without Love," I withstanding not too well the calumny of the Saias & Whites. Katherine Hepburn acts like a poor caricature of herself; Elliot Nugent was lispy & occasionally dull; Audrey Christie vibrant. Dialogue poor, not even relieved by its attempt at "timeliness." Pursuit for 8 scenes trying to get each other into the bedroom—new angle being that they've been married for a year.

Midnight snack at the Eat Shoppe—met Salzmans.

SATURDAY, JAN. 2

Bank business; bought snow shoes.

Spent an hour and a half with Nat talking—his new philosophy being that it's not living to sit beside a girl & listen to music. Had to break appointment with Burton for concert to appease Nat. Then Burt & I ate at Kavkos, a Russian restaurant, saw a movie, walked, past midnight chocolate, and a good-bye kiss. He's unhappy & pessimistic—his last fling, perhaps?

SUNDAY, JAN. 3

Breakfast with Handlers—not only pleased but honored by this emissary. Second breakfast with Henkens & Whites. Orchids on train from Judy, Clarice, & Larry.

Roy Harris (1898–1979) was an American composer. His Symphony No. 4, *Folksong* Symphony, was particularly significant in the music world; it featured excerpts from traditional American songs, including "When Johnny Comes Marching Home" and "The Streets of Laredo," in a classical composition.

Daddy helpful in shipping off luggage & buying foodstuff.

Long, neck-aching ride to Chicago.

MONDAY, JAN. 4

Walk along the Chicago Lake Front—trees thickly top-crusted with ice, & gleaming in the sun. Visited Chicago Art Institute—Seurat, Picasso, Renoir, Monet, Degas, Soutine, Toulouse Lautrec all well represented. Good exhibit of backgrounds of Dutch painting.

Visited Orloves—slept well.

Train to Spring Green, looking as if it will never start, & certainly never arrive. But it did—almost two hours late, with David, Kenn, Marcus, and Curtis all waiting at the station for "our sweetheart."

TUESDAY, JAN. 5

Began cooking for the supper meal: tomato aspic, buttered beets, deviled eggs; Bavarian cream. I seemed to talk endlessly—so much to tell.

WEDNESDAY, JAN. 6

Lunch: Roast pork, roast potatoes, rutabagas and apple sauce, watermelon pickles. Chicken timbale for Mrs. Wright.

Supper: Southern corn pudding, stewed tomatoes, cheese blintzes; Vienna tarts.

Saw the Magnificent Ambersons in Spring Green—accompanied by Jack, Johnnie, Curtis, Kenn, Marcus. Went to Marcus' home afterwards—popped corn. His sentence postponed indefinitely. (Possible time off to try Mr. Wr. for sedition?) Marcus' attitude stubborn, I fear, almost as much as conscientious. Full of rationalizations for his stay-at-home.

THURSDAY, JAN. 7

Lunch: Sauerbraten, baked potatoes, carrots, crabapples. Swiss steak for Mrs. Wr. Baked bread.

Supper was Kay's party—for which she used chicken I had prepared for the Fellowship and Ruth did all the dishes. David pulled the bad cold act again because he didn't want to appear (an act earlier tried at his Bar Mitzvah—probably had conceived it but wasn't ready to work on it by his Bris). I had lots of explanations to make to everyone, including the Wrights—but I carried it off with good grace, possibly because I have learned to lie without blushing.

Kenn came in after for a short talk and some drinks.

FRIDAY, JAN. 8

David & Kenn hauled logs. They also visited Marcus who will probably return soon, until the indefiniteness of his postponement is defined.

Lunch—Bitki; brown rice; baked squash; sweet pickles. Wrights—hamburgers, pea timbales, crabapples.

Supper—cheese soufflé; frozen vegetable & chicken salad; crabapples; tomato rice soup; sour cream cake with chocolate icing. Wrights—roast chicken; mashed potatoes; string beans; peaches.

Kay told me that the squash & bitki were both raw—"it's a pity you had to have two things uncooked in a single meal." She makes me think of words no nice girl ought to know.

Curtis, Kenn, Johnnie came in for a little salami, liquor, date, nut & fig, & chatter party in our room.

SATURDAY, JANUARY 9

Cooking is still composed of so many little events and no big event. Lunch: spareribs and sauerkraut (excellent!), boiled potatoes. Wrights—peas, egg soufflé, potatoes, peaches. Supper—roast beef, gravy, delicious pickles (their trade name not a commentary), mashed potatoes; wax beans, strawberry mousse. Mrs. Wr., who has decided that none of the meat we can offer her is any good (after we have about 6 animals killed), asked for 2 soft boiled eggs.

The movie directed, produced, & written by Sergei Eisenstein—Alexander Nevsky—was excellent. The photography was beautiful—suitable for framed stills, and the theme almost an abstraction. Music by Prokofiev was throbbing.

SUNDAY, JAN. 10

Evjue spoke about appointed judges, Wright, Marcus, & the Fellowship on the radio. We keep on phoning Marcus but can't get in touch with him. Is it possible that his parents try to prevent communication with us?

Lunch for Wrights had to be completely recooked and re-prepared because they decided to eat an hour and a half later. Fortunately, it was a vegetable platter: baked potatoes, stewed tomatoes, fresh peas & beans.

Supper—roast chicken (and a quail that bashed its head flying against a window for Mr. Wr. The lady wouldn't eat it because it had committed suicide), gravy, dressing, cranberries, whipped potatoes, carrots, pickles, hot mince meat pie, coffee. Mrs. Wr. said it was a very good dinner, but she hoped my cooking till Tuesday wouldn't throw everyone off schedule. The things she worries about!

Concert good—duets (Brahms) —Johnny & Curtis; trio & quartet—ditto, Svet, Ruth.

Marcus' trial postponed from 12th to 14th. Shall I see him again?

Lunch—pork chops; potatoes on half shell whipped with giblet gravy, creamed carrots au gratin; pickles. Mrs. Wr.—grilled livers, peas.

Supper—scalloped tomatoes, corn soufflé, cottage cheese, chocolate pudding, kisses. Add chicken soup for Wrights.

Rendered lard today, too.

Hans told us that the famous Smolensk Institute which Mrs. Wr. always boasts of almost entering, is nothing more than a glorified finishing school for mistresses of the nobility—and that the Jugoslavian nobility she boasts of, were nothing more than bandit "princes."

Howard was excellent kitchen help last week; Jack in one morning already accused me of being sullen. Are other people mirrors in which we see ourselves reflected?

Curtis and Kenn came in for an informal nosh & chat.

TUESDAY, JAN. 12

Lunch only and my cooking week was over. Roast kid, boiled potatoes in jackets, rutabagas mashed with applesauce, pickled red cabbage.

After a well-deserved scolding last night by Mr. Wr. directed at all the boys for not working more in the studio, a studio hour of from 3-4, before tea, has been added, going into operation today. A good thing, too.

Iovanna has decided that the car must call for her at 2:20 so that she can cut English—the teacher's moronic. (Actually the little dear seems to be having trouble with composition.) Yesterday Mrs. Wr. called across the tea table, "Iovanna, are there any intelligent children in school besides you?" "No, mother." Daddy, "Well, I don't know about the village children, but it seems to me the farm children should have some intelligence." "But they don't, Daddy." Now that I've finished Thurber's delightful "My World—and Welcome to It," it occurs to me how perfectly she could niche herself into one of his cartoons, perhaps the one captioned "She says she's burning with a hard, gem-like flame."

Phoned Marcus who received our "American Songbag." His cheerful optimism is one of the saddest things I've met. Completed T. S. Eliot's Collected Poems.

Humorist **James Thurber** (1894-1961) was best known for his short stories and cartoons in the *New Yorker*. Published in 1942, *My World and Welcome to It* contained a collection of these works. The cartoon Priscilla refers to here appeared in the magazine on June 18, 1938. A teenager sits upright and still in a chair, while her mother remarks to a friend, "She says she's burning with a hard, gemlike flame. It's something they learn in school, I think."

WEDNESDAY, JAN. 13

This same optimism—half-hearted this time, is reflected in Marcus' letter to us, half thank you, half farewell. We're all making arrangements to go to the trial tomorrow. Jack made some insinuating remarks to me about why go to the trial since it doesn't matter to me.

Salzmans sent the fluorescents. More puttering around for David.

Studying under David's tutelage the principles of mechanical drawing. There's such a big mind block to overcome first. Did a little more tracing on the Leigh Stevens house. Beginning the penciled tracing of the Arch Oboler guest house.

Mr. Wright very solemnly asked us after supper to go to the trial but to say nothing to anyone. There would be reporters around eager to point out the boys to the FBI. He likewise said the judge might be lenient with Marcus, but that he had his own dignity and authority to maintain at no matter what cost. Marcus will be the cost. The rest of the boys will be personally introduced to the judge to prove that he had mis judged them. Probably won't be at all convinced.

Read Amy Lowell's "A Dome of Many Coloured Glass." Keats certainly was her beau idéal. So many of her lighter poems remind one of "I stood tiptoe on a little hill."

Kenn, Ruth, and Howard came in to visit us.

JANUARY 14, 1943

Marcus was sentenced to 3 years in a federal penitentiary today. That's all that matters, no matter what else I write. And the writing of this would be a tale of endless blunders, all adding up to the fate of a sensitive boy who wept while he fought.

Blunders! From the very first Marcus should have pleaded C.O., instead of taking Mr. Wright's advice that he hope for deferment on physical grounds—the same advice he gave to Curtis only a few weeks ago, and similar to that given Howard to declare himself necessary as a farm laborer. Then, none of the boys knew about form 47 till rather late to be demonstrative of one's conscience. Anna May Davies, a lawyer, a Socialist, secretary of the FOR was edged out of the case because a woman did not figure in this man's world. And in her place was Holmes—arrogant, pompous, well-fed, absolutely unconvinced about anyone's conscience, especially Marcus's, angry at him because he had not asked him for advice (why didn't he guard the man it was his duty to protect?), eager to get back to his business which meant more money. He never advised Marcus he was on trial his two previous times, nor that today was a continuation of the trial. All anyone knew was that it was just a sentencing. The D.A., prosecuting attorney was more effective in

Marcus' behalf than the defense attorney who was obviously collaborating with the judge and pushing affairs quickly. Incidentally, the judge read the sentence from a prepared document—the only hopeful factor being the reduction to 3 years from the usual 5, due partly, no doubt, to public pressure. Marcus made one excellent suggestion to Judge Stone (at Curtis's instigation) namely that the FBI complete investigation of Wright & then see whether he was influenced or not—and then determine whether it is fair to be prosecuting Mr. Wr. with Marcus as scapegoat. The manifesto was brought up, too. Marcus refused to give the authors (he should have been counseled about this), but said the ideas had been discussed at work and at table, and therefore were generally acceptable. Signing was voluntary.

Mr. Wr. said Marcus had done the boys a favor by forcing them to fight. Jack had a squeamish backing out look; Davy & Wes are not opposed to war, just this war; Johnny's probably soft; Curtis & David will probably remain adamant. After Mr. Wr.'s talk at tea about never belonging to a movement or following a party, Curtis remarked to me, "I think FLW will come out of this all right, but what will happen to us?" I thought FLW would probably preserve his own integrity, inertia causes him to forget about making this a CPS camp (Internal Revenue Department already recognized this as an educational institution) —while Marcus is in prison.

Stone said the manifesto smacked of seditious character; grimly amusing to hear his confession that "this case concerned me more than most."

The beautiful Japanese vistas of dawn—blue, yellow, pink in layers—was ineffective to prevent my tightened knuckles. Marcus, when we arrived, clutched my hands tightly, and then got up & wept. He turned white when sentence was pronounced. Howard, Ruth, & I ran after him for a block while the marshal escorted him to the county jail. We tried to give him some words of encouragement—but he didn't dare turn round—probably afraid of giving vent to his emotions.

Rev. "Shorty" Collins, Baptist minister, was there with words of encouragement for all the boys—and probably definite help thru the FOR, in spite of the fact that Stone hoped this sentence would not only be punishment in itself but a deterrent to the other boys. Marcus can be freed at any time he wants to join the army.

Rev. George "Shorty" Collins (1892–1991) was a campus minister at the University of Wisconsin, known in particular for his work with peace groups and conscientious objectors. Collins later moved to San José State, where he helped found the San José Peace Center. He was influential in the civil rights movement in the 1960s and continued to work with conscientious objectors during the war in Vietnam.

In the meantime, David wrote to the WRL. FLW wired Llewellyn for a good lawyer—David suggested Roger Baldwin or Arthur Garfield Hayes, a friend of Mr. Wright's.

Curtis came in, letting down his hair, and showing all his communications with the Selective Service Board. He's intelligent and quick-witted—good company.

David fought madly at tea time against all the inertia. Here's praying he wasn't batting his head against a stone wall.

Clouds rolling over ice-gleaming hills on the way home, more poignant reminders of Marcus in jail. To come a thousand miles to shed real tears for someone I've known only three months. They quickened when FLW referred to him as "this carpenter's son who has made the way easier for all of you boys. You ought to be grateful to him—if a man has only one life to live, he could live it in no better way."

Received a letter from Sylvia S. today, writing of 7 glorious months with her husband—why hadn't they met earlier?—and his going off to war Jan. 8. She closes with the only enduring wish for any of us—Victory & Peace. So we fight on all fronts.

All the evidence Judge Stone gave of his personal interest in the case was his teetering back & forth on his chair, and his eyes flashing. Otherwise a self composed business man.

Marcus didn't want his parents there—"why should I hurt them of all people? I've hurt them enough already." The D.A. described him as sensitive, reliable, cooperative, religious, with no un-American sympathies.

Kenn helped David & me do the dishes, & then came in to chat.

FRIDAY, JAN. 15
Davy and Jack have been re-classified as 1A. Went to the Dodgeville Board to consult their files—at David's suggestion.

Typed David's Form 47 clearly. Read. Had 2 hour conversation with Mrs. Wright today—all based on fact that toes of Kay's authoritative ego had been stepped on because Ruth & I consulted Kenn more than her. Ironing out, plus incidental discussion of my religion, why she thinks I'm wasting my time teaching (I can't think of you as a teacher—I always have such a low opinion of them), of the Gurdjieff Institute, of how she met Mr. Wright, of Kay's efficiency, of Eleanor's weak will and a fault so bad "I can't tell it to you," etc., etc., etc. She told Ruth to read more to keep her husband.

Roger Nash Baldwin (1884–1981) was a founder of the American Civil Liberties Union (ACLU) and its longtime executive director. A pacifist, he had been jailed as a conscientious objector during World War I. **Arthur Garfield Hays** (1881–1954), was a prominent lawyer in New York City and general counsel for the ACLU.

FLW's son Llewelyn is sending Scher, a lawyer, to appeal Marcus's case. Llewelyn is assistant to Thurman Arnold, solicitor-general of the U.S. Weston parents phoned today to find out what had happened—nobody had notified them. 3 column spread in the paper. FLW irritable & touchy—husband & wife flying off the handle at each other, & Iovanna suggesting non-combatant service, being nurses, & binding up the wounds of suffering humanity.

Social visits from Hans, Kenn, Ruth, and Howard. Even Davy came in for five minutes.

Mrs. Wr. prides herself so on her influence in the lives of young people.

SAT. JAN. 16

Read. Cleaned. Recordered. Worked on plans of Oboler stable and cottage. Helped sort eggs to ship to the folks. I certainly wish David would try some plans of his own on anything. He's busy going thru Architectural Forums now—useful, but they should employ not his best but his petered energies. Wrote to Nat, George Brody, & Saias.

Wes saw Marcus thru heavy glass & mesh doors—he was quite cheerful because he was in the same cell block with several other C.O.'s. Bob Scher, the lawyer, came in today. He's a corporation lawyer who may be technically good but won't be able to fight this on idealistic grounds because he himself is for the war. So what's the good?

Movie's—Artkino—Wings of Victory—cinematic story of flight of 3 Soviet fliers in 1938 to San Francisco.

Played our records to Kenn, Johnny, & Curtis up in Kenn's room.

SUN. JAN. 17

Breakfast discussion till 1 P.M. with Scher questioning each of the boys individually. Evjue spoke of the Weston case & the double standard of ethics which permitted big business to get away with murder, & Marcus wasn't even granted a conscience. Spoke of him as "sensitive, reliable, modest, self-effacing." This may be the making of Marcus—he may find himself now; overcome his unworldly innocence.

Walked down to the bridge—nearly frozen before we returned. Curtis & Kenn came in to nosh & chat.

Talked all Sunday night instead of concert. FLW's confidence in the lawyer was encouraging. The name Marcus Weston I have heard so much recently, seen so

---

Thurman Arnold (1891–1969) was a lawyer and, from 1938 to 1943, served as assistant U.S. Attorney General at the Department of Justice. Arnold was later a judge in the D.C. court of appeals and cofounder of the law firm Arnold & Porter LLP.

MARCUS WESTON, 1943.

often in print, that it has gained an entity of its own and divorced itself from him—the way words lose their meaning that have been repeated too often. I almost expect to hear of him giving testimonials for commercial products. That Marcus Weston who has become a national figure can hardly be, it seems to me, the same who ran laughingly down cold corridors, played a hushed guitar, danced folk dances, rumbled uphill in a tractor, and chatted with us for long delightful hours. I have to keep braiding together the threads of memory to revive these images of him. And Evjue speaking of him as an idealist with a misdirected idealism, pushed him still farther away. We all feel that this will be a vital factor in his growth—and that he will find himself. My only regret is that in finding himself, we will be lost to him—or at least temporarily shelved.

Wes is hot-headed and short-sighted. He was born several hundred years too late—should have been a feudal lord with an empire of his own, or a knight riding a white charger—under no one's domain.

MON. JANUARY 18

Wrote to Marcus. David got lots of cards out for affidavits as to his conscience. Continued tracings of Oboler Gate House and Cottage. Read Erskines, "Solomon, My Soul"—Interesting interpretation of the Biblical story, especially Solomon's lack of prowess with women, and Bathsheba's murderous tendencies.

All of us seem deeply beset with a feeling of uselessness & frustration. Perhaps the cold makes you tremble so, you have no desire to do anything else.

Curtis was given a 4E presidential classification. His spirits were dampened, however, by the fact that he needs another eye operation. Kenn has the restless blues. Scher has decided the best thing to work on in Marcus' case is executive clemency.

Worked on some more orthographical projection. Cheered me with my recorder. Served & washed dishes.

TUESDAY, JANUARY 19

Snow crystals gleam like fireflies. The drifts are so deep your tracks are obliterated by the time you've walked ten feet further on.

Burton has been re-classified 1A. My cup floweth over.

After running around asking for permission, waiting for Wes & FLW to return

---

Orthographical projection is an architectural and mechanical drawing term for drawing three-dimensional objects in two dimensions.

with the money, waiting for Davy to write a letter to Hershey to be reviewed by the lawyer, waiting for Mrs. Wr. to write a note, we finally started off to visit Marcus— and immediately got stuck in a snow drift at the entrance and had to be pulled out with the tractor.

U.S. Marshal Comfort gave us permission to visit Marcus in jail—visiting booth blocked by wood, glass, and bars. It was the most frustrating thing to see part of his face—if you stood on tiptoe you could see all of him, and not be able to touch him, to have to speak thru a grill. What <u>torture</u> it would be if the people were married or in love! A visit from his father in the morning was very disconcerting because he was seen in position of a jailbird. He thinks of himself as a martyr—he should be convinced he's a pioneer. He places no hopes in the lawyer, and expects at best to be paroled for good behavior—three years is a long time. We tried to comfort him on that score. His roommate is Laurenson, an intellectual objector to the war, who, Marcus says, has him as completely analyzed as I had, and is trying to straighten him out. Marcus is a real objector, but vaguely, because he knows there's something wrong with war, but can't place his finger on it. I told him the same, he feels, when I asked him to write and clarify his thoughts. He said his pessimism resulted because he was facing reality; I asked him to think of Taliesin and me too as reality.—"But you belong to someone else." Wareham, exponent of Gesell's philosophy, heard his name mentioned as one of the current names in the field of economics discussed here, at Marcus' trial. He thought we take courses in it here, and visited Marcus to discuss Gesell with him. He's trying to persuade him to take 1A-O service so that he can propagandize the army; he'd be useless in jail. I can see the return army marching across America, with a New Economic Order in their minds, and Marcus their prophet. Howard gave him a few words of cheer on FLW's confidence in the lawyer, and plans for making Taliesin "work of national importance." He reads a lot, talks with Laurenson, plays cribbage, walks a mile for exercise (around the cell block 48 times, tho there's a party that contends only 42 times are necessary). Pallid in his drab prison-gray coveralls, but wearing a nicely laundered shirt and his own tie underneath. He explained he's trying to forget Taliesin (perhaps because remembrance is pain?)

Freezing ride home in marvelous winter sunset, the whole landscape blue white with snow, trees and shrubs etched against it.

Lewis Blaine Hershey (1893–1977) was director of the U.S. Selective Service System from 1942 to 1970.

Gesell's philosophy Silvio Gesell (1862–1930) was a German-born economic theorist and author of The *Natural Economic Order.* With a strong belief in the motivation of self-interest and a reliance on personal abilities, he was both anti-Marxist and anti-establishment.

Davy has decided David is a phoney C.O. because he knows all the answers. Davy, I figure, is probably phoney, because he knows none.

Curtis came in to chat with me, and later Kenn with both of us.

Did I forget to mention Marcus' delight in seeing Howard and me?

We haven't quite decided whether Taliesin is boycotting Royal Blue because the storekeeper told the FBI Marcus was so influenced here that he no longer associated with the townspeople, or because we have run up a high debt. All the ramifications of this episode would make an interesting chapter in a pirated sub rosa biography of Wright.

Amusing the way the Capital Times wrote up our running after Marcus, & his not turning around. "Taken in charge by a federal marshal, he asked as he was going down the steps of the building whether he could go back and say goodbye to his Taliesin friends, but the marshal said this would not be permitted. Several members of the fellowship, however, ran after him down the street & walked with him to the Dane county jail."

Marcus is suffering a good deal thinking of all the things he might have said— what is for most of us the life-long frustration of remembering the brilliant repartee one might have used after the party is over.

WEDNESDAY, JAN. 20

Letters from George & Mom; letter to whole fellowship from Marcus.

Played recorder; more orthographic projection & tracing. Read D. H. Lawrence's "Pornography & Obscenity" & "The Virgin & the Gypsy," both fully illustrative of his thesis. Room visits—Curtis & Kenn.

Long talk at tea with Mrs. Wr. in re the Czarist regime, the Russian Revolution, political prisoners, her following Gurdjieff, her teacher, from the Russian dramatic Art School to Constantinople, Berlin, and Paris.

THURSDAY, JANUARY 21

Letters from Anne Williams, Judy, & Paige still backing out of payments. Typed vehement letters practically all day on this score for David.

Recorder-ed. Finished Lewis Mumford's Technics & Civilization—amazing analysis of the effect of machines on civilization—fresh approach—a book I'd like to own.

Tracing still on Oboler house—my line is truer, but I'm still hasty & careless.

Richard E. Paige was David's employer at the Display Finishing Co. and at Richard E. Paige, Inc. in New York City.

Long evening visit by Hans. Told us how impressed he was by Sandburg and how the boys actually lacked the spirit & enthusiasm to enjoy him. His money is saved, not for sham man-of-the-people posing, as Wes insinuates, but to provide for an epileptic son who couldn't otherwise provide for himself. Hans was introduced as a German. Carl asked, "A German from the Germany that is?" Hans answered, "No, a German from the Germany that will be." And they embraced in true European style.

Am I lacking the direction I accused Marcus of lacking? Or am I in that period of hiatus when I can't concentrate because I don't know what direction fate will take for the lives of those I love? What of David's re-classification? Burton's 1A? Marcus's jail sentence? Where is Julia headed? And I?

FRIDAY, JANUARY 22

Continued tracing, but was interrupted by Davy's angry outburst—"If you hadn't been so g— d— inconsiderate & selfish, I could have seen Marcus Tuesday, and wouldn't have to go today." —All because David wanted to go so badly that he even asked Kay to sit on his lap to make room for one more. I can still scarcely recover from the nastiness & insinuation—"you didn't even apologize. All you could talk about was Marcus & you." I couldn't even answer with justification of lack of time, that he could walk as well as we could, and that he really went to see his lawyer about his letter—Marcus was a second thought.

Well, the boys went down and were disappointed—Marcus was taken to a reformatory or corrective school, at Sandstone, Minnesota. Farming work, & no walls.

Walked for an hour and a half in this wonderful deeply piled, thin-crusted snow— 45° above—sun gleaming—it was rejuvenation.

Read Wright's Disappearing City—a "social, economic, & esthetic analysis"— also plans for Broadacre City. Also his "Experimenting with Human Lives"— seismography and architecture & skyscrapers.

It was Davy who suggested to FLW what the consensus of opinion was about Marcus's friends—and gathering from Mrs. Wr.'s looks, some lewd insinuations about me. So the storm clouds gather. Curtis & Kenn are furious. David's letter of explanation to Marcus why we may never write to him again is sufficient unto itself & unto me.

Puny people can never understand a whole friendship. I hope never to "measure out my life with coffee spoons." There should be more generous giving of self in true

---

Sandburg's eldest daughter, Margaret, had **epilepsy**, for which there was then no seizure-stopping medication.

coffee spoons: from T. S. Eliot's "The Love Song of J. Alfred Prufrock."

ICICLES HANGING OFF THE ROOF OF TALIESIN, winter 1942–43.

FOREGROUND: FRANK LLOYD WRIGHT AND DAVID HENKEN. BACKGROUND: KENN LOCKHART, CURTIS BESINGER, TED BOWER, undated (1942–43).

friendship—perhaps my Waterloo—certainly my joy.

Curtis, Kenn, & Johnny came in to visit. It's always a joy to have them.

SATURDAY, JANUARY 23

Yesterday's upset left me with such a splitting headache that I slept right thru breakfast today.

Continued tracing Oboler House for about 4 1/2 hours—the concentration was pleasant. Work always is.

Supper table talk about Sherwood Anderson's Memoirs, which FLW said "smelled of whiskey, sweat, and underwear." Told of his experiences with the "darkies," their recognition of him, desire to shake hands with him, describing him as one of those "face-cards," but a smiling one. Described meeting Gertrude Stein in Madison on lecture tour—they were invited to her hotel room—she said Wright was familiar to her but she couldn't tell why. Alice B. Toklas sat behind her like a kind of guardian angel, and when they invited her to the Fellowship, she hesitated, & said, "But we like to fly. We want to fly to Milwaukee." And they nudged and pinched each other, and Alice said, "yes, we like to fly."

Picture was Artkino's "General Suvorov," famous before & during Napoleonic campaigns. Much too long drawn out in spite of some bits of good acting. Kenn came in to talk after the movie.

SUNDAY, JANUARY 24

Dull, misty, drizzly day, yet warm.

Long talk with David aided & abetted by Kenn about why David came here, his rôle in the Fellowship, the extent to which he must cooperate, & the extent to which he can let things go hang. A pleasant, refreshing walk couldn't stave off further revelations of extraversion & introversion & our effect on other people. David can't seem to calculate it—viz. Davy's considering him a phoney C.O. because he talks too glibly; or Howard's telling him that several of the boys, including Wes, were equally angry at him & Davy for starting that row about seeing Marcus on Friday, because each considered Marcus's friendship his own especial property. David's also gone on a new crusading campaign (God spare me when I wind up in the Fiji Islands)—so I typed a letter written by him to Franz Werfel inquiring into the why and wherefore of his conversion to Catholicism.

Franz Werfel (1890–1945) was an Austrian Jew who escaped the Nazis and was inspired by the Catholic shrine at Lourdes in France. His novel *The Song of* *Bernadette* described, among other things, the healing power of the water at the famous grotto.

Concert good tonight. But it would be interesting to know why Jack sat out the singing of Do ye ken John Peel, with his hands over his ears. Freud could give an interesting explanation. Or perhaps Jack could give a better.

My heart turns somersaults every time Davy or Kay come near me. Their insinuations & self-righteous anger make me want to run away, as if I wouldn't have to take me with me.

The plucking of the violin strings in the Beethoven trio pounded in my solar plexus.

FLW read from some Chinese philosophers tonight—Kung Fu Tse (Confucius), Cheng Sui and Laotse, the great Chinese spiritual leader, equivalent of Jesus.

Have to do the Oboler house again. My plans are correct according to the working drawings, but Oboler made his own changes, & the boys are trying to remember them. So every time they remember, there I go with a new tracing. Curses!

MONDAY, JANUARY 25
Well, nothing ever happens here! So they make things happen. The Wrights had a heart-to-heart talk with Kenn. Summary: Kenn influences Ruth & me against Kay; Kenn influences David & me against Kay & Davy; Kenn is "toadying" to me for naughty, naughty reasons; we couldn't be too friendly with Marcus because we've known him so short a time. So it must be sex! Curtis suggests I go to Madison once a week, bite my nails, & send wild telegrams to Marcus begging him to give the child a name. It would be ludicrous if we weren't so subjectively involved in the whole affair.

More tracing, reading, recorder-ing. Helped David with tea & brownies. He was busy most of the day chopping ice off the steps.

Curtis is going in for his eye operation Thursday—will last 10 days.

Tea guests—Franz Aust, head of Department of [Landscape] Architecture in U. of Wisconsin—delightful personality. Mrs. Wr. wouldn't have liked her husband's teasing Aust to introduce him to a widow who owns 2000 acres of land in Mt. Vernon so that they can join their property, buying up all the land between here & there for Broadacre city. He twinkled at the suggestion. She farms her land with the help of C.O.'s—they therefore protect & support each other. When 6 boys, 14 to 16 years old, destroyed some of her trees by rolling a stone over them, she punished them by court order, by having each one plant a thousand white pine trees. Her name's McDonald.

Kenn came in to chat, altho he was accused of spending all his time with us; & Ruth & Hans. Incidental information: FLW told Kenn in this long afternoon's talk that David & I are both intelligent, even tho he had to put David in his place for talking out of turn at tea.

FLW badly upset by Woollcott's death, & wanted to go to his funeral, but it was held in the McMillin Theater of Columbia U. "I'm going to miss Alec," he said.

TUESDAY, JANUARY 26

Character affidavits from Paige, Bischof and Dave Wertman make me want to look up and say to David, "Are they talking about you?"

Life's quieter today after yesterday's scandal mongering. Finished Oboler house. Finished Dali's autobiography, "Secret Life of Salvador Dali," fetishes, libidos, ego, crutches, soft watches, telephones, sadism, masochism, surrealism, et al. Also kicked my ankle so hard, I can hardly walk—I, too, look Daliesque now—icebag filled with icicles tied around my ankle with a rope.

Helped David make spice cup cakes for tea. Cards from Judy, Julia, & Burt. Marcus' civilian clothes seem to have been sent home to his folks. Davy is making friendly overtures again—he approaches & recedes like the tides.

FLW at tea read from Sherwood Anderson's Memoirs. Said he's an interpretive, & not a creative artist. Added that "fame & shame come to the same thing in the end. Don't desire to be famous unless you like to suffer."

Mrs. Wr. always smiles as if her lip were split.

FLW comment on using any but planes in this war, "Using battleships and men conveyed by their own foot power is like taking your mother to battle and trying to protect her at the same time."

WEDNESDAY, JAN. 27

Swept studio & walks. Laundered. Prepared hors d'oeuvres for tea. Read Carter Dickson's "The White Priory Murders." Relaxing dawdling work. Fun hanging clothes on the line & watching them stiffen ad rigor mortis while lifting them out of the basket.

THURSDAY, JANUARY 28

Played recorder. Swept halls & studio. Sanded entrances. Helped David with tea. Laundered. Pressed. Mangled. Planned ménus.

FLW left for Chicago to lecture at the Art Institute.

Salary earned for income tax accounts received from all high schools.

The Davisons left for Sandstone to visit Marcus—a deep secret lest anyone should decide to accompany them. I hope they see him. Their personal triumph will make them forgive my "selfish" seeing him on Tuesday—I think. They were sent on a mission by the Wrights, probably all expenses paid.

FRIDAY, JAN. 29

Cleaned bathrooms & studio. Read Sergei Eisenstein's Film Sense—good explanation of synchronization of senses & his technique in "Alexander Nevsky." Wrote letters to Frances, Bonawit, & Sylvia Shlimowitz. Served & washed dishes. Mrs. Wr. complained about our indifference to whether the Davisons see Marcus or not. If I evince too much interest, I'm lascivious; if I react the way the others do, I'm indifferent. So what's a girl to do?

Gene annoys me—a professional smiler; an impenetrable glassy surface, the "perfect secretary."

SATURDAY, JAN. 30

Long walk to get the mail—gray, etched morning. Branches thickly crusted with snow. Our mail yielded a card from Burton disqualified for meteorology & hence subject to "private" duty; affidavits from Sam Verne & Abe Kaufman; our letter to Marcus returned because we're unauthorized correspondents. Jack & Davy received their induction papers. Davy & Kay were not allowed into Sandstone because Marcus is still in quarantine, & even if he weren't, only his parents could see him once a month by appointment.

Read Robinson's "Captain Craig."

Washed & waxed studio. Played recorder. Heavy, drugged sleep in the afternoon—am I losing my élan vital?

Picture was very poor and exaggerated—"The Frontier"—very Russian; very shouting for normal speaking.

SUNDAY, JAN. 31

Joan, Ted's sister, is a vacation guest. Henning & Gene are hovering. Mr. Wr. returned from his Chicago lecture, & Wes from his Milwaukee business.

Cooking was tiring as usual, especially since La Belle Dame decided on a beautiful tray sent down to her with complete change of ménu at 6:45. David, as my K.P., and I were nervous & irritable. Lunch—roast beef; baked potatoes, stewed tomatoes, green beans, jello. Supper—roast pork, mashed potatoes & gravy; mustard pickles; apple sauce; carrots, apple pie with top corn flake crumb crust (delicious!), coffee.

FLW spoke of his plan to ask Washington for $30,000 to work on Broadacre City for a year and a half, with 24 of his hand-picked men, even those who have to be pulled back from the army. I felt sorry for his optimism & our youthful pessimism & lack of enthusiasm, & I felt like crying out, "Old man, old man, you're much too young for us."

Everybody went sleigh riding pulled by horses, except me. I was Cook Cinderella—and very jealous.

MONDAY, FEB. 1

I'm tired. It seems I never left the kitchen, especially with her deciding on special meals for <u>her</u> "illness." At lunch she didn't want chicken timbale, but canned baby food; after lunch she complained she hadn't been getting enough chicken lately, tho I roasted one for her yesterday which she was too cranky to eat; so I roasted a chicken for this evening. After it had been going for two and a half hours, she decided she wanted baked pike. A woman can smile and smile, and be a villain still.

Lunch: chicken à la king with dry wine; biscuits, baked potatoes, kohlrabi, mustard pickles. Supper—cheese soufflé, green beans, frozen vegetable salad, boiled dressing, steamed ginger pudding. Wrights—Chinese cabbage, baked pike, rice gruel, green beans, farina pudding.

Everyone has gone off to see "Now, Voyager."

FLW spoke of his Broadacre plans again at tea. A man's reach should exceed his grasp, or what's a heaven for?

David has been reclassified into 3B, which would mean no worries for a few months for me, except that my darling is pushing straightforward to a head-on collision. He wrote them asking why he isn't 4E. Am I so damned unattractive?

Charming letter from Julia; day's yield—Paige, Joel, Judy, Newtown, storage company, draft board. The compass of our life. . .

Chat in the room with Kenn.

TUESDAY, FEBRUARY 2

FBI man came around to investigate Wright on Stone's accusation. Davy made several incriminating statements because no one thought of asking why they had come. Davy then went to Dodgeville—out of the kitchen 9 hours!

Lunch—sauerbraten, mashed potatoes, gravy, watermelon pickles, pickled beets. Wrights—roast chicken, beets, potatoes, chicken soup, baby food desserts. Supper—tomatoes stewed with bread and onions, onion soup with croutons and grated cheese, salad of grated carrots, apples & raisins with boiled dressing, baked potatoes, sour cream cake with chocolate icing. Wrights—baked potatoes, salad, tomatoes, carrots, mushrooms, celery, chinese cabbage, jello, apples baked with honey.

David's moved our double bed into Marcus' room, & his bed into ours as a couch.

---

smile and smile: from Shakespeare's *Hamlet*.

He drafted all day—plans for Ausgefuhrte Bauten.

Is Joan Bower making a play for Johnny after Gene and Henning have been on her trail?

Kenn came in to chat in the evening.

WEDNESDAY, FEBRUARY 3

Lunch:—pork steaks, Brabant potatoes, raisin carrot apple salad, rutabagas and apple sauce. Mrs. Wr. commandeered roast chicken & jello at 10:30! And she got them.

Supper:—potato salad with Taliesin dressing, corn, cottage cheese, cauliflower timbales, frozen coffee pudding. I also baked nine loaves of Scotch oatmeal bread and 2 of corn bread.

Saw slides of Taliesin & Taliesin West in the evening.

Letters from Muriel, Judeth, Dr. Melamed, and George Schottenfeld, and strudel from Mom.

Davy and Jack were notified by Scher that his appeal to the Selective Service commission was unsuccessful.

When I went down to Mrs. Wright to ask her about her meal, she sidetracked via an article by Ben Hecht in Readers Digest to the "Jewish problem." "Why don't the Jews get a great military leader who is also an idealist & fight for a land of their own! They could conquer any country they wanted to." When I suggested Herzl & Zionism and Arab Jewish unions & the opposition by feudal lords instigated by England, she ranted, "There you go again like all Jews, only intellectualizing. You have no creative urge & no initiative. Your only initiative takes the bad form of aggressiveness. I told a Jewish friend of mine that the only reason she's creative is that she's part gentile." Etc. Etc. Etc. She has the floor—it's her show—and she only returns arguments by discussing personalities. I gather up my dislikes like a gathering storm.

Wes saw the Westons—they're very bitter and hate everyone & everything connected with the Fellowship.

Often called the *Wasmuth Portfolio*, after its publisher, ***Ausgeführte Bauten und Entwürfe von Frank Lloyd Wright*** (Executed Buildings and Designs by Frank Lloyd Wright) was the first major compilation of Wright's work. Published in Germany in 1910, it documented his projects from 1893 to 1909 and introduced Europeans to Wright's uniquely American architecture. A modified version, *Frank Lloyd Wright: Ausgeführte Bauten*, was later published for the American market.

Hollywood screenwriter **Ben Hecht** (1894–1964) published an article, "Remember Us," in both *American Mercury* and, in condensed form, in *Reader's Digest* in February 1943. The piece is credited with alerting Americans to the massacre of European Jews in Nazi concentration camps.

Theodor Herzl (1860–1904)—for whom David Theodore Herzl Henken was named—was a Zionist leader who helped set the stage for the establishment of a Jewish state in Palestine. In 1942, Palestine was under British rule; the mandate expired in 1948 and Israel declared independence.

David saw Mr. Weston in Spring Green—couldn't include any of our note to Marcus except our wishes for his birthday because he can only discuss members of the immediate family.

Lunch:—New England beef stew with carrots & onions; whipped baked potatoes, watermelon pickles. Wrights—chicken stew, jello. They ate none of the chicken altho it was "delicious" & asked that it be put away for tomorrow. Also celery & olives.

Supper:—Beans & corn, cheese blintzes with whipped sour cream, tomato rice soup, cabbage & beet relish, bread pudding with blackberry syrup. Wrights—celery, olives, lettuce, beans, rice, farina pudding.

Movies after supper—The Czar Wants to Sleep—amusing satire on the mad Paul I. Kenn came in afterwards to nosh & chat.

Read Steig's The Lonely Ones—clever cartoon abstractions, obsessions and clichés.

FRIDAY, FEBRUARY 5

Pre lunch conversation with Mrs. Wright yielded the following choice morsels: My soup last night which the Fellowship thought was excellent, she said was bad. When I asked her why, she said, "It's your ignorance. You're an amateur. One meal's bad, another's good. I'm surprised that we grow fat & have rosy cheeks in spite of our amateur cooking." David suggests that I quit & tell her that I'd hate to endanger the health of the Fellowship, & further injure her poor invalidism.

Lunch: Wrights—lamb chops, spinach, potatoes, olives, rothe gruetze ("Kay put it into the cook book & it's been coming back like an old ghost. It's very muddy. Never make it.") Fellowship—spareribs & sauerkraut, boiled potatoes, apple sauce. I rendered lard today.

Henning, Ted & Joan had a party this evening in place of my cooking supper. — Suki Yaki, shrimp tempura, glacéd oranges. I got delightfully drunk—happy, gay. Kay & Gene kept kissing & kissing.*

David was notified by the Spring Green Bank about his note for Mr. Wright. He logged wood all day with Kenn. *[Davy snored off soundly. Jack was clever & witty. Johnny & Joan disappeared together—so did Henning & Svet. But it was lots of fun.]

SATURDAY, FEBRUARY 6

David & Wes settled with the bank temporarily until his notes come from Paige.

My hatred for La Dame is burning with a hard gem-like flame. Steak approved by Kay & specially prepared for her was too dry, jello too hard. It's some comfort to know that FLW yelled, "Damn it, woman, that's the way I like it." When I told her that she would have beef shortly because they had butchered yesterday, she whined, "Now I won't eat the meat. Don't you know I can't have personal relations with the animals. I'm too sensitive." Damn her.

Baked muffins for lunch—I didn't realize that the bread supply could disappear since Wednesday evening & baked bread in the afternoon.

Lunch—pork pie with carrots & onions; cole slaw with boiled dressing thinned with sour cream.

Supper—roast pork; mashed potatoes, gravy, frozen vegetable salad with tomatoes, carrots, eggs, olives, onions, Chinese cabbage, celery, lemon juice & lemon gelatin; corn souffle; grandmother's apple cake, coffee. The Wrights had Swiss steak & Indian pudding. I was glad to tell her that she couldn't have any cream for her pudding because Iovanna had used it all. Incidentally, the boys spent a good part of the day decorating the studio for her party; the servers had to do the dishes for her, & they wanted me to prepare the meal, but Kay helped instead; afterwards the boys were asked to dance with the girls. David, of course, got that stubborn look which said, "I won't dance at a time you choose. I won't dance with a person you choose. I won't dance in a place you choose. In short, I won't dance." So after helping Kenn a little, we went to bed. Incidentally, exhausting as the day was, I wanted to dance.

Pictures were Russian—Adventures in Toyland, & the Czar Duranday, & other fairy tales.

SUNDAY, FEBRUARY 7

Dull breakfast. Cold chill in the room—a sick personality who returned everything, perhaps the cause? I think FLW's complimenting me on yesterday's fine supper was to forestall his wife's remarks. He can notice her not too subtle working on me as on a psychological study. After all, someone who keeps herself informed of what the best minds are saying via Readers Digest, & refers to herself as reading "medical books" when she means Hygeia, is bound to have a not too charming smattering of ignorance. "Too sensitive to have personal relations with animals," she doesn't hesitate a fraction in her corkscrew probings of people.

David's making things easier, too, by threatening to disappear again tonight—his excuse dishes. I have given up counting the number of teas & Sunday evenings for which I've had to explain his absence to FLW. Mr. Wright is sensitive about non-appearance because that's his personal relationship with the boys. I either have to hurt him or David, or explain—and lie. David's excuses have been paper thin. A bad morning & afternoon with his telling me again for the nth time that our marriage was a mistake—not for him but for me, because he could never make me happy.

Long walk in the beautiful sunshiny clearness, with crisp snow underfoot. Movies in the afternoon—The Great Awakening—a Russian film on the beginnings of the collective farm movement, an important picture historically because it shows the departure from the Marxist principle of dividing equally, and the rise of Stalinist principle of division according to the labor given.

Two guests from the University. Mrs. Wr. in a chummy little corner with her clique including Joan. Joan & Ted recited the scene with the 'milk of human kindness' speech in Macbeth. I was embarrassed.

Long talk with Wes & David on the historical period of the Nazarene.

"Czar Duranday" was the only copy the U.S. had—here in the exclusive possession of Taliesin. Richard Hovey wrote a poetic drama about this place called "The Masque of Taliesin."

The Welsh bard, Taliesin, is one of the original sources of the Arthurian legends.

Read Ameringer's Life & Deeds of Uncle Sam—brilliant brief "little history for grown up people."

MONDAY, FEBRUARY 8

Played the recorder. Traced a plan from Ausgefuhrte Bauten. Read George Meredith's "The Tragic Comedians"—Victorian novels of frustrated love almost always give me a headache. Wrote letters to Mom, Judy, Nat, Burton, Chic-ngai. Letter from Abe Kaufman gave advice for Marcus & told David not to protest his non appealable 3B classification. How he got it, only God knows & He won't talk. However, the manna tastes good while it lasts. Also letters from Julia & Nat.

The Fellowship is disgusting me again. No one's going anywhere, & such petty insolences, I get to feel more & more as if David & I are a lonely island.

Cornelia & Peter are returning as apprentices; two boys, 16 & 17 years old are coming too. One lives in a wealthy section of Detroit. "That's good," said Kay. "Better classes," said Mrs. Wright. The girl stenographer from N.Y. Mr. Wr.

The poem is "**Taliesin: a Masque: Voices of Unseen Spirits**," (1896). The song, by Richard Hovey (1864–1900), is not actually about Wright's Taliesin: "Here falls no light of sun nor stars;/No stir nor striving here intrudes;/No moan nor merry-making mars/The quiet of these solitudes."

Cornelia Brierly (b. 1913) joined the Fellowship in 1934 after studying at Carnegie Tech in Pittsburgh. In 1939 she married another fellow, **Peter Berndston** (1909–1972), who had arrived in 1938 after two years at MIT. After the birth of their first daughter, Anna, in 1940, they moved to Spokane, Washington, where Peter was stationed during the war, but returned in 1943 after their second daughter, Indira, was born. The couple then moved to western Pennsylvania where they practiced architecture together, but later divorced; Cornelia had remained close to the Fellowship and returned in the late 1950s. The drawings from Peter's practice, nearly one hundred projects in all, are housed at Carnegie Mellon University's Hunt Library. Cornelia has been instrumental in preserving Wright's legacy and was a long-standing board member of the Frank Lloyd Wright Foundation. Her memoir, *Tales of Taliesin,* was published in 1999.

wants, but not the two leading women: "Let's have no more intellectual girls." Mrs. Wr. didn't like her sending her picture—"We don't do things that way here;" didn't like the expression in the left corner of her mouth—but probably will take her, money in advance—and use her for dirty work so that she leaves of her own accord.

Curtis returned from the hospital, came in for a short visit, & stayed till 12:30. He explained to us why most of the senior apprentices left two summers ago. There was a system whereby an apprentice could bring in a client of his own & get half of the architect's usual 10% fee, and half would go to the Fellowship. The plans were signed Taliesin Fellowship, John Doe, Architect. The boys would help in the supervision, tracings, etc. Not in all cases did the architect supervise (probably the reason Benny Dombar left). FLW gave his approval or made corrections, & then he called the whole thing off. Possibly he was tired of work which did not reach his own standard & yet was associated with his name, or he may have disliked the mêlée of ideas when he did warmed over work so that the result was neither fish nor fowl. With no direct opportunity of working as architects, many of the men & women left. Also, FLW's promise of 10 acres of land per apprentice for building Broadacre City & living right here on the grounds never materialized. Hulda & Blaine, & Cornelia & Peter wanted to buy farms in the valley here—perhaps the latter two will, now that they are returning with their two children.

Kenn came in too—very blue & lonely.

TUESDAY, FEBRUARY 9
Played recorder. Read Walter Duranty's I Write As I Please—a little late for ramifications of the last World War. Traced plans from Ausgefuhrte Bauten. Touched up Ardmore plans.

FLW embarrassed us by coming into the room when it was such a mess. Didn't like David's radiator sticking out into the room. Ted's room & our two will be taken away to make room for a three-room apartment with bath & outside closet for

---

Benny Dombar (b. 1916) joined the Fellowship in 1934.

Blaine Drake (1911–1993) joined the Fellowship in 1933. Drake married another fellow, **Hulda Brierly** (1911–1992), who joined the Fellowship in 1935.

Ardmore, Pennsylvania, was the site of the Suntop Homes (1938–39), an ambitious test of one of Wright's Broadacre City housing models consisting of clusters of small houses in compact, pinwheel-shaped arrangements. Originally planned as federally funded

housing in Pittsfield, Massachusetts, the project was moved to Ardmore, where only one of the planned four sets was built. Priscilla's comment that she "touched up the Ardmore plans" may indicate that Wright hoped that the project would be completed. The concept for this type of housing was included in the *Ausgeführte Bauten* (plate XIII), illustrating what Wright called a "Quadruple Block Plan" and offered as a "new scheme for subdividing property."

Cornelia & Peter. I don't know how soon we'll be asked to move out nor where we'll go, but it's all very disturbing.

FLW left for Washington on his mission—then on to N.Y. by next week. His letter to Davies, a personal friend, ambassador to Russia was a pathetic appeal. His letter to Kennedy, ambassador to England, was returned unopened. He'll be disillusioned to know he's persona non grata in Washington.

Hans came in for a long talk—his discussion of the reasons for failure of other community farm projects on which he's worked and idealistic Utopian experiments sound very much like the reasons for the potential failure of Taliesin. As human beings, we're still not sufficiently civilized to live together.

Most of FLW's houses cost too much to run—hence the reason most of his clients don't remain on friendly terms. He almost always goes beyond estimated costs, but to his credit, frequently supplies the difference from his own pocket rather than let his principles of architecture suffer.

WEDNESDAY, FEB. 10

Took care of Tal while Davy & Kay went in to Madison.

Practiced recorder; tried to learn lettering with rico pens & stencils; traced some more on my plans; read "Immortal Bachelor" by Penn & Burnett, a biography of Burns with emphasis on the loves in his life.

A frightened white possum wedged its shivering way in between our primex can & the vinegar barrel in the cooler, frightening Joan, Ruth, Mrs. Williams, and me— but not our stalwart Howard who carried it out to the road & sent it scurrying. Of course it played possum—went absolutely dead & Howard was able to carry it out limp by its tail which was as long as its body.

THURSDAY, FEBRUARY 11

When the breakfast gong rang this morning, David went in to our own room to dress, ran out yelling "Fire," which I mistook for "quiet" or a choke, & came back with a pail of water. I mistook the clanking sound of this for Howard's method of waking us as K.P. duty. That's why I was calm. A column of fire rose in the middle

---

Over the years, Wright wrote letters to many Washington politicians and bureaucrats in the hope of influencing them with his ideas. **Joseph E. Davies** (1876–1958) was a former ambassador to the Soviet Union who, in 1943, was chairman of President Roosevelt's War Relief Control Board and still involved in Soviet politics. **Joseph P. Kennedy** (1888–1969) was former chairman of the Securities and Exchange Commission and ambassador to the U.K., but by 1943 he had resigned his political posts and left Washington. Hence the returned letter.

Primex was a brand of vegetable shortening.

of the room burning a hole about 5 feet square. Opening the door allowed a draft
for smoke which sent our helpers out retching. Everyone helped carry water, or
move Hans out of his room, or chop up the floor with an axe, or squirt the fire
extinguisher. Nothing of ours was damaged except two of David's sweaters & two
of his plates which both of us had just completed with painstaking energy—but no
one was hurt. I shudder every time I think we might have been sleeping in the room,
too overcome by smoke to do anything.

Hans, Curtis, Ted, Kenn, David & I worked on repairs this morning—I wielding
a saw not too straight & a hammer, missing the nail at least one blow out of five.
The two theories are: 1) mice in a nest between the flooring nibbled away at the
insulation, causing a short, & a slow smoldering fire for hours or days, until it
reached an outlet, draft, & flames. 2) cracks between the fireplace bricks allowed
flames to touch the wood joists beneath. Certainly learned a lot about house
construction with no classroom instruction—and more than I had bargained for.

Three kids were born last night to an oldish goat—one crept out into the cold
and froze to death; the others are too weak to nurse from their mother. They topple
on their legs & occasionally slide over. Their weak little baby cries are pitiful, and
there's no one here who knows too much about how to feed & keep them warm.

Traced plans of the River Forest Tennis Club.

Read James Thurber's "The Middle Aged Man On The Flying Trapeze"—a definite
forerunner of the type of short pieces he chose for "My World—And Welcome to It."

Slept in the guest room that was our original room when we first came here—and
will probably be our room from as soon as we move out.

Our clothes were permeated with smoke—and a refrain ran thru my mind all day.
I kept on wondering whether Millay's description were true—"the blue bitter smell
of smoke."

FRIDAY, FEBRUARY 12

Lincoln's birthday—and no vacation, shucks!

The weaker of the two kids died this morning. We hope the third will live. In the
meantime, two other kids were born. Howard's feeding the possum in the chicken
coop. Will he get a complex and lay eggs?

Wright designed a clubhouse for the **River Forest
Tennis Club** in River Forest, Illinois, in 1906, after a previous facility burned down. It is a long, low building typical of his Prairie Style, with broad eaves and clapboard
siding. When the club's property was appropriated

for a forest preserve in 1920, the club moved the
Wright-designed building to its current site. It was later
expanded under the supervision of other architects.

the blue bitter smell of smoke is likely a reference to
the Rupert Brooke (1887–1915) poem "The Great Lover."

Finish tracing, perspective, & foliage of River Forest Tennis Club.

Read D. H. Lawrence's beautifully written "The Man Who Died" and his so-what "Triumph of the Machine." Also Robert Nathan's "A Winter Tide" in which I like particularly Sonnet II and A Note to Politicians.

Hans and David rebuilt the fireplace, and then we made a vague and almost futile attempt at getting the room in order.

Got a letter from George Brody—says nothing about his whereabouts—is very sarcastic in an attempt to pass censorship.

Svet and Wes gave a party in Joan's honor—or perhaps Carrie's-Frances'-Tor's—a buffet supper. We played "Murder," an amusing game, but I was frustrated—when I was murderer, the victim committed suicide before I had a chance to get my hands on anyone's throat. Then we danced folk dances (Henning my partner while David changed records), and social dancing (David, Jack, & Kenn). Joan was wavering between Curtis and Johnny, but clung to Johnny. Hans says "Johnny withdraws." Amusing and sad to be objective about another girl's search. David says I called Burton's name several times at night.

Tried to make method out of the charred madness in our room.

SATURDAY, FEBRUARY 13

Johnny received his 1A classification. So it begins again. We already have two criminals on our premises who refused to report for induction. Scher asks the boys to let him know when the blow comes, and the best he can offer is that when they all go to jail, at least the jail will be Sandstone where they can all be together. There are 374 C.O.'s there out of 473 prisoners—the whole place to be turned into a C.O. camp.

Letters from Mom and Irv Weingarten. Julia has a job working for a doctor. So we have a new professional breadwinner in the family. Wrote to Julia, Burton, Anne Williams. Washed my hair. Practiced the recorder. Finished the second volume of Stendhal's "The Red & the Black." Received six boxes of Halvah from the Henkens. Served and washed dishes. Also read D. H. Lawrence's "Psychoanalysis & the Unconscious."

Carrie-Frances-Tor: Jesse Claude "Cary" Caraway (d. 1994) joined the Fellowship in 1934; Frances Fritz Caraway (1917–2009), joined the Fellowship in 1942. The two married, had two children, Tor and Caren, and lived and worked in Chicago. After retirement, the couple returned to Spring Green.

Kenn says that Johnny told him he's really deeply affected by Joan but restrains himself because war and the imminence of jail would otherwise check him. Like Burton, perhaps, thinking you can preserve life by bottling it up?

Hans revealed that in a talk with Lloyd Lewis, he was told of Mr. Wright's confession that his wife is becoming more difficult and more sensitive. We can attribute it to either one or both of these theories: 1) change of life 2) a constant brooding fear that she will be left unprovided for and unprotected. Even Taliesin is a white elephant, never fireproof, and when mortgaged, the bank was willing to settle for 50% of the total cost. Lewis also said that Mr. Wright's fifth volume lacks the fire of the first four—too much has been deleted or altered for his wife's sake.

Saw Claudette Colbert, Joel McCrea, Rudy Vallee, and Mary Astor in "Palm Beach Story"—an intermission from our Russian season—frothy & delightfully amusing.

SUNDAY, FEBRUARY 14

David, will you be my valentine?

Quiet morning—reading Lawrence's "David" and chatting, and Olive Moore's study of Lawrence, "Further Reflections on the Death of a Porcupine," & Lawrence's "Mornings in Mexico."

Went skating with Howard, Kenn, and Davy—skating in a manner of speaking. Slid down hill in sitting position. I learned how to get up after you've fallen; how to stand, ankles turned in, while waiting for someone to push you; how to walk slowly & deliberately as if there were pebbles in your shoes; and how to scream loudly for help. David, all this time, was quietly drawing foliage & reading Thurber—a leaf, a chapter, a leaf, a chapter. . .

All went well until evening—I'm beginning to feel superstitious about Sundays. Mrs. Wr. was in a vicious mood—scolded Kay because she was disrespectful—she had called her into an empty living room. Then the fun began for us—she was lonely and Ruth and I sat down next to her at her request. She asked David to—twice—and he told her he was taking advantage of his man's prerogative to stand with his back to the fire. And then she launched into him about his being disrespectful when a lady asks him to sit down next to her, etc., etc., etc. He sat in stony silence like the grim god of vengeance for the rest of the evening, & got no consolation from me. I told him that I regretted he was rebuked publicly, but that it was a rebuke he should have gotten some time in his life—(I'm glad my memory hasn't retained all the times he asserted his male independence by refusing to sit down, or stand up, or dance, or walk, or anything when I or another person has asked him to.) Of course, now he's convinced either that I'm stupid in a female way that has nothing to do with a college education, or that I'm in league with the evil ones. I, too, am disgusted with his disregard of the human element in tackling the logic of a situation. So Taliesin has revealed the worst as well as the best in our marriage, as such close confinement is bound to do. One must almost pray for the spring thaw—not that it solves the basic problems. It's just a headache tablet that doesn't get at the root of the ill.

MONDAY, FEBRUARY 15
Played recorder. Read Gelder & Lawrence's "Early Life of D. H. Lawrence." Traced plans from Ausgefuhrte Bauten.

Letters from Mom, WRL about Marcus' parole, & Burton. The warden of Sandstone explained about constructive education for Marcus, tests during quarantine period, possibility of working on model of his church, visits by parents, letters by seven "harmless" people of his choice.

After buying sheep last Friday, Henning was classified in 1A. Is he buying sheep to pull the wool over the draft board's eyes?

Actions toward Mrs. Wr. & the other members of the Fellowship in the past, present, & future were the subject of a long heart to heart quarrel with David. This place certainly is a trial to marriage.

TUESDAY, FEBRUARY 16
Traced plans of Dana House. Played recorder. Mended trousers—all very domestic, to which Kay added more by telling Ruth that she & I henceforth in our non-cooking weeks would alternate between mangling (Mrs. Williams doesn't like the idea) and weaving.

Ruth started to teach me the piano—CDE flat—very tuneful. Letters from Julia, Harry Handler, & Epstein.

WEDNESDAY, FEBRUARY 17
Practiced piano and recorder. Traced plans of Usonian Ellinwood House.

Laundered—Mrs. Williams got an official countermanding of the mangling order—all Kay's bright idea. Skated with Kenn and Curtis for about two hours, frequently beginning and ending in the sitting position, but better when Kenn

---

The **Dana House** (1902–4) in Springfield, Illinois, was designed for Susan Lawrence Dana, whose husband Edwin L. Dana had been a prosperous mining engineer. Wright's work consisted of a total renovation of, and substantial addition to, a nineteenth-century Italianate house that had been owned by Susan Dana's father.

The result was one of the largest and most elegant of Wright's Prairie Style houses, replete with Wright-designed furniture and art-glass windows, doors, and light fixtures.

The design for the Alfred **Ellinwood House** (1941), in Deerfield, Illinois, was never built.

hummed the skater's waltz to give me the rhythm of skating. Helped David with the dishes. Visits from Kenn & Ted in the evening.

THURSDAY, FEBRUARY 18

Practiced piano and recorder—not too much transfer because I used the soprano clef. Completed plan of Ellinwood House Sheets. Mangled Fellowship laundry (yes, countermanded orders) and our own.

Skated with Kenn and David who moved pretty upright from as soon as he got on the skates. I remember the way we used to talk about ice skating, hoping against hope that it would be a mild, slushy winter. I can now rise gracefully—and frequently—from the sitting position, stand in the middle of the pond, ankles practically parallel with the ground, take several tentative steps in either direction depending upon which way the pond slopes—& not scream for help! David sat by on a log giving logical advice on equilibrium, the science of skating, body posture, until someone handed him a pair of skates. Lord, how I prayed, but he moved forward, not too erect, but not prone either. So now I hate him. I manage to move on the ice alone, but it would be a downright lie to say I cut a pretty figure—or any at all.

Sweet letters from Nat and Judy—and a wonderful recommendation from Bonawit for the exam—all 5's and this extra word of cheer: "particularly fine sense of responsibility and cooperation in helping with departmental work. Intellectual alertness and curiosity, understanding of students."

Read Clark B. Firestone's "Coasts of Illusion," a study of travel tales—particularly interesting account of the lost continent of Atlantis.

Standing in the middle of the pond, the sky seemed a deep cloudless blue, the trees russet hued as if autumn's leaves had dyed the branches, the moon rose clear and full. Sparklingly beautiful.

Read D. H. Lawrence's Essays—Reflections on the Death of a Porcupine.

FRIDAY, FEBRUARY 19

Mr. Wright is seeing Hershey today; conferred with Archibald MacLeish; may be endowed by Carnegie—all half threats and vague promises, it seems to me.

Wes may try to get some of the boys off as vital to the farm in which case they may have to waive their conscientious objections. E.g. 1 milk cow = 1 farm unit; 3

Wright continued to meet with influential people to discuss and appeal for funding for his plans. **Archibald MacLeish** (1892–1982) was a poet and Librarian of Congress and worked for the War Department during World War II. The Carnegie Endowment for International Peace had been founded by **Andrew Carnegie** (1835–1919) in 1910.

WES PETERS AND BEN GRAVES WORKING WITH A HORSE-DRAWN SLED, January 1943.

FRANK LLOYD WRIGHT AND OLGIVANNA SITTING AT THE TEA CIRCLE WITH THE FELLOWS, undated (1942–43).

acres of corn—1 unit; 5 sows—1 unit, etc., etc. From 8 to 16 units need one man depending on the degree of mechanization of the farm.

Practiced piano and recorder. Took long walk with David. The premature thaw has melted the snow down, uncovering wide horizontal brown ridges of moist earth. Saw Henning's sheep huddled together, and the little goats scampering about. Traced plans.

All the boys may be excused as necessary to the farm except for Davy & Jack, because so much of their cases has already gone under way.

Read Xenophon's Hellenica, a history remarkably similar to ours. Little phrases shoot out, like "This is a democracy, not a tyranny," or "After the 35 years service list was exhausted, they chose to enter into active service those who had occupied government offices."

Finally convinced Howard with the aid of Webster-Merriam that I am entitled to pronounce my final r as I wish, and then gave a brief lesson in phonetics to an admiring Curtis, Svet & Johnny.

SATURDAY, FEBRUARY 20

Ruth gave me another piano lesson.

Completed Sheet 2 of Ellinwood House—mat and framing (heating plans).

Letter from Bert Slanhoff—a mournful tale of loving not wisely but too well—and the army.

Read Robinson's "Merlin" and "The Town Down the River." Merlin is an excellent psychological version of Malory's tale.

Picture was "Nazar Stodolya"—revolution of the Ukrainian serfs in 1861 based on poem by Taras Shevchenko. Also a short of the Red Army Chorus Song and Dance ensembles.

Mrs. Wright left the supper table in a huff because Hans, David, Jack & I were talking—and she wanted individual attention. An imperious woman trying to command adults with an elementary school teacher's manner. Her lovableness must have long since rotted.

SUNDAY, FEBRUARY 21

Read Sparks' "Light on the Leaves." Cleaned the room thoroughly. Three of Henning's sheep have lambed—4 lambs. Between us, David & I wrote ten letters. Pleasant recorder quartets in the evening—and finally, charades with all sorts of violent and bitter feelings. Adult games are dreadful.

MONDAY, FEBRUARY 22

Practiced piano and recorder for almost three hours. Completed Sheet 2A—Details of the mat and framing plans of the Ellinwood House.

Letters from Whites, Wilbacks (a baby boy), more fuss with storage company, and Judy.

Went with Kenn to feed the bees their sugar-water. They were busy fanning the hive with their wings to cool it, and throwing out the dead bees as Item 1 on their spring cleaning schedule. A house bee tore off the wings of a robber bee (visitor from the next-door hive) to prevent his flying—nasty punishment. Unless otherwise fed, the bees eat their own honey—and why not? —so they must be visited frequently if you're to profit from the venture. The hives are well protected against winter cold by a thick padding of straw, and against summer heat by boards which allow for the passage of air.

The hills are now washed brown with ridges of white by the February thaw. Mild and spring-like weather which if I were younger & happier would set me a-flutter.

Read Aeschylus' "The Suppliants"—story of the 50 daughters of Danaus & 50 sons of Aegyptus. Discovered that willy-nilly comes from will-ye nill ye (whether you like it or not.)

TUESDAY, FEBRUARY 23

Bright, cheerful letter from Julia. A gray, humid day—wonderful for the pathetic fallacy. Completed sheet 3—Elevations and 1/4" Intersections—of Ellinwood House. A difficult job tracing it from the pink print. Read Robinson's "Lancelot" and cried— you must have reasons for tears inside you to be moved by a story of people dead before history was born. Enjoyed practicing the piano (picking out the notes of simple pieces) and the recorder. Served & washed dishes.

Kay added to the festivities that Ruth & I are now tea-makers, beginning today. David was furious at this imposition and refused to help or come. So I made honey drop cakes and served them to a lonely five.

FLW via phone has given Wes full approval to work on the farming angle, and drop the CO business if necessary. I'm full of malice when I think of Marcus, a real CO, in jail, and these draft-evaders becoming essential to the nation's agricultural work.

Read Max Beerbohm's "A Christmas Garland," clever parodies of English authors popular in 1912, the date of publication. Also read Buchan's "The 39 Steps," excellent suspense of the chase.

Completed lettering of Ellinwood Sheet 3.

Practiced piano and recorder—really a joy.

Read D. H. Lawrence's revelatory (of author as much as of subject) sketch of Maurice Magnus for the introduction to his "Memoirs of the Foreign Legion," called the "Portrait of M.M."

Letters from Chic-ngai (scholarship under Mr. Wright's good <u>and</u> respected friend, Mies van der Rohe); WRL discussing bill for women's conscription; Murray Rubin (in Groton, N.Y., "soulmate of Spring Green"), and Leo Steinlein (obsessed with school, war, and slow convalescence.)

Made a delicious apple sauce cake for tea.

THURSDAY, FEBRUARY 25

Practiced piano and recorder, the latter in the group with cello, violin and 4 recorders. I play the four lowest notes and can scarcely hear myself, but I suppose I'm there. David tells me now I can appreciate the story of the musician who spent his vacation in the Carnegie gallery, & told his friends "you know the part where you go boom-boom-boom & I go ta-ra-ta-ra, ta-ra, well it doesn't sound like that at all. It sounds like . . ." and he hummed the Habanera. This is a Russian folk song from which the Andante Cantabile was taken.

Walked for the mail. Frost fell so quickly on yesterday's light snow, that you can practically see each separate crystal. Letters from Saias, Coronet (Irwin Stark's "We Advertised For a Family" appears in the March issue), Elsie Sproge, and George Brewster. Wrote to Julia, Saias, Whites, Starks.

Deputy sheriffs or marshals took Davy & Jack to Madison today, but didn't put them in jail because they may possibly be classified as agricultural workers. They were taken to the post office & bailed out by Wes—$1000 each. So they're back tonight. Arraigned by Judge Stone.

Made brownies for tea.

Johnny & I went to look up a line in the Snyder & Martin Ted borrowed from us— and we got his permission to go into his room. As I leaned over his drawing board

---

Ludwig Mies van der Rohe (1886–1969), German modernist architect and head of the Bauhaus school from 1930 to 1933, moved to the U.S. in 1937 and established a practice in Chicago.

women's conscription: The Austin-Wadsworth bill, introduced in the Senate in 1943, would have added women without dependent children to the mandatory draft; other wartime bills suggested a nurse draft. None passed.

A reference to the anthology *A Book of English Literature*, edited by **Franklyn Bliss Snyder** and **Robert Grant Martin**, first published in 1916.

my eyes fell on our names—evidently a letter. The gist of it was that "Priscilla & David Henken have been here for 4 months & all they think about is the morning's mail, and the first thing they do is sit down & answer all the letters they've received. They think of nothing but New York, are interested only in their old life, & in nothing else." I'm deeply hurt by this, but am even more shocked by the lack of perception which prevents his seeing how actively we've participated in everything here. Perhaps this is Henning's opinion originally—but if not, it is so now—and consequently shared by the Wrights. Not calamities—but these pettinesses are the things that try men's souls.

Hans came in for a visit—his rebelliousness & his intelligence and independence are refreshing. Kenn joined us later.

FRIDAY, FEBRUARY 26

Went to Spring Green about withdrawing $220 from my postal savings account. Davy & Jack made the front pages.

Made lemon wafers for tea. Practiced recorder & piano almost tirelessly. Letter from Burton telling of a mild flu, a black mood, and the ides of March.

Read Robinson's "The Three Taverns."

Hans & Kenn came in for evening chat. Hans's character perception is very keen—told us of Betty Barnsdale, a millionairess apprentice here, of her influence on Kay, of Mr. Wr's incorrect estimates of his houses, frequently putting the contractors in a hole over extra costs.

Told Kenn & Curtis about Ted's appraisal of us—and they're amused. I've decided to do a sleepwalking scene for Ted—"Will all the perfumes of Taliesin ne'er wash this little mind clean?" or "Brooklyn, The Bronx, New York creeps in this petty pace from day to day, Till the last syllable my lips can mutter."

Planned next week's ménu.

SATURDAY, FEBRUARY 27

Walked for mail—a gleaming inchoate spring day.

Practiced piano & recorder. Answered Burton. Threaded Mrs. Wright's loom—she's making a tweed suit for herself of gray wool, coral, gold, teal blue, lemon and chartreuse rayon threads. Typed ménu and presented it for approval to the Czarina.

Betty (Aline Elizabeth "Sugartop") Barnsdall (b. 1917), one of the first fellows at Taliesin, started in June 1933. Her mother, Louise Aline Barnsdall, was a client of Wright's and commissioned the Hollyhock House in Los Angeles. Betty married another Taliesin fellow, Irwin Shaw, who joined the Fellowship in 1932. She subsequently remarried.

the last syllable: from Shakespeare's *Macbeth*

Sweet, understanding letter from Sylvia S. She can see her husband weekly—stationed at Fort Dix—weak eyesight—no military training.

Eleanor's letter to Kenn says that she has prospects of a good job & is teaching nights at Cooper Union.

Movie was "Gypsies"—excellent music, dancing, & photography.

Mr. Wright came home with all sorts of stories to tell. His petition for a Broadacre City grant has been signed by Erich Mendelsohn, Einstein, Robert Moses, Walter Lippmann, Frederick Delano, Thurman Arnold, Robert Sherwood, Thornton Wilder, Archibald MacLeish.

He & Robert Moses, N.Y.'s commissioner of parks, are cousins thru marriage. Moses' wife is FLW's cousin from Dodgeville. Moses told Wright he was a mole while Mr. Wr. had wings. Wright turned the tables by saying, "You mean you're blind, burrow underground, & leave tracks obliterated by the first rain but damaging the country." However, Moses signed.

FLW went to the Rev. Harry Emerson Fosdick, but was told by his secretary that Fosdick could see only those in need of spiritual comfort & encouragement. Wr. sent a note back—"I have no need of spiritual comfort & encouragement, but thought you might need some. I wanted to preach you a sermon. Signed—Jenkin Lloyd Jones' grandson, Frank Lloyd Wright." Fosdick sent after him with explanations & apologies.

He & Walter Lippmann went into the Carlton in D.C. —very, very exclusive with tables reserved. FLW hadn't done this, but since Lippmann was his guest, he proceeded ahead, not knowing what it would lead to. The head waiter greeted him very effusively, & said, "We have a table on the side for you, Mr. Arnold." He had dined with Thurman Arnold, & now he was mistaken for him.

Einstein told him he liked Gropius' wife, but not his architecture, but he signed Wright's petition anyway, thru Erich Mendelssohn.

---

petition: Seeking funding for his Broadacre City plans, Wright met with people across the spectrum of cultural and political influence.

Robert Moses (1888-1981), among the most influential people in New York City for infrastructure projects, later claimed he was instrumental in getting the city's planning board to approve permits for Wright's Guggenheim. Moses's wife, a second cousin on Wright's mother's side, was Mary Louise Sims (d. 1966). **Walter Lippmann** (1889-1974), a journalist, wrote about liberty and democracy, among other subjects; **Frederic Delano** (1863-1953) was a railroad executive; **Robert Sherwood** (1896-1955), a screenwriter, Oscar winner, and Pulitzer Prize winner; **Thornton Wilder** (1897-1975), a poet and playwright; **Harry Emerson Fosdick** (1878-1969), a noted liberal clergyman who was active in ecumenism, race relations, and the peace movement. A committed pacifist, Fosdick was vocal in his opposition to World War II.

Walter Gropius (1883-1969) was a leader of modern architecture and a founder of the Bauhaus School in Germany who later taught at the Harvard Graduate School of Design and was influential in bringing modernism to the United States. Einstein perhaps referred to Gropius's second wife, née Ilse Frank.

FLW walked in Washington buildings for miles looking for elevators that worked, & finally found himself on the outside of the building, still wearing a badge.

After "Skin of Our Teeth," he told Thornton Wilder he thought the play was excellent, but he was surprised at the spoofing at the end. "In that part, I was serious," Wilder told him. He felt Tallulah was a little too pert for him.

Scher has 2 men lined up for Marcus' parole, & now needs a third who's on his way, but a CPS Camp will be almost as bad, & Mr. Wr. is disappointed unless he can get him here for work of national importance—which is unlikely.

Henning's farm was bought for $8000 on a foreclosure of Cousin Dick's farm (Mr. Wright's cousin), and he sponges on their hospitality, & capitalizes on his having done them a good turn—i.e. not chasing them off their property.

Joan Bower was asked by Mr. Wr. to be an apprentice here, but her father disapproves—he believes in formal education & degrees & she feels she's not getting as much out of college as she would be here. Perhaps she'll compromise by being a summer apprentice. Probably his ¶ about us was an appraisal of Fellowship members for his father.

SUNDAY, FEBRUARY 28

Cooking again. Lunch—baked potato, asparagus, cottage cheese, corn bread, jello.

Dinner—roast beef, mashed potatoes, gravy, Southern corn pudding, pickles, apple pie with corn flake crumb crust, coffee.

Mrs. Wr. had a long talk with us on spoiling "classic" recipes like classic apple pies & classic ham & eggs. However, she told me to go ahead & she'd be the first to tell me if the apple pie were good. She told me it was delicious but we'd have to call it by a different name—apple flake? apple delight? apple corn crust? cherry cake?

She & Mr. Wr. both told me how lovely, elegant, delicate, Priscilla-like I looked in my guimpe, blue blouse & evening skirt.

MONDAY, MARCH 1

Lunch—Swiss steak, baked potatoes, sauerkraut baked with caraway seeds (but good!) garlic pickles

Supper—beans, cheese soufflé, tomato aspic, boiled dressing, left over pie, & jello. Wrights—Indian pudding—approved very highly.

Letter from Julia—the family certainly isn't in bouncing good spirits.

---

spoofing: At the end of this play, an actor announces that the other actors have taken ill and cannot continue to act.

Cousin Dick: Richard Lloyd Jones (1873-1963) was the publisher of the *Tulsa Tribune* in Oklahoma. Wright designed a house, Westhope, for his cousin in 1929.

Looks as if Wes & Courtney will make most of the boys vital farm workers unless classified safely otherwise.

Henning, K.P., displeased Mrs. Wr. with "his bare unwelcome table setting," & he left the kitchen in a huff. T-t-t-t.

TUESDAY, MARCH 2

Curtis asked Henning whether March came in for him cold and lamby. He's having trouble feeding them—they freeze in these unsheltered winds, & topple when they stand.

Lunch—New England boiled dinner, buttered beets, tomato aspic relish, boiled potatoes. Wr.—steak, beets, potatoes, rice pudding.

Supper—stewed tomatoes, potato salad, cauliflower timbale, apple sauce cake with whipped cream. Wr's.—chicken soup (a navy blue chicken, I swear, & one of our layers, too, more's the pity, & Kenn cursed soundly), beans, spinach, rice gruel, peach tapioca.

Read relaxing mystery, "The Red Widow Murders."

WEDNESDAY, MARCH 3

Letter from Nat.

Lunch—excellent meat loaf even if I do say so myself, baked potatoes, rutabagas & apple sauce, garlic pickles. Wr's.—baked fish, etc., apple sauce pudding.

Supper—cream of lima bean soup with paeans of praise, Spanish rice, macaroni & cheese timbale, sweet pickles, frozen coffee pudding with whipped cream. Wrights—grilled livers, spinach timbales, cottage cheese, farina pudding, blackberry sauce.

Played in the recorder group—my début is Sunday—Händschen, & few charming Elizabethan lyrics. It may be an interesting experience if I don't have to go to the toilet at the same time.

Mr. Weston phoned to tell us that Marcus has already gotten thru the jail the parole information we sent him thru the WRL.

THURSDAY, MARCH 4

Lunch—hamburgers, sweet pickles or Spanish rice, Brabant potatoes, carrots; Wrights—Lamb chops, etc., & baked pears.

Supper—potato soup, stewed tomatoes, beans, American cheese, gold layer cake with lemon filling & whipped cream.

The pears were soundly berated because there was water at the bottom of the pan—"don't try to improve on me" and the soup was "the best we've had." So we go up & down, down & up.

Recorder for Sunday is over—She didn't like the way we sounded—angry at Kay because she hasn't learned anything in two years, and she has plenty of time, etc., etc.

Letter from Dr. Bonawit—my most faithful correspondent.

FRIDAY, MARCH 5

Lunch—noodles & chicken, rutabagas & apple sauce, baked potatoes, pickled grapes. Wrights—steak, potatoes, beans, baked pears.

Supper—lentil soup, deviled eggs, buttered beets, pickled pears, Vienna tarts. Wrights—Rice Gruel, lentil soup, beets, spinach, Indian pudding. We asked the Wrights to wait a half hour & it still remained syrupy. Finally they phoned & we served it with apologies—"Delicious" they sent word with Henning. We served them with trays all week because Mr. Wright has a bad cold. In the anxious period, Johnny joked, "Tell Mrs. Wr. Priscilla is on the hill garden committing hari kari with a bread knife."

Read "The Chinese Orange Mystery"—Ellery Queen is good relaxation.

SATURDAY, MARCH 6

Letter from Eleanor (full of opinions of Taliesin), Honey, & Dave W. on another of his ship testing trips.

Lunch—Chili Beans, Ginger bread, baked sauerkraut with caraway seeds, pickled pears. Wrights—baked eggs, potatoes, spinach, bacon, vegetable soup, jello.

Supper—Baked Livers (Baked Halibut), mashed potatoes, beans baked in tomato sauce (peas), tomato aspic, strawberry mousse (crème Duchess*) *approved highly.

Picture was a dreadful Ukrainian folk opera—Natalka Podolka—without titles, or visible plot, but some good music. As Johnny put it, "If it had only been in Russian & not in Ukrainian, we would have understood it"—Mrs. Wr's usual answer to a question about a Russian movie.

SUNDAY, MARCH 7

Mr. Wr. is still dreaming wildly his Broadacre City pipedream, plotting what land Davy should buy, what statues should be erected (e.g. a <u>free</u> design by Carl Milles for an 80 foot statue of a pioneer), overpasses (300 of them) & underpasses, etc.

Baked bread so as not to leave Ruth in the lurch now that her mother is visiting her.

Mrs. Wr. kicked up the stupidest fuss because croissants Gene made for breakfast weren't the crescents Henning once made & which she expected. She told Gene he didn't take cooking seriously (and after he baked grapefruits with vermouth & spent hours on preparation) & Henning that the least he could do is remember the book & page of his recipe. Mr. Wr. laughed & she left. My personal theory is that she spends most of her time between the kitchen & bathroom investigating digestibility.

Piano and recorder practice. Read D. H. Lawrence's "Widowing of Mrs. Holroyd." Wrote home.

At concert, FLW scolded the trio because they put so much concentration & effort on a third-rate composition by a third rate artist, Dvorak's Trio in B Flat. However, he liked the reverence & sincere emotion in the cello solo, Walter Kramer's "In Memory of His Father."

MONDAY, MARCH 8

Practiced piano & recorder. Read D. H. Lawrence's "Touch & Go" & Wright's "Broadacre City—The New Frontier," the Taliesin magazine of 1940. Spent some exciting time working on plans for a school for Broadacre City, embodying Wright's principles and my ideas of visionary education. So far I've worked on an octagonal unit two stories high, with the center square in a cluster of 4 octagons used as corridor on the first floor & projection booth (movies, slides, radio, phonograph) on the second. It bears working on.

Curtis went for his third eye operation today. Letters from Mom & Judy. Wrote to Judy.

David had a big blow-up with Jack. David asked Jack to leave enough cookies (he was washing as usual) for tea. (David & I made old fashioned molasses cookies.) Jack called him a fat slob, a bastard, how can you talk with your table manners, etc., etc. Said to me, "Thank God at least you're an asset to the Fellowship." What crime that personality irritations make life so miserable here.

Snow helped warm 16° below weather slightly.

David's busy ordering from Sears Roebuck & filling out income tax returns.

More repercussions about Jack—he ran to tattle to Mr. Wr. saying something ought to be done about David. After "The Gypsies" he told Wes & Howard he's "like to do something sneaky to hurt that dirty kike who's always monopolizing the conversation." There's no place on this earth free from race prejudice, I'm convinced—and bitter.

Taliesin Magazine was a journal published irregularly over the years by Wright and the Fellowship. The 1940 issue, planned for many years and issued as "Vol.1, No.1," served as a catalogue for Wright's 1940 retrospective exhibition at the Museum of Modern Art in New York.

TUESDAY, MARCH 9

Went for a long walk after the mail—snow falling steadily. Eleanor returned our trunk key; Julia writes with undertones of sadness; Burton writes in detail of his efforts for enlistment, with voluntary induction après tout on March 11.

Tried to roll on the loom for a few minutes but Mrs. Wr. stormed in that I was tangling it still further, & that Henning should complete his responsibilities & how dared he ignore her command that he come down to the studio & go off to the Graves. FLLW kept on "now-nowing mother," but it didn't help.

Completed sheet 4 of Ellinwood House. Washed a heavy laundry. Wrote to Julia. Piano & recorder.

WEDNESDAY, MARCH 10

Piano & recorder. Mangled laundry. Check from Paige arrived—now David can pay note for FLLW. Finished warping loom for Mrs. Wr. with Kay's help. FLLW asked me why Gene hadn't worked me in on the typing of the 6th volume which he was busy correcting. Made butter thins & had cider for David's tea.

Read Maugham's "Cakes & Ale" which I had read before, & Arnold Bennett's amusing "Buried Alive."

Mrs. Wr. in the study told Ruth & me (invited down to taste her corned beef hash) the story of a Jewish apprentice here married to a Chinese boy, Goa, & her serious flirtations, out till 2 o'clock in the morning with other men, etc., etc. "I don't mind flirtations—they're pleasant to see—but . . ." Anyway, the dear thing is in China with her husband now, & settled down. Was it told to point a moral to me? If so, the woman flatters me. Also, the picking-up-the-cane incident in The Servant Mind chapter of Vol. V refers to Ted & Chic-ngai. Mrs. Wr. never airs her dirty linen publicly but what she labels each garment too.

THURSDAY, MARCH 11

Went to Midway twice—once for shuttle & wool for Mrs. Wr. & once to weave. Brilliant blue western sky; blinding snow; bird-calls; but so cold indoors, the snow did not melt off my pants cuffs for an hour and a half.

Finished Grahame's "The Golden Age," in Woollcott's second Reader, a good anthology of stories & novels.

Piano & recorder. Wrote to Nat. Began tracing sheet 5 of Ellinwood House—furniture and ceiling elevations.

Hans came in for a short talk.

Helped David with tea—toasted marmalade sandwiches & blackberry snow ice-cream (Ted's idea—snow, whipped cream, eggs, confectionary sugar, blackberries).

FRIDAY, MARCH 12

Air mail letter from Burton—temporarily deferred for eyesight until limited service list is exhausted—2 weeks to a month. He seems quite set on going into the army. Letter from Bert S. in hospital with pneumonia, & of course involved with army nurse.

Piano. Recorder. Weaving. Tracing. Walking. Helped David with tea—jam cupcakes & Jah-vah-au-lait.

Crisp, sunny day with a hint of spring—but I would have been happy anyway about Burton.

Mr. Wr. in a cheerful, reminiscent mood. Spoke of Ben Davis who could swear so that it was a magnificent spectacle—put in a curse word between every syllable of the word—e.g. (mild) "absogoddamlutely." Urged Davy what land to buy, & then if he didn't like it for farming, they'd make an exchange with some Taliesin land. FLLW said there'd be big doings here within the next 5 years in re Broadacres, & that we ought to keep diaries. David & I smirked.

SATURDAY, MARCH 13

Sad letter from Judy—farewells from Burton, Jocko an air cadet, & Murray.

Reference "for the applicant" from John Adams—2-5's & 3-4's—not bad for only 3 months of service.

Piano. Recorder. Weaving. Tracing—Completed Sheet 5 of Ellinwood House— Workspace & Furniture Layout. Wrote to Burt & Muriel. Spring must be on its way. Yesterday, the snow covered hill stretched away with the infinite sense of the sea; this morning the snow crunched underfoot, breaking a block of snow for a fresh footprint; at noon, the mud was so deep & swampy my snow shoes were half pulled off my feet; and the smell in the air was the smell of pavements after a spring rain.

Picture was "All that Money Can Buy," the cinematic version of Benet's "The Devil & Daniel Webster." Huston excellent; the picture very American in spirit.

SUNDAY, MARCH 14

Piano for two hours. Saw "All That Money Can Buy" again. Hear Mr. Wright's broadcast as the "architect of the future" on Cooperative Houses.

In the local idiom, "the day was wonderful overhead, slushy underfoot." But we were too busy even to walk in it.

Traced typical heating diagrams for Usonian houses.

At concert, FLW spoke of the Detroit cooperative houses—wants to experiment on emulsified cement or asphalt mixed with the rammed earth. The earth may not be topsoil because the organic matter will cause the walls to deteriorate, nor too much clay, but in between. Program: choir, Arensky trio, Bach Church cantata #161, Vivaldi—Nachez concerto.

David, serving, was notable chiefly for his non-appearance. When will he draw the line between sullenness & silence, between unobtrusiveness & unfriendliness?

Read Mukerji's answer to K. Mayo, "A Son of Mother India Answers," and finished Horace Wyndham's, "The Mayfair Calendar," some society causes célèbres, famous trials.

MONDAY, MARCH 15

It's pouring—a real warm spring rain. Ruth gave me piano & recorder lessons.

Letter from Mom along with Julia's dress & Purim Haman Taschen. Muriel's sick; Alice Gr. is in the hospital; Daddy's tired; Julia knows too much for her co-workers—family portrait.

Traced sheets 1 and 5 (pink hectographed copies) of Barton "Oak-Shelter" Cottage—General Plan & wardrobe & closet details. Regular tracing of sheet 2—Elevations.

Wrote to Murray, George Brody, Hilda, Esta, Rose, & Mom.

Kenn & Hans came in the evening for chats & beer & Haman Taschen. Hans said he respects Wright as a genius & as a personality, but not as irresponsible regarding financial matters & as an "exploiter." FLLW is an altogether lovable personality in almost all respects. Hans also said that the baby changed Svet for the better—from a vicious, quick-tempered, tale-bearing girl to a sweet & gentle person.

TUESDAY, MARCH 16

Long walk for mail. The pond overflowed on the road, leaving a thin crackling icy crust. Real March winds & snow flurries that don't light on the earth. Wove in numbing cold at Midway. Completed Sheet 2 of "Oak-Shelter" Elevations. Piano lesson. Recorder. Served & washed dishes.

WEDNESDAY, MARCH 17

Gusty March, howling winds. Washed laundry. Piano & recorder. Read William Rose Benét's, "The Dust which Is God," one of the best books I have ever read—an autobiography in blank verse & lyrics.

Purim, a joyous Jewish holiday, is often celebrated with Hamantaschen, traditional triangular-shaped pastries.

The design for the John Barton Cottage (1940), **Oak-Shelter**, in Pine Bluff, Wisconsin, was never built.

Customers came about reconstructing flooded Spring Valley. FLLW adamant about costs. Says the town's banker hasn't stopped earning money—why should he? But he's undertaking plans to rebuild the whole city—stores, churches, schools, roads, homes. These will then be submitted to the local boards for approval, & then fingers are crossed.

Completed tracing Sheet 3—Framing Plan of Oak-Shelter Cottage for the Bartons.

Read Robinson's grim Avon's Harvest.

THURSDAY, MARCH 18
Traced. Piano lesson. Recorder. Read Buchan's "Mountain Meadow." Visits from Curtis & Hans. Letters from Julia, Judy, Harry Handler. Hans is leaving Tuesday. Wrote to Bonawit. Spring Valley will use nothing old but the inhabitants. Has even selected a new beautiful site up in the hills. Mangled laundry.

FRIDAY, MARCH 19
Heavy snow fall. Letter from Burton. Piano & recorder. Tracing. Walked to Graves' barns—yield: the minorcas consort easily with the leghorns; da lambs is droppin'; the piglets is huggin' Mama; the peacocks have the creamiest plumage; 12 deer were spotted on a nearby hill—one of them white. I suspect it was a unicorn, but there was no way of testing it—the virgin of Taliesin was at school.

Wrote to Burton, Julia, Sylvia.

Played duets with Ruth & recorder a total of 3 3/4 hours.

FLLW very upset that Hans is leaving.

SATURDAY, MARCH 20
Piano. Recorder. Traced Sheet 4—Elevations of "Oak-Shelter" Barton Cottage. Very gay supper—everyone in good humor. Movie—"Parson of Panamint"—to Mr. Wr.'s question why it wasn't more successful, Kay said, "They can't stand seeing the picture, because they're (the American public) more interested in gold than in spiritual values." What sanctimonious hypocrites we are—or what superior people. Each one of us at Taliesin is superior to the next. Davy sued his father for money, too!

Read Aeschylus'—"The Persians" & "Seven Against Thebes."

Spring Valley, Wisconsin, experienced a particularly devastating flood in September 1942. In 1943, Wright offered to design a new town, but the plan was rejected.

In the 1960s the Army Corps of Engineers built a dam to protect the village.

SUNDAY, MARCH 21

Officially spring is here. Actually, it was agonizingly cold so that walking from one part of the room to the other was a major expedition.

Read Aeschylus'—"Agamemnon" & "The Choephori."

Piano and recorder. Movies instead of concert—Chekhov's "The Bear"— very amusing.

MONDAY, MARCH 22

Letters from Muriel & George Brewster. Weaving. Piano lesson. Recorder. Traced Sheet I—General Plans—Watkins Studio, New Jersey. Kenn still avoids us so as not to give credence to the Snooks story. How childish! Henning teased about planning to sue his mother for money, probably a throwback to Davy's maneuvers.

TUESDAY, MARCH 23

Letter from Marcus addressed to Mr. Wr. —tells about prison life & his carpentry & missing Sunday evenings. Stilted, pass-the-censor tone.

Weaving almost all morning. Piano & recorder. Room party for Hans as farewell— Ruth, Howard, Curtis, Kenn.

WEDNESDAY, MARCH 24

The white swirls of snow in the furrows are gradually melting exposing a brown renascent earth.

Weaving, piano, recorder, traced Sheet 2—Elevations—of Franklin Watkins Studio in N.J. Letter from Frances Salzman.

Hans left today on the evening bus, going to Lloyd Lewis's in Libertyville first for repairs there, & then on to his dentist in the east. Mr. Wr. repudiated him completely, would have nothing to do with him, "deserter," "traitor." Of course, he had no money to pay him the hundreds of dollars he owes him, & Hans had to borrow bus fare from Wes. Long talk in the room with Hans & Howard before he left.

Tea outdoors in the tea circle—spring is almost icumen in.

THURSDAY, MARCH 25

David butchered today—I'll have either a very sick boy or a vegetarian on my hands shortly. "For all experience is an arch . . ." Last week he hurt his hand with one of the

---

Watkins Studio: In 1940, Wright designed a studio and residence for the painter Franklin C. Watkins in the seaside town of Barnegat, New Jersey. Never built, the structure was sited among the dunes and nicknamed "Windswept" for its dramatically angular profile.

bolts of the electric saw, & was confined to drawing most of the week (not that he minded), but this week it's been wiring & butchering.

Weaving at Midway—I'm really going at lightening speed these days; but never before was I as cognizant of the meaning of "bogged down by mud" and the dogs pawing me muddy too. Piano, but too severe a headache for recorder.

Traced Sheet 3 of Watkins Studio—Framing Plans of Roof & Floors. Laundered. Wrote to Muriel. Letter from the Whites.

The day was so lovely we had tea outdoors again, but when the March winds began getting gusty, & Jack explained that it's so long since we last sat outdoors, he thought we should now, Mr. Wr. said "That's what I call wishful sitting."

Wes & Svet left for Chicago.

Hans & FLLW finally parted on friendly terms, & Mrs. Wr. came down especially to Hans last night before he left to thank him for being a man about saying goodbye to Mr. Wr., even tho there was tacit understanding that the older man had been childishly grumpy.

Served & washed dishes. Davy got money from his Dad finally to buy the farm.

FRIDAY, MARCH 26

Weaving. Recorder & piano lessons. Planned ménus, but Kenn whom I consulted was definitely gruff in his bending over backwards to be un-snooks.

At tea, Mrs. Wr. asked me if I had done something to my hair because it looked so lovely. "No," I answered, "a clever woman always chooses good lighting effects, like the sunlight." Mr. Wr. said I was married to a lighting expert, so why not?

David & I went to Midway Hill to take pictures—the swirls of plowing, Taliesin from all its glamor angles, the blue Wisconsin, etc.

While I mangled, David got FLLW's permission for us to Easter at home.

Read Constance Roarke's "Davy Crockett."

SATURDAY, MARCH 27

Typed ménu. Recorder trio. Piano. Diddle-dawdled. Went to Richland Center with Howard & Ruth to get back our smoked hams. It's Mr. Wright's birthplace & his German Warehouse is there too—very Mayan looking, but I don't like his angular

Wright designed the **A. D. German Warehouse** (1915–1920) in his hometown of Richland Center, Wisconsin, for a distributor of coal, grain, and other basic commodities, for free in order to settle his debts to the company. He crowned the simple brick building with an elaborate cornice made of decorative concrete blocks, prefiguring his textile-block houses of the 1920s in Los Angeles.

buttresses. But it is old period—1914. Flat tire 12 miles from home—Ted rescued us & late for dinner.

FLLW told a dream he had in which Hitler invaded the U.S.A., got Mr. Wr. at the entrance as he was about to phone "the Taliesin C.O. Militia" (David's table quip), & proceeded to walk down the road with him. But FLLW said to him, "This is just the opportunity I've been looking for—a chance to discuss this war with someone who knows what he's talking about." As he was shot, he awoke.

Picture of U.S.S.R. dancers was good; documentary film about the Danube frontier very obvious propaganda, tho some of the kerchiefed women & gesticulating men were so familiar, they might have been our relatives.

Letter from Mom. Jack talked to FLLW about David's opening or closing valves. David got the story straight, however. He wired in the living room today. Mrs. Williams was egged on to quit today—opportune when Svet was away so she couldn't appease her, tho Mr. Wr. tried to. "The apprentices can clean from now on," said guess who.

SUNDAY, MARCH 28
Cooking with Curtis as K. H. Lunch—hamburgers, stewed tomatoes, baked potatoes, baked apples. Supper—roast beef, potatoes, beans, pickles, cream puffs, coffee. Last minute upsets of course, but that's life. Concert good with FLLW moving furniture most of the time. David did wiring for a good part of the day—a great man's whims. . .

MONDAY, MARCH 29
Lunch: Pork Chops—braised with tomatoes, southern corn pudding, baked potatoes, apple sauce. Wrights—swiss steak, carrots, cornstarch pudding, pot. Supper—scalloped cauliflower, spaghetti with Napoli sauce, carrots, apple sauce cake w. whipped cream. Wrights—Welsh stew, rice gruel, peas, farina pudding. And quiet flows Taliesin. Of course, we're feeling the butter shortage, but not so it hurts.

Letter from Nat. Piano. Recorder. Walked with David.

TUESDAY, MARCH 30
Letter from Burton—brimming with friendliness & low spirits. Letter from Marcus to the Wrights, telling of vague parole possibilities.

---

and quiet flows Taliesin: A reference to Mikhail
Sholokhov's novel *And Quiet Flows the Don*, the first part
of his sprawling epic *The Quiet Don*.

Lunch—spareribs & sauerkraut, boiled potatoes, barbeque sauce; Wrights—swiss steak, brabant potatoes, carrots, peaches. Supper—macaroni, cheese, & tomatoes; creamed fish with eggs & asparagus, buttered beets, cream of lima bean soup; raspberry & lime jello w. whipped cream. Wrights—cottage cheese, asparagus, beets, soup, jello.

Read Howard Fast's "The Unvanquished"—good, human portrait of Washington.

A day that made this run thru my mind as I worked:

Shall I compare this to a summer's day?

It is more temperate & more lovely.

WEDNESDAY, MARCH 31

The Fellowship still leaves with bellies distended as much as skin will let them, but grumble, grumble Mrs. Wr. Damn! Lunch—bitki, rice, rutabagas & apple sauce, pickles. Wrights—hamburgers, rice, stewed tomatoes, kissel. Supper—stewed tomatoes, molded cottage cheese salad, potatoes au gratin, strawberry mousse. Wrights—asparagus, baked eggs, cottage cheese loaf, apple tapioca.

Piano. Wrote to Burton. My feet are tired, my eyes bleary, & my wrists protest under Hanon's treatment. Johnnie, who makes kitchen life pleasanter, is being taken out to work on Mr. Wr.'s rooms. He considers nothing but the whim of the moment. David's working on telephone repairs.

THURSDAY, APRIL 1

Letter from Dave Wertman—he's marrying Frieda! Let's hope she makes him as good a wife as he deserves.

Piano. Recorder. Read Sigmund Spaeth's Words & Music A Book of Burlesques.

Lunch—roast pork, potatoes au gratin, franconian parsnips, hot apple sauce. Wrights—chicken soup, boiled beef, potatoes, plums. Supper—almost everyone was at Gene's party for Wes & Svet's anniversary, so a very quiet supper. Beans baked in tomato sauce, beet & cabbage relish, frozen vegetable salad, potato soup, mocha tier cake with mocha frosting. Wrights—Porters came unexpectedly, announcement at 6:35 grilled livers, peas, beans, farina pudding, blackberry syrup, salad, baked potatoes.

---

shall I compare: A reference to Shakespeare's Sonnet 18.

Jane Porter (1869–1953), one of Wright's sisters, lived with her husband, Andrew, and son, Franklin, at Tan-y-deri (Welsh for "under the oaks"). Built in 1907, though some scholars (William Allin Storrer, for one) think it was designed as early as 1901, this house is on the Taliesin property.

Franz Aust, who was here, had to resign his professorship at Wis. U. because he was caught in a hotel with a young girl—both married. FLLW wrote a wonderful letter in his defense & to protest newspaper scandalmongering.

Svet's peeved because the Davisons are spending all their money on the farm & won't have a cent left for stock & tools, & she thinks they're probably counting on her & Wes to supply the lack—which they probably are.

FRIDAY, APRIL 2
Lunch—Beef Stew, celery, carrots, onions, potatoes, frozen veg. salad. Wrights— Ditto, peas, jello. Supper—Tomato Rice Soup, deviled eggs w. curry sauce, baked potatoes, head cheese, hot pickled beets, coffee bavarian cream. Wrights—chicken soup, chicken, fish, Indian pudding.

At 5:30, I was hastily summoned to the loggia. Mrs. Wr. advanced these charming accusations at me: "your mind must be elsewhere; you pay no attention to the cooking; everything is oversalted or flat; you have no sense of taste, and it all comes from your wisecracking attitude. It's all right in a man, but bad in a woman. Whenever I give you a compliment like a lovely bouquet, you destroy each petal. You have a lovely, graceful figure, & you spoil it by your raucous wisecracks. It's not wit. I know what true wit is. Alexander Woollcott was one of our best friends—& he was the wittiest of wits. He represents good N.Y.; you represent bad N.Y. Your friends probably all sat around & wisecracked & you had to do it to keep up with them. And you do it out of embarrassment. It's all right to be embarrassed—but you should blush & stammer & be demure. Everybody is so embarrassed (& I've asked other apprentices) when you make your cracks that they all hang their heads or have forced smiles." Etc. Etc. I preserved a stony silence, so that she kept on winding herself up, & interrupting "Do you understand?" Mr. Wr. knew what was going on, & came in to show me his sulphur & molasses mixture— "You see, Priscilla, I'm a cook too," but she shooed him out quite gruffly. Heaven forbid that anyone should steal her scene. She's jealous of any youth, & any esprit besides simpering female silliness.

I let my hair down for Curtis—he understood—but we're all hopeless as to how to handle the situation. She meddles more in people's lives than parents would dare to.

Sulphur & molasses was a traditional spring tonic
recipe to clear the system after a long winter.

SATURDAY, APRIL 3

Lunch—boiled potatoes, pickled beets, spareribs & sauerkraut, franconian parsnips. She prepared her own. Supper was superb: Roast beef, gravy, mashed potatoes, cottage cheese & celery balls, beans baked in tomato sauce, excellent pumpkin pie with whipped cream, coffee. Svet prepared the Wrights' supper. Shall I feel rebuffed or be pleased that I had an easier day than usual?

Picture was "We Are From Kronstadt"—a few very moving scenes.

David cleaned studio & bathrooms, helped w. wiring, fixed the refrigerator, etc. My little handy man-about-town.

Letters from Florence, Mom (George is returning to the U.S. on leave), Judy.

SUNDAY, APRIL 4

David & I climbed the high Bryn Mawr Hill—birches gleaming white against the blue sky & bluer Wisconsin River. Sun wonderfully warm & invigorating. And then the week & the climb took toll of us & we slept the mid afternoon away after some mild—very mild—housecleaning.

The whole evening was a tacit apology, with Mrs. Wr. complimenting me on my dress, my hair (you're the only one in the Fellowship who can wear it that way), & Mr. Wr. saying "That's because she has such pretty ears," & he asking me how we pronounce rations, & she how Roosevelt, & leaning over to tell Mrs. Porter I'm a teacher of English, etc., etc.

Concert—Corelli's Sarabande; Mozart's Trio No. 4 with David the only one knowing what the Kochel cataloging was; Handel's Alexander Fest. & Choir.

Oh yes, Mrs. Wr. told me my cream puffs were better than Ruth's. Ach, du lieber Augustin.

MONDAY, APRIL 5

We rose at 6:00 today—the ponds & river curved in blue-green shimmering patterns, russet high-lighted—a chiaroscuro with the dark land shadows.

Piano. Recorder. Cleaned studio & entrances.

Gardening for 4 hours—tying up the vines in the vineyard—cloudless, sunny, cool—occasional visits by plump robins and creamy orange meadow larks and a few swallows. Wes furrowed double rows for potatoes between the vines. David dug parsnips in the vegetable garden.

The **Köchel Catalogue**, first published in 1862, is a complete listing of Mozart's work.

Ach, du lieber Augustin is a melancholy Viennese song about the trials and tribulations of dear Augustin, for whom "all is lost."

Letters from D. Bonawit & Nat—but wonderful!

Davy & Kay signed the deed to their new farm—and are very anxious to evacuate the tenant. Henning is planting 2 acres of strawberries so that he can get 2 more units to be exempted as a farmer. A pretty pack of C.O.'s!

Read Claude Bragdon's "The Frozen Fountain," essays on architecture & the art of design in space.

Mr. Wr. went to his Madison doctor again—just getting old, doesn't want to eat—year full of frustrations, & he can't expect to do the things he always used to. A summation of age.

TUESDAY, APRIL 6

Still tying vines fanwise in the vineyard, but the cold was too numbing for long activity at a stretch.

Piano. Recorder. Cleaned studio. Traced color perspective of Franklin Watkins Studio. David K.P. today for Howard who is butchering.

WEDNESDAY, APRIL 7

Worked in the vineyard 4 1/2 hours—Johnny says I ought to sing "Come This Lovely Hour of Tying." The day changed from a diademless mist to emerging sunshine and breeze, thru to a parching heat. The birds renewed their chirping with much effort of the sun to make itself felt. A sweet grassy odor, with a hint of flowers.

Piano. Recorder. Washed skeins of wool in preparation for dyeing in Nacconol NR.

Davy made an attempt to throw the tenant farmer off his new farm today—otherwise how can he be deferred as a farmer. May be balked by the unwritten law that a farmer who has begun planting can't be evicted till harvest. Also has trouble about who will help him work it—needs Fellowship help & Wes's machinery.

Howard had his final type physical today—Ruth low spirited—David K.P. again, & I took over for supper.

Letters from Julia, Muriel, Henry Saia, Sam Verne

Fred Benedict, ski troop officer who visited us here (former apprentice) is now in a psychiatry ward suffering from nervous breakdown. So is Burt Goodrich, a former apprentice, who may be returned here so that he can recover under conditions most nearly approaching normal. So the war wreaks vengeance on the sensitive! I wonder how George Brody will impress the family when he returns this week.

Nacconal NR was a synthetic cleaning solution developed in 1930, used to help hold the dye to the strands of wool.

Burt Goodrich (b. 1911) joined the Fellowship in 1934.

WES PETERS PREPARING THE GROUND FOR POTATO PLANTING, April 1943.

MIDWAY HILL, April 1943.

PRISCILLA ENJOYING THE SPRING THAW OF 1943.

146

THURSDAY, APRIL 8

Worked in the vineyard again under a warm April sun. Mrs. Wr., Toggie, & Kay went fishing while FLLW walked up & down commenting on Wes's plowing, & on my tying—"good knots because women's fingers are so deft."

Henning rode to & from his farm on horseback looking like lord of the manor, graciously waving his hand, back straight, horse reined in.

Letters from Murray & Judy. Recorder and piano just barely squeezed in because I helped Ruth for a while in the kitchen this morning. David still K.P.

This dream I had very indicative & characteristic: Davy said something nasty to David who passed it off as a joke, but I lost my temper, & Jack threatened to have it out once & for all before Mr. Wr. Jack & Davy prepared mimeographed sheets for a week, raking their memories for every incident in which we figured unfavorably. Jack was opposed mainly to David, but when I became involved, he said, "Listen, I think you're cute, but if you're going to start up, I can find plenty against you, too." At the trial in Mr. Wr.'s study, with him, Curtis, & one other judge, I asked Davy why he needed the duplication of so many mimeo'd sheets—was it to blackball David for future clients, & he said yes. Mr. Wr. counted this revelation as against Davy, & thus scored points. I awoke before the decision.

Planted potatoes this afternoon from a tobacco planter. The machine was run between the vine poles by Davy; Johnny & I sat in the back dropping the quartered potatoes in the hole created every time the ratchet clicked. Amazing how much coordination is required for so simple an act.

Mrs. Wr. scolded David & Ruth for serving the white bowls on the plates—and said that David had never been willing to learn anything about the kitchen. When he protested, she called in Johnny to verify that he had told her so when he was showing David the ropes. He was dreadfully embarrassed, but lacking in courage as we knew he'd be, & answered, "Whatever Mrs. Wr. says, is correct." She told David he's only interested in intellectual learning. He answered that skills interested him too. She said "Do you learn easily?" "Yes." "Just as I thought—that means you forget easily."

At tea, she was very offensive to Mr. Wr. because he asked her why she dragged Ted away to go fishing. "I don't like to be questioned. You have no right to question me, etc. etc." He got up, bowed slight[ly], "I forgot. One must never question the hostess," & left.

The Davisons gave a cocktail party before supper to celebrate the buying of the farm. David with his usual aplomb, & as usual leaving me to bear the brunt of explanations or casual (& to the Wrights, therefore, an indifferent wife) shoulder shrugging.

Card from Dave W. welcoming us to Washington.

Piano. Recorder. Read Dorothy Parker's real & bitter collected stories, "Here Lies." Cleaned bathrooms.

Tied vines in the vineyard practically all day, aided by a new apprentice from Texas, Jay Glass. He seems intelligent, & amazingly well informed on Mr. Wr. and asked several shrewd questions on financial status, management, building in operation, favoritism, Mrs. Wr.'s influence over Mr. Wr., etc. After tea, Curtis, Jay, David & I walked over to the Porters' house (built in 1907 by FLLW), over stiles, across Michaels' farm with views & pines & birches such as give ample excuse for Mr. Wr's desire to buy it, past the first crocuses (lavender—furry cupped, & bright yellows), over barbed wire across the ridge to Wes's farm, visiting all the animals, including the beautiful curled fur Hereford cows.

Of course this was immediately reported, so that Davy when Johnny, Curtis, Jay, & David were sitting in the tea circle, obviously called Jay away to show him some more of Taliesin.

Howard later reported that Mrs. Wr. asked him where David was so he could fix a fuse, & when he answered, "Probably helping him carry down his luggage," she screamed, "Why, of all people, is he helping him?" & Howard answered "Because he's the only one who volunteered most likely." But that's the way the wind is blowing. I predict gradual ostracism for us, & fatherly warnings to Jay. But I'm pretty heavy-hearted.

SATURDAY, APRIL 10

My heart is even heavier than yesterday. Jack told Jay first thing after chorus, that "there are some people here longer than you who don't know what the fellowship stands for—avoid them as much as possible." Jay told me this as well as that Davy took him aside last night to give him similar advice—& not to show him anything. So, as I predicted, after ten minutes of helping me in the vineyard, he was called to help in the vegetable garden. He had no sooner returned after garden hour, & tied two vines, when Svet called him to help in the flower garden. The wheels of injustice move swiftly.

Discouraged, I left the vineyard early, & traced Sheet 6—Details—of Watkin Studio. Piano. recorder. Cleaned studio. Served & washed dishes.

Jay Glass was a Taliesin fellow briefly in the 1940s.

David finally chose today—now or never—to see Mr. Wr. about his status here, a talk he had long delayed. Conversation ran pretty nearly as follows:

Mr. Wr., I think that I'm persona non grata with some people here.

Well, I guess you are, David, but not with me.

I've been to movies & laughed when damnyankee was used as one word, but never till I came here, did I hear Jew bastard applied to me in the same way.

Not here! (violent tempered). You should have beaten him to a pulp, & I would have backed you up completely. That sort of thing has no place here, & never had.

I don't believe in answering that way, Mr. Wr. I'd like to know why I'm resented here.

Well, for one thing, you know more than any of the boys here. You have more experience of the world, more information. You have a very keen mind. They resent you knowing too much. Why, even I got angry at you once for that.

I know. I was sorry, & tried to change.

I noticed that.

I try to speak as little as possible—my silence resolving itself almost into sullenness.

Well, don't do that. I like you to speak. Only try moderation. It's not necessary to go the opposite extreme.

You see, Mr. Wr., you're so provocative. You make a statement at tea, & I have to answer you.

That's why I make those statements, & I want answers. But the boys think you've been here so short a time, you shouldn't speak up.

Then why don't they? They all sit back in silence.

Because they don't have the information or the erudition.

What else?

Wes thinks you're lazy.

I assumed as much, but it isn't true. You told us that it takes apprentices three months to relax sufficiently to get into the swing of things, but Priscilla & I tried to dive into work as quickly as possible. The first day I was out hauling gravel, & Priscilla was busy doing other work. But as soon as it became known I was a "specialist," I was called in to do wiring and nothing else. For weeks I wasn't visible as working because I insulated boilers. Even if it's to change a fuse, they call me in. After chorus, when work is assigned, I'm forgotten because I don't attend chorus.

Why don't you?

Well, I have one of those voices—like Wes's, I guess, that just don't carry a tune.

Oh, I know what you mean.

I want to learn all these skills—if I didn't, I wouldn't have come here. I don't drive well, so they don't use me. The first week I drove the car under Wes's supervision, & the tractor under Howard's, but not since then.

Yes, I guess you're right. You should be learning all these things, & I'll see to it from now on that you do. The only trouble is that you're the first person who's been here who knows so much about electricity. I don't know why that should be so, but it is. But I'll see that you learn anything you want to, even that stonemasonry over there. Light is most important for effects, & I never studied it too thoroughly. But I should. I should. (This in answer to David's explanation of his company's work in theatrical, store, home & World's Fair Lighting).

Now another thing the boys resent may be your laughing easily—they think you wisecrack too much & you're too sarcastic. We had another boy here, Edgar Tafel, also Jewish, & from New York—everybody liked him, & yet they couldn't get used to him, because he laughed so readily they thought he was laughing at them.

What do you do when you don't go to chorus?

I draw in my room, or read on architecture.

I don't like that. Why don't you draw in the studio?

In the morning, chorus is going on & it would be an intrusion. In the evening, it's too cold & lonely.

But doesn't Priscilla disturb you in the room?

No, because she draws, too. You know two of her plates were accepted for the Arch. Forum.

Yes, I know she's a very talented girl. What does she do in the 3 weeks when she doesn't cook? You know, she must be kept busy, or she'll get into mischief.

But she is busy. She's learning to play the recorder & the piano. She works in the fields for several hours, draws a few hours each day, & has taken over most of the weaving.

Edgar Tafel (1912–2011) joined the Fellowship in 1932 as one of the original core group of apprentices. He worked with Wright on some of his most important buildings, including Fallingwater and the S. C. Johnson Wax building. After serving as a photographer in World War II, Tafel moved to New York City to start his own practice and worked on more than eighty houses, dozens of religious structures (including the airport chapel at Kennedy International Airport), and several college campus plans. His book about working with Wright, *Apprentice to Genius,* was published in 1979.

She is very talented. She ought to be doing some literary work, as on the magazine, but I can't get Gene to turn any of it over. You know how some people are—jealous of the work they do. But that's what she should be doing. But I want to know who called you that name.

SUNDAY, APRIL 11

Our visitors were Joe Jones, director of the Chicago Art Institute, & his son, David. No great pronunciamentos about art, but maybe they'll all be in the book he's writing.

Traced a little. Piano. Went riding with Jay & the Ten Brinks, & visited Herbert Fritz's house—amusing application of Taliesin even to sandstone statuary plastered into the stone walls, but charming & comfortable. He looks as if he belongs in the Village's bohemia.

Direct repercussions of yesterday's talk—David ran the tractor for 2 1/2 hours, & Kenn (to whom Mr. Wr. had spoken) told him he shouldn't let those things worry him.

Concert—Viracini Sonata in D minor was the only new offer—good, too—Svet & her violin.

MONDAY, APRIL 12

In discussing Franz Aust last night, FLLW remarked "Well, you can't blame him— he's 58—at the dangerous age, & he's been there for 18 years." Otherwise, Mrs. Wr. seemed to take an almost lewd interest in the case.

Laundered. Served tea (filled cookies). Piano. Completed tracing. Sheet 5— Section B B of Franklin Studio. David K.P. with Kay. Recorder. One row in the vineyard. Long walk. The bluejays gleamed & burnished blue in the chill sunlight.

Spent the evening playing records in Gene's room—all of ours before we take them home. Invited those who'd like to hear them—Kenn, Gene, Johnny, Jay, Ten Brinks, Curtis. Kay & Davy came in unexpectedly. All we wanted was the use of the machine, but Gene embarrassed us by serving beer, pretzels, crackers, popcorn, & I brought down the last of the Halvah. So an unplanned evening became almost a "snooks party."

Herbert Fritz (1915–1998), an apprentice from 1937 to 1941, farmed in Wisconsin through the 1940s. His sister, Frances Fritz Caraway, was also a fellow. His father (also named Herb Fritz) worked as a draftsman for Wright and survived the 1914 massacre. The younger Fritz and his wife, Eloise, later opened their home, Hilltop, as a summer camp and retreat for visitors.

TUESDAY, APRIL 13

Traced. Began packing. Mangled. No farming—there's snow on the ground! Kenn & Jay visited in the evening. Herbert Fritz is returning to the Fellowship. Tea—cookies & cocoa. Recorder. The Wrights left on a brief vacation for Chicago.

WEDNESDAY, APRIL 14

Traced sheet 4—Section A-A of Franklin Studio, and so completed the set. Finished packing—luggage in the station. Completed another row in the vineyard. Pressed shirts. The room still has to be cleaned for absentee browsing.

Meeting of Wes, Johnny, Ted, Jack, Davy to be questioned as to their farmer ness before the Dodgeville board, holds decision still in abeyance. Davy's tenant farmer won't get off until he's paid $800, the equivalent of a year's earnings.

1900 pounds of models were sent off to Cambridge for a comparative exhibition there of modernity: Wright, Picasso (who's never mentioned in the same breath), etc.

Made party fudge cake for tea.

THURSDAY, APRIL 15

Felt very ill—3 hours of bending & stretching in the vineyard, but finished the stint I set myself.

Completed Hesketh Pearson's biography of Shaw—"G.B.S.—A Full length portrait."

Piano lesson. Made Spanish buns for tea. Cleaned the room. Completed last of packing.

FRIDAY, APRIL 16

Left for N.Y. —Kenn drove us down. Train reservations cancelled even though they were made 2 weeks in advance. Waited 4 1/2 hours in Chicago for next train— terrific muscular aches—doped myself with aspirins—sat up for 22 hours in a train so crowded, many slept on their valises in the aisles & on the platforms.

SATURDAY, APRIL 17

All our wonderful plans about breakfasting with Nat, Burt, George, & Judy abrogated by our wild telegrams & late arrivals. Up to the Henkens—wonderful family reunion with both our families—the family bosom is capacious. Party in

---

This **comparative exhibition** took place at the Fogg Museum of Art at Harvard University. Called *In Memory of Frederick Randolph Grace, Masters of Four Arts,* it opened in May 1943 and featured Wright's work alongside that of Aristide Maillol (1861–1944), French sculptor; Pablo Picasso (1881–1973), Spanish painter; and Igor Stravinsky (1882–1971), Russian composer.

the evening—George, Burt, Saias, Weingartens, Nat, Horowitzes, Esther, Pearl, etc. David & I both bubbling to talk, showing plans, prints, color slides with projector. Julia came up with George, very silent about his Midway & Solomon Islands experiences. Burt properly indignant about some Taliesin injustices—funny inconsequentialities after what George went thru.

SUNDAY, APRIL 18
Central Park Walk—Nat, Burt, Saias, Judy, and kept on collecting people all the way, like the man with the goose under his arm in the fairy tale. Then in to Du Barry's for very expensive pastries, creams, & drinks (inflation with a big boom!), to the Saias to admire their apt. & capehart, & to the Jussims for dinner. Muriel so grown up; Jared sophisticated E.E.B. type; Daddy dog-tired.

MONDAY, APRIL 19
Visited A.J.H.S.—lined up job for the fall—emotional upheavals that make teaching more difficult, the about to leave sadness. Passover Seder at the Henkens with Palestinian wines, still, strangely enough. Beselah cold & hostile in the car—still thinks we're slackers, probably.

TUESDAY, APRIL 20
Second seder at the Jussims. Saw Disney's "Saludas Amigos" and "Talk of the Town": Still rainy, with hints of spring.

WEDNESDAY, APRIL 21
Saw Dave & Frieda Wertman at the Taft for breakfast & the Champlain for lunch. (They were married yesterday.) Rapid fire talking until train time when we saw them off for their Florida honeymoon. Saw the Lucioni and Berlin exhibits at the AAA Galleries, and the "Art of our Century" at the Peggy Guggenheim Galleries. Dinner with Judy at the Barbour, and on to see "The Doughgirls," a play about overcrowded Washington. Slightly risqué, moderately funny.

Midway and Solomon Islands were sites of American-Japanese naval battles in the Pacific region during 1942.

Peggy Guggenheim (1898–1979), opened her gallery, **Art of This Century,** in the fall of 1942 and, for the next five years, displayed a rotating collection of European and some American abstract expressionists, cubists, and surrealists. The gallery spaces themselves were striking, with curving walls and with one area painted black. Every so often, the lights were turned off completely. Paintings were hung by wires from the ceiling, or on adjustable arms jutting into the rooms.

THURSDAY, APRIL 22

Lunch with Sylvia Shlimowitz—delightful, quick exchange of news. Visited Mom, & Dad at his place—still plugging for David to give up his C.O. principles. Supper with the Steinleins—worried about his slow recuperation, and imminent drafting on May 15. Evening at the Henkens, visited by Nat.

FRIDAY, APRIL 23

Biking out to Tuckahoe (about 40 miles all told) with Nat, David, and Burton. As usual, we lost Burton right near home—just like Boston. Burton, Julia, David, & I visited the Brewsters in the evening—magazines, music, hobbies. A delightful day— spring is even in my heart.

SATURDAY, APRIL 24

Daddy home, tired & ill. Latin-American exhibition at Museum of Modern Art with Burton; dinner at Shinia's in the village with Judy, David & the Saias. They went to see Skin of Our Teeth which I already saw, & Burton & I walked, stopped in for drinks, & walked. Ended at the Saias, greeting the Whites, etc. Met Burton's uncle on the way; he omitted the Mrs. so uncle could think he was out with a "glamour girl." Funny boy.

SUNDAY, APRIL 25

Spent the day at Henkens, & walking in the park with the Saias & Whites. More reviewing of plans & pictures, discussion of personalities way into the evening. Felt very blue—again the same feeling of lack of direction, not knowing what will happen to us, plans for September, nullification of 3B classification, etc.

MONDAY, APRIL 26

Dentist's. Reservations made on Trailblazer. Supper at Mom's. Ballet with Burt, Judy, David, Milt & Margo. Petrouchka, Princess Aurora & The Three Cornered Hat given—Markova, Argentenita. Slept at Mom's.

TUESDAY, APRIL 27

Completed dental work—two fillings. Dinner at Prof. Bischof's—very much interested in Taliesin. A charming evening.

The **Latin American Collection** of the Museum of Modern Art (1943) was one of the first major exhibitions on Latin American art in the United States and a landmark show in this field. It comprised 270 works based on purchases made in South America in 1942 by consultant Lincoln Kirstein.

WEDNESDAY, APRIL 28
National Orchestral Association Rehearsal—Leon Barzun conducting—David liked it better than any concert. A 70 year old woman in her début followed a 12 year old. Visited Dad in the factory. Met Frances Salzman—ate & talked—she's disillusioned & looking for hope, probably communism. Met George Brewster—showed us the new cardboard tarp. Bessie Henken took us to dinner at Farmfoods then to the ballet—Luba, Blanche, Sophie & Arthur (of camp), Pas de Quatre, Pillar of Fire, Capriccio Espagnol, Apollo. Markova magnificent.

THURSDAY, APRIL 29
Handlers—breakfast. Visited Mom's. Packed. Visited Julia in her place—her doctor seems quite taken by her. Dinner with Eleanor—all enthusiastic about her job at Princeton—post war planning commission. Party at Burton's with Nat & George— evidently some family dispute dampened Burton.

FRIDAY, APRIL 30
Visited Dad in factory. Dinner with Mom. Saw "Oklahoma" in the evening—Saias, Medwins, Luba, Judy. Burton met us after the show—took me home—imminent departure permitted us to say lots we would not have, ordinarily. Parting was sweet sorrow, for tender was the night.

SATURDAY, MAY 1
Farewell to New York. Greetings to Philadelphia—relatives the same, city greatly industrialized. Visited Bubbie, Itzie Henkens, Witkins, Bernie, Whites. Up schmoosing with Clarice & Larry till 4:30 a.m.

SUNDAY, MAY 2
Visited Whites, Max Henkens, Witkins. Train to Chicago. I'm scared to death about reproaches for a long vacation.

MONDAY, MAY 3
Visited & lunched with Orlovs in Chicago. Nasty, windy day—movies. Train to Spring Green—greeted by Curtis & Kenn. Kenn arranged room with wild plum blossom & box alder. Sat up late talking. A sweeter reception than we anticipated.

Rodgers and Hammerstein's *Oklahoma!* had just opened at the St. James Theatre on Broadway on March 31, 1943.

for tender was the night: a paraphrase mixing Shakespeare's *Romeo & Juliet* with John Keats, "Ode to a Nightingale."

TUESDAY, MAY 4

Evidently my not appearing on schedule for cooking upset everyone. Mrs. Wr. greeted me faintly, Mr. Wr. cordially. When I explained that I would make it up, he said, "That's what I told <u>them</u>." Filed wood to simulate brick for Sundt House model. Gathered 4 bushels of dead wood with Johnny—it resembles the inside of baked sweet potato, at least birch does, & is used as fertilizer for wild flowers. Jay came in asking advice about bringing his wife, & what she could do here. (She's pregnant.) Curtis came in later—he's to appear for his final type physical May 15. Ted was run over by the tractor—more shocked than hurt—and is now in the hospital. David was given a 2B classification (work of national importance) until Oct. 19. An evasive board, but thank the Lord for these favors.

WEDNESDAY, MAY 5

Piano. Recorder. Began tracing plans of Bernard Schwartz House. Mrs. Wright's faintness in greeting us still makes me feel ill at ease. Peacocks hooted down the chimney flue. David's tearing down stone piers & wood trusses for remodeling the living room & Iovanna's roof. Organization very poor, and materials lacking—work therefore pretty unsatisfactory. In the two weeks we were away, they planted onions, peas, lima beans, okra, chard, lettuce, spinach, and tomatoes (covered with little white cotton rags as if they were individual hot houses). A magnificent thunderstorm, but David, unperturbed played the records to Jay, Wes, & Kenn down in Gene's room, and Wes rounded out the evening by showing his tricks of magic.

THURSDAY, MAY 6

Completed tracing Ground floor plan of Schwartz house. Piano. Recorder group playing Mozart & Hayden with Ruth, Kay, and Jack. Gardening today consisted of clearing away dead stalks, pieces of wood, match covers & tin cans from the upper court. A clear, sweet, post-rain smell, with the hillside white with wild plum blossom, the trees burgeoning greenly. Walked to the Unity Chapel graveyard with Jay and David. Jay's wife is not coming—wants to be near her family, doctor, & hospital—but someone explored his room & discovered a picture of her. Pretty soon no secret. Started planning ménus—bored still. Still carpentering for David.

Bernard Schwartz House: In 1938, *Life* magazine commissioned eight architects to design "dream houses" for "four representative families earning $2,000 to $10,000 a year." Two architects were assigned to each family, one asked to design a "traditional" house and the other, a "modern" one. Wright was assigned to the Blackbourn family of Minneapolis, but they were unable to build either project. In 1939, Wright prepared a modified version of the design for Bernard Schwartz, a businessman in Two Rivers, Wisconsin. Dubbed "Still Bend" for its location at a point where the adjacent river slows to form a broad marsh, the house was completed in 1940.

FRIDAY, MAY 7

Letters from Mom & George, plus a shell necklace from him—very sweet note and thought. Davy & Jack's trial scheduled for May 17. Played recorder with Kay & Jack—Ruth on cello, Kenn on bass fiddle, and Curtis on viola—loads of fun & it sounded good too. Planted potatoes over at Hillside with Henning and Davy. Completed ménu planning—a sorry thing with only canned tomatoes left, and most of our root cellar vegetables gone. Completed tracing Sheet 1—Improvements—Plot Plan of Bernard Schwarz house. A gray cold Decembery day which still couldn't repel the pink apple blossoms. Served and washed dishes.

SATURDAY, MAY 8

Weeded vineyard where radishes and onions are growing. Planted potatoes again at Hillside with Henning and Johnny. Ted's back from the hospital, but life is always exciting here—some shingles fell off the roof and made a direct hit on to David's nose—he feels woozy now.

   Sighted some cardinals and orioles today, plus a beautiful pastel gray and yellow snake, known with logic as the "blue racer."

   Movie—"Laburnum Grove" at Hillside.

SUNDAY, MAY 9

Jack and Davy were summoned to appear for trial on Tuesday, May 11 instead of the original May 17. Both were very busy getting their mental & financial status in order. Jay was assigned as my K.P. instead of Jack, which will be very hard on both of us—he as a new, and therefore slow, beginner—I as a far from efficient cook. Lunch and dinner went off fine today, with all sorts of compliments—a little hard on cook and servers since it was all buffet style. Lunch: creamed codfish, boiled potatoes, celery and olives, carrots, jello. Dinner—baked ham (cut in diamonds just as in a House Beautiful ad and all stuck with cloves and Mr. Wr. cut a slice off for himself right then & there), mashed potatoes, carrots, spiced apples, cream puffs with hot chocolate wine sauce. "I thought it was beginner's luck last time, but these are excellent." (From Mrs. FLW) Mr. Wr. said I looked very pretty & very French, apron over black evening gown & all I needed was a pointed cap. Later when I removed the apron after all the fuss & flurry of serving, he remarked, "Now that you've changed your clothes, you're in your right mind again."

WASHING DISHES AT A TALIESIN SINK, undated (1942–43).

Guests were Mr. (California architect) & Mrs. McCarty, on their way to South America, building for gov't. rubber plantations on a thousand miles of the Amazon. Also Mr. & Mrs. Boss & daughter Ruth—Marcus's mentor, and head of the Methodist Peace Congregation—here to look over place as possible apprenticeship for Ruth. He wanted to give Davy & Jack advice, & found that they had disappeared from the breakfast table too bored with his conversation to remain. He was very well informed on politics and political nuances.

Concert: Beethoven—Trio, Opus 3, and Cello duet in G Minor; Charpentier—Melody; Chorus; Mozart—Little Trio #1.

MONDAY, MAY 10

A minor miracle has happened—thru Saber's intercession, the trial has been postponed indefinitely pending action by State Draft Board to declare them vital farm units! Davy & Kay off to Chicago to convert several thousand dollars worth of securities into cash.

David teamaker—sandwich spread on crackers.

Lunch: Roast kid, spiced apples, baked potatoes, asparagus (freshly picked by Wes), stewed rhubarb.

Dinner: Parched rice with tomato & cheese sauce; pumpkin custard pudding; ham à la king (eggs, asparagus, carrots), green beans.

Wrights: Harvard beets; ham; glazed carrots; pudding. Baked bread which they said tasted like cake.

TUESDAY, MAY 11

Jay complained about Henning's not washing the milk can last night, & Henning answered, "Oh, I better I guess, or the snooks will get after me." So quickly are we labeled. Jay, of course, nearly flew into a fist fight with him.

Lunch: Roast chicken; carrots, brabant potatoes; plums—Wrights.

Fellowship: sausage, brabants, harvard beets ("simply delicious!"), Virginia chunks.

Dinner: Franconian parsnips; cottage cheese; stewed tomatoes; potato soup; rhubarb pie. People are still raving about the meals. Jay says they're the best he's had here—& as K.P. he should have lost his appetite.

To try and avoid reliance on Asian rubber, American corporations (such as Ford) and the U.S. government invested in **rubber plantations** in Brazil in the 1920s-40s.

WEDNESDAY, MAY 12

All is still calm. Hooray! Lunch: kid stew; boiled potatoes; rutabagas & apple sauce; cucumber pickles.

Dinner: spaghetti with Napoli sauce; cauliflower au gratin; tomato rice soup; deviled eggs with mustard sauce & ripe olives; Vienna tarts. Wrights—smoked fish, caviar, Hollandaise potatoes; carrots; farina pudding.

Read Dalton Trumbo's "The Remarkable Andrew"—charming and clever.

David's been planting pine trees—there'll be a total of 2000 done this spring.

THURSDAY, MAY 13

Lunch: Wrights—baked fish, mashed potatoes, baby beets, grilled parsnips, cornstarch pudding. Fellows—roast kid, mint sauce, mashed potatoes, gravy, Virginia chunks.

Dinner: Wrights—rice gruel, cheese soufflé; stewed tomatoes, jello. Fellows: Italian rice, soufflé, baked lima beans, spiced apples, jello with fruit & whipped cream.

In re tea: Tuesday, David produced layer cake cracking hard shelled American walnuts for over an hour; Wednesday, vanilla wafers; today, angel food cup cakes—all solitary labor & all delicious.

Jay & I took an hour off today to go walking & resting in the sun. Spoke of his disillusions & the mediocrities.

Letter from Burton—friendly & cycle-ly. Walked with David in the evening.

FLW's speaking at Spring Valley Monday & at Sandstone Tuesday—Marcus must be on pins & needles.

FRIDAY, MAY 14

A smooth day. Lunch: liver stew, ovenfried potatoes, sauerkraut (carrots), mustard pickles (crème duchesse). Dinner: whole wheat muffins, potato salad (stewed rhubarb), cold sliced kid, mint jelly, asparagus, coffee & chocolate custard pudding (Indian pudding). Jay & I work well together and between us, we always leave a clean kitchen. Comments on supper: "A wonderful meal," "the best supper in a long time" (Jack), marvelous salad, delicious desert.

David planted Norway pines on Midway & Bryn Mawr hills, & prepared lemon wafers for tea—good, too.

Aline Barnsdall phoned FLLW before tea from Santa Fe, and he fell into a train of reminiscences. Said she had a round, startled face, & the smallest hands & feet you ever saw—might have married her himself if he hadn't been otherwise engaged. Said 3 out of 5 women whom you build house for, fall in love with you—can be turned to good advantage for the family if you keep your wits about you & make no false moves. Aline was the mother of Ordinsky's (director Metropolitan Opera House) daughter, but wouldn't marry him, because he was too European, & would take all her money (6 million). Her house, on a high hill in the exact center of Los Angeles, is making all her neighbors mad, & the city wants to take it from her & turn it into a public park—the gates all around are decorated with sentiments by such Los Angeles favorites as Lenin, Marx, & Nietzsche.

Wrote to Mom & Burton. Letter from Judy.

SATURDAY, MAY 15

A rainy day—so no picnic & no rolls. In fact, small puddles are forming in our room right now.

Lunch: baking powder biscuits & Welsh rarebit (broiled lamb chops), beans (peas), boiled potatoes, (apple cornflake pudding).

Dinner: cold sliced ham, creamed asparagus, baked potatoes, pickled crabapples, coconut cream pie, coffee.

Movies—Crossroads—French—good involved plot.

SUNDAY, MAY 16

Breakfast conversation revolved around the superiority of whole wheat bread, and the Graves family type and Fellowship type as builders of the future order.

Read Silone's biography of Mazzini & his selected works.

Picnic lunch at the Porters: Everyone there including Cousin Charlie, Cousin Dick, Mary—all the Lloyd Joneses, it seemed—& the Graves family. FLLW, of course, set his cousin Charlie (prizes for Wisconsin model farm) at ease by saying, "Well are you too rich or too much of a snob to visit us any more?"

Aline Barnsdall was heir to her father's oil fortune and a feminist with progressive artistic interests. Her relationship with Richard Ordynski (1878–1953), a Polish actor at Barnsdall's theater in Los Angeles, produced a daughter, Betty "Sugertop" Barnsdall (b. 1917). Barnsdall hired Wright to design a private cultural center on Olive Hill, a 36-acre site in East Hollywood overlooking central Los Angeles, to include artists' studios, theaters, shops, and a dormitory for actors. The centerpiece was Barnsdall's residence, Hollyhock House (1919–21), a Mayan-inspired structure named for its stylized floral ornamentation. Only the Hollyhock House and two other structures were completed. In 1927, Barnsdall donated the entire site to the City of Los Angeles. It is now known as the Barnsdall Art Park.

WRIGHT WITH FELLOWS AT A PICNIC, undated (1942–43).

PRISCILLA AND OTHERS HOEING IN THE TALIESIN FIELDS, undated (1942–43).

Both the Wrights, driven by Burt, left for Spring Valley today. Early supper, & everyone off to the movies, except us—we had seen the picture already.

Piano. Traced. Read Silone on "Mazzini" & "Love & Ethics" by Ellen Key, translated from the German by Frank Lloyd Wright and Mamah Bouton Borthwick!!!

MONDAY, MAY 17

Piano. Recorder. Traced Sheet 2—Plans and Details—Improvements for Schwartz house. Planted onions in the lower garden. Washed very heavy laundry. David still working on house remodeling. FLLW lectured at Eau Claire today. Lack of official supervision is putting everyone in a holiday mood. Noted catbird calls, and blooming of the yellow mustard plant. During the week, David brought me little nosegays of wild rose and violets—today it was the exquisite apple blossom. Whole fellowship went to see Spring Green High's Senior Play, "Hobgoblin House," starring our own Ross Graves. Amateurishly amusing with everything in it as well as the kitchen sink.

TUESDAY, MAY 18

Trip to Racine with Howard, Ruth, Jay, Curtis, Ted, & David in Howard's car. Taken thru the Johnson Wax Office Building and Wingspread House by Eleanor Moritz, Johnson's secretary. Critics compared Office to a "beautiful woman swimming naked in a pool." Warm coloring and lighting. House near Wind Point is magnificently opulent and is better and near[er] the human scale than its photographs. Passed Alberts House designed by Edgar Tafel, apprentice. We brought our own picnic lunch up to their elegant cafeteria but the secretary smoothed over beautifully the initial embarrassment. Also visited the Jacobs and Pew Usonian houses near Madison. Wonderful sunset view of Lake Mendota with the salt smell of the sea in the air—from Pew House, which is really a jewel of a house. A good, informative day all round.

Wright's S. C. Johnson & Son Administration Building (1936–39), in Racine, Wisconsin, colloquially known as the **Johnson Wax Building**, is famous for its open-plan office area punctuated by a grid of treelike structural columns. Skylights and clerestories composed of Pyrex tubes rather than plate glass notoriously leaked (though recent renovations have apparently solved that problem). Wright also designed a distinctive research tower, clad in alternating bands of brick and glass, added to the complex in the 1940s.

Wright designed **Wingspread** (1938–39), also in Racine, for S. C. Johnson & Son president Herbert F. Johnson shortly after beginning work on the company's administrative headquarters. Johnson and his wife donated the sprawling house to the Johnson Foundation in 1959, and it is now used as a conference center.

The **John C. Pew House** (1938–40) in the Village of Shorewood Hills, now part of Madison, is reminiscent of the more famous Fallingwater in that it is cantilevered over a ravine.

WEDNESDAY, MAY 19

Weeded quack grass & clover from strawberry patches in lower court. Mangled laundry. Walked. Traced. Filled room with torquoise chinese bowls of yellow dandelions. Lilacs are just blooming. Eight white-ruffled-petaled strawberry blossoms coming up. Violets and mustard blossom pleasing contrast. Noted wood thrush (rust colored, white margined tail) and catbird (slate grey, speckled black, with at least 20 different calls). Evening visits from Wes (who asked David & Jay to be in charge of lawn mowing this summer—and who spoke at length on birds, bees, bulls, and house building contracts), Jay, and Kenn, who brought us some blackberry liquer he had made. Session ended at midnight.

THURSDAY, MAY 20

Weeded mallow, milkweed, dandelions, dock, clover, thistle and quack grass out of main strawberry field in court below the house.

Flowers now blooming around the house: tulips, sweet william, choryopsis, bleeding heart, lady's slipper, canterbury ivy, rue and anemone, violets, lilacs, shooting star.

Tea lasted till supper time with the Wrights discussing their lectures at Eau Claire, Spring Valley, and Sandstone. Saarinen sent in drawings to Spring Valley too, but they rejected them because he put all the buildings on top ridge of hill where they'd be blown off by the terrific winds (in collaboration with son-in-law Swanson). At Sandstone, Marcus seemed tanned & healthy, but afraid of having lost his outside contacts. The jail is extraordinarily clean, well staffed with doctors, psychiatrist, & teachers, but the discipline is severe, tho not harsh. The prisoners were an intellectually hungry, keen, alert audience, and FLL was very enthusiastically received—the jail's only outside speaker ever.

Worked on essay for birthday box—school in transition. Piano. Recorder. Read Rupert Brooke's Selected Poems.

FRIDAY, MAY 21

Piano. Recorder. Planned ménu. Thinned radishes in vineyard—greens used for salad. Long talk after tea with just David, Mrs. Wright, and me—lasted till supper— war, and the hypocrisy of the change of line, Alexander Woollcott, Lloyd Lewis, & Franklin Porter. David mowed the lawns and hoed. I have my first sunburn of the season—Hooray, spring is here!

Wright's **birthday box** was a Taliesin Fellowship tradition, similar to the Christmas Box: One apprentice designed the box, which was then filled with drawings and other items from the other fellows.

SATURDAY, MAY 22

Piano lesson. Played recorder near goat-studio. Worked on birthday essay in the sunshine of our little bedroom balcony. Hoed area near asparagus & gooseberries. Thinned radishes again. Cleaned theatre with Henning—we gathered mustard blossoms on his hills, and lilac, and apple blossom, and violet. A charming arrangement in yellow, pink, and shades of purple. Picnic on Davisons' property—lots of fun, with the Wright girls dressed in ruffled garden dresses, and I in culottes. Davy & Jack called to trial on Wednesday. FLLW kept on criticizing Davy for choosing the wrong building site and for planting firs where they would block the view. Movies—"Magnificent Dope" with Henry Fonda—pointed and amusing.

SUNDAY, MAY 23

Mrs. Wr. more upset than FLLW about Clifton Fadiman's New Yorker criticism of the Autobiography—"dismaying egotism," "overwritten." Svetlana—"How dare they criticize Daddy Frank?" Johnny—"He's just a cheap radio entertainer," etc.

 Johnny & I picked asparagus for dinner. Lunch: creamed codfish (Mr. Wr. said it was perfect—just the way he likes it), boiled potato, lettuce, olives, rice pudding (perfect—just the way she likes it). Dinner: baked ham basted with wine, asparagus, mashed potatoes, radishes with Taliesin dressing, sour cream muffins, pumpkin pie, coffee. Mrs. Wr. "Everyone's raving about your meal"—Mr. Wr. ditto on "gems"; Mrs. Porter—gems & muffins, etc. Virtues of amateur cook extolled. Johnny & I had a pleasant, slow-paced day.

 Beginning of summer visitors. Concert good.

MONDAY, MAY 24

Well, Johnny said this was the easiest day he ever spent in the kitchen. The Wrights left in the afternoon for Chicago to buy drapes for Svet. Lunch: veal paprika (lamb chops); Harvard beets ("put them in the Taliesin cook Book"); baked potatoes, (plum crème duchess). (Mr. Wr. lectured at Dodgeville before the Kiwanis Club

---

Clifton Fadiman (1904–1999) was book editor of the *New Yorker* from 1933 to 1943, and established the Book-of-the-Month Club. His May 22, 1943, *New Yorker* review of Wright's *Autobiography* noted, "He is a man about whose supremacy there can be no doubt, least of all on behalf of Mr. Wright himself . . . There is not the slightest doubt that his ego and eccentricities are part of what makes him a profound artist in wood and stone and concrete. It is just that this ego and these eccentricities should be reserved for his private enjoyment, not broadcast in this blatantly overwritten autobiography . . . Yet somehow not even his most humorless pomposity can quite disguise the central magnificence of his professional thought on the subject he knows best. His office buildings and his houses, and the liberating vision of which they are the product, will stand when his crotchets have long been forgotten."

at noon.) Dinner: cream of tomato soup, creamed potatoes, wax beans, cottage cheese, brown sugar loaf with mocha icing.

Yesterday, in discussing Jens Jensen, landscape architect, Mrs. Wr. attacked him as having no feeling for building architecture against Mrs. Porter's defense. "Don't feel sorry for him. Feel sorry for the underdog, the man in no man's land, out in front of the firing-line—your poor dear brother." (This last in quavering tones.)

Jack & Davy are arraigned, but definitely not on trial Wednesday—that may take place in July.

Worked on plans for school room cluster. Recorder.

TUESDAY, MAY 25
Recorder ensemble. Four and a half hours off from cooking—a good day! Lunch: Lamb stew, beans, carrots, onions, celery, potatoes, pickles. Dinner: stewed tomatoes, ham à la king, cottage cheese vegetable salad, pumpkin custard pudding with whipped cream. Worked on plans again—and still. Difficult, but excellent for mental exercise, and appreciation of what a plan means. New apprentice— Phil—from California. Kittredges are coming tomorrow for an indefinite vacation— he's ill*—excellent typographer and illustrator; Quietly generous. *Blood clot on brain—always seems slightly tipsy, finds it difficult to remember what he's saying—amnesia.

WEDNESDAY, MAY 26
Davy & Jack arraigned today—trial set for June 9.

Lunch: roast veal; gravy, brabant potatoes, baked parsnips, pickles & radishes, (rhubarb pie).

Dinner: potato salad (ham à la king), asparagus, cheese soufflé, jello with whipped cream & peanut butter cookies (lemon pudding). Wrights returned from Chicago.

Letter from Nat. David still "improving" house.

Lady had a colt that wobbles when it manages to rise at all. I suspect Mousie will kitten under the stove.

Long walk in the evening with David and Jay. The sun rose just long enough to set—& the woods were purple with Canterbury ivy.

Jens Jensen (1860–1951), a Danish American landscape architect who designed numerous parks and private estates in Chicago and elsewhere in the Midwest, moved to Ellison Bay, Wisconsin, in 1935, and established The Clearing, a retreat where city dwellers might renew their connection to nature. It remains in operation as an educational center.

THURSDAY, MAY 27

Lunch: Tifselki, mashed potatoes, rutabagas and apple sauce (carrots), peaches.

Dinner: Veal and noodle casserole, steamed sauerkraut & caraway seeds, stewed tomatoes (asparagus), chocolate pudding (orange & egg). Ted & several others said that the chocolate pudding was the best ever served in the Fellowship. Mrs. Wr. told me that last night's dinner served to her & the Kittredges was astounding. Most cooks lack imagination by the evening meal, but this was a creation, the work of a chef, as if an artist were in the kitchen, etc., etc. and more praise for the work of amateurs.

FL in speaking of his exhibit at Cambridge of the four masters—Wright, Stravinsky, Maillot, and Picasso—said he never thought much of the other three.

He also told Mr. Kittredge to leave the city and live in the country for 3 years, listen to the songs of birds, watch clouds, even hear the flowers grow, and he would be completely better. Then he turned to Jay, David, & Burt, who were listening in almost themselves convinced, winked and, "Maybe I'll try that myself some day."

Recorder. Read.

FRIDAY, MAY 28

Letters from Mom & Judy. Recorder.

Lunch: Paprika veal, Harvard beets, baked potatoes (rice pudding).

Dinner: Potato soup, baked bacon, cottage cheese, wax beans (carrots), strawberry mousse, (Indian pudding), scallions and radishes (of which FL eats handfuls to the complete disgust of his wife). Served on hill garden.

Walk with Jay in the afternoon. I'm tired & irritable.

SATURDAY, MAY 29

Lunch: biscuits, creamed eggs & asparagus, stewed tomatoes, (apple cornflake pudding).

Dinner: Served as picnic outside the theater. Everyone commented on the lushly lavish appearance of the heaped up trays, best picnic dinner ever served, tastes as good as it looks—even better, not trying to make you feel good, but it's wonderful, etc.

Salami and cheese, hamana white and brown bread, scallions and radishes, cottage cheese and vegetable salad, olives, potato salad, virginia chunks & sweet pickles, boiled coffee, spice cake, jams, peanut butter.

Movies—"Harvest"—wonderful & touching scene of the gift of bread.

Well, my week ended with a bang, not with a whimper.

Warm breezes coming in thru open doors—heavy odor of lilacs, heat lightening so frequent, it affected closed eyelids like candle flickerings.

Structural perfection of bleeding heart & lady's slipper. Owl & whippoorwill calls.

SUNDAY, MAY 30

Walk on quarry hill—took along all sorts of paraphernalia & then it grew threatening. Finished Gilbert Seldes', "The Seven Lively Arts," recorder, wrote letters. Phyllis & Ellis, former apprentices are visiting for a week on his way to the army. Phyllis came in attracted by David's cardboard manipulations—and now he has a potential pupil—two, as a matter of fact. Ellis joined them too. David played some of the records at the concert tonight—which filled in a bad spot when Curtis lost his temper & dismissed the chorus because they were doing a miserable job. Mrs. Wr. flew up & off, but Mr. defended him quickly— he understood.

Ellis & Phyllis dismissal exact repetition of Eleanor Kenn "immorality" charge. Ellis' complaint—you were trained for years to be an architect, & then couldn't go off to practice (see "senior apprentice departures" herein previously discussed). Interested in cooperative building ventures—he in arch.; she in sculpture; two in laws in ceramics & textiles, with a place for Marcus as a builder to which he can return from jail unstigmatized.

FL discussed Fadiman criticism with David, Jay & me—it still rankles tho he takes it with much more levelheadedness than his females. Says his chief trouble is that he can't write with a wrinkle in his eye.

MONDAY, MAY 31

Walked to Hillside to get groceries. Picked radishes, scallions, asparagus. Laundry. Worked on birthday box. Piano. Recorder. At tea, FL asked Curtis if he felt any remorse (no) or whether the end justified the means (yes). Then he asked Curtis to play some Beethoven for him because he reads so beautifully, & this was their tacit handshake in spite of la belle dame. Alternating sun & showers—I changed 4 times.

TUESDAY, JUNE 1

Picked asparagus, rhubarb, scallions, radishes. Played recorder with Ruth in the sun. Jay was moved up to Marcus' room because "you're friendly with the Henkens

---

Ellis Jacobs (1921–2008) joinded the Fellowship in 1937. He married another Taliesin fellow, **Phyllis M. Wesley** in 1942, and, after serving in WWII, started an architecture practice in California.

& they won't mind," and we spent all morning moving, vacuuming, and cleaning. Mangled a little. Read Untermeyer's "Food & Drink." Worked on birthday box plan—Curtis thinks it's good, but that FL's criticism depends on his mood. He sometimes gets very moody on his birthdays because of the passing of the years, & because the boys never do anything except then & for Christmas.

Visitors today—wife of Prof. Reese—German—U. of Wisconsin, her daughter, & niece & nephew, children of Schmidt, German architect.

Sunday, when David sat on one of the music chairs designed by Mr. Wr., FL asked him to sit on the sofa because the proportions of his figure didn't suit those of the chair—and the chair didn't look so good.

David's been doing stonemasonry—& Curtis may be relieved from the kitchen to work on it too, because FL thinks he does even better stone work than Phil himself.

WEDNESDAY, JUNE 2

Typed essay for box—now I have to work on plans. Fifth day of rain—and today after a beautiful orange sunrise that made me jump out of bed to see the way it gilded the valley, tho directly opposite were thick grey clouds & ominous thunder.

Ruth & I gathered asparagus, rhubarb, & leaf lettuce, and for the souls' delight, some wild geranium.

David was still working as a stonemason and I cleaned out the laths (de nailing them) and plaster from Iovanna's room.

Recorder out in the orchard. Played Mozart duets. Letters from Ada & Bonawit. Wrote to Nat.

Grace Volkman, new apprentice came. Seems eager to work, quite friendly, & endeared herself to FL by saying "a soldier is not quite a man."

Read "Rockwellkentiana"—bibliography, writings, drawings, engravings, woodcuts.

FL announced at tea that Luise Rainer phoned from N.Y. about getting a house built, & that Katherine Cornell on her way thru Madison in "Three Sisters" will stop from Sunday noon to Monday noon, with Carleton Smith, musicologist, & assistant librarian of the Library of Congress.

THURSDAY, JUNE 3

Letters from George B. enclosing very biting criticism of Autobiography by

---

Grace Volkman joined the Fellowship in 1943.

CURTIS BESINGER PAVING A COURTYARD AT TALIESIN, undated (1942–43).

Wm. Lescaze in N.Y. Times; Bert Slanhoff actually flying alone; Florence (Sol's had his physical).

Picked asparagus, radishes, scallions, leaf lettuce.

Still shoveling plaster—I hate the grit and fine dust it makes. I'm going to put muscles where they don't belong on women, I guess.* Played piano.

Typed carbons of "sincere C.O." letters for David.

*FL was rather cute about it. I stood around aimlessly wondering how I could get the plaster down, & he said, "Well, the first problem is to get you up." Later I picked up branches as he trimmed the hedges, & we discussed the review. He said that Wm. Lescaze tried to come here, but he wouldn't have him, & that 5 times in N.Y. Lescaze invited him to dinner, but FL refused. "I've tried to be friendly, but this is the last time." "That's up to you." This was his way of getting even this personal venom that shone through. FL said "That's what you're always to expect from your disciples."

Mrs. Wr. is thinking of weaving table mats, so she's dyeing, & I made a warp, chained & threaded it today—two blistering walks to Midway.

Worked on some of Curtis' suggestions for my plan. David's still struggling with his, but the idea is good. He is also a good enough stonemason now to work on a wall alone.

FRIDAY, JUNE 4

Gardened scallions, radishes, asparagus, with Grace.

Made 10 pounds of soap in the afternoon. To a can of lye dissolved in 2 1/2 pints of water cooled, add melted fats, stir, mold. I kept water & vinegar handy in case of burns, which are acid.

Recorder. Piano. Worked on school plans—can't get the classrooms in proportion.

Square-knotted new warp & old on loom, & rolled warp on—now Mrs. Wr. is ready to proceed.

FL went to Washington today to see Biddle personally about Jack and Davy. An interesting speculation for some of us, a minor hell for others. (Cornell visit naturally postponed.)

Swiss-born architect **William Lescaze** (1896–1969) immigrated to the United States in 1920. Working in partnership with architect George Howe (1886–1955), he designed the Philadelphia Saving Fund Society (PSFS) Building, completed in 1932 and widely regarded as the first major International Style building in the United States. In a *New York Times* review of Wright's autobiography, Lescaze criticized him for, among other things, ignoring the contributions of other architects to his work and mentioning the two world wars and the Great Depression only in passing.

Francis Biddle (1886–1968), a lawyer and judge, was attorney general of the United States in 1943.

RUTH TEN BRINK, SVETLANA PETERS, AND HENNING WATTERSON PRACTICING RECORDERS OUTSIDE, undated (1942–43).

FRANK LLOYD WRIGHT AT A PICNIC WITH THE TALIESIN FELLOWSHIP, undated (1942–43).

Chorus voted and asked Curtis to lead them again; Ted & Henning refused to come as protest—they wanted Svetlana, and are waiting for a Sunday show down.

Norman Thomas answered David's invitation that he would be glad to come here in August at the time of the Socialist picnic in Milwaukee.

Svet and Wes had a house-warming, which could have been great fun after all the chicken & champagne, but we played charades. From that point on, Iovanna became petulant, nasty, & vicious, directing all sorts of remarks at me in the mood of the eternal feminine. Disgusting display—and Jack was going at Kay for all he was worth, & cracks were flying. It's such fun to be people.

SATURDAY, JUNE 5

Letters from Mom & Judy–ambiguous advice about my returning home.

Grace & I gardened barefoot, gathering scallions, radishes, lettuce, asparagus, cleaning them & our feet at the lawn pump.

Pressed the tag-end of Monday's laundry.

Set up the theater, showing Phil around. Movie was a Joe [sic] Pal puppetoon, "Tulips Shall Grow," and a mawkishly sentimental "The Great Man's Lady," based on Senator George Hearst's life (Wm. Randolph's pop).

Several people commented on Iovanna's rudeness, & thought I should have demanded an apology—but what can one expect of a spoiled, petulant child.

SUNDAY, JUNE 6

FL phoned he might not be back by Tuesday—probably getting hold of Biddle is not too easy.

Worked on my own plans & sheet 3 of Schwartz House. Picked asparagus. Wrote to Bleiberg about returning to school in Sept. Served & washed dishes, with David. Visits from Ruth, Curtis, Jay.

Concert excellent, especially César Franck trio, opus #1 and Hayden cello trio.

MONDAY, JUNE 7

Completed sheet 3—Farm unit plans of Schwartz house, and wrote letters to Mom, Burt, Bonawit—all while keeping office for Gene. David worked on his birthday box plans all day.

Norman Thomas (1884–1968), a leading socialist, involved with the Fellowship of Reconciliation, was one of the founders of the American Civil Liberties Union and was a six-time presidential candidate for the Socialist Party of America. Milwaukee, home to several socialist mayors between 1910 and 1960, is the site of a picnic hosted by the Socialist Party, still an annual event after more than a century.

Read Huxley's "The Art of Seeing." Piano—very little. Picked scallions and radishes.

Spring Green gossip about us: We're building a big landing field here for the Japanese. Earlier, they said two Japanese from Taliesin blew up the Spr. Gr. Bridge, & the only Japanese here at the time was Chic-ngai.

TUESDAY, JUNE 8

Mr. Wright's birthday—and he brought good news from Washington:

1. Dept of Justice ordered trial dismissed & Davy & Jack classified 2C. Of course, Stone may refuse this since he's not under their jurisdiction, but he probably won't.

2. Marcus is free on parole, & working in a hospital (or similar service) in California—not sent to a CPS camp at all.

Watched office for Gene & practiced my recorder & piano at the same time. C. Smith called from Chicago about visit with Cornell, as did FL arriving happily, & the Wisconsin State Journal twice.

David spent most of the day completing his perspective. Me—piano & recorder & office girl.

High tea with the launching of the Davison rowboat as birthday gift to Mr. Wr., which he promptly gave as a gift to the Fellowship over their protests.

Gala party in the evening with Johnny reaching new heights in his fruit & flower arrangements at the theater. Picture was a brand new Russian musical comedy, "Spring Song." Gifts of glassware, slippers, ties, antique Chinese iron pot & kettle, fruit basket & scarf, 1811 cognac & flask. Mr. Wr. threw cherries at all of us—very gay mood.

Jay, Ellis, & Phyllis came in later to hear some Porgy & Bess, and join us in some beer & salami.

WEDNESDAY, JUNE 9

Birthday breakfast and opening of box: Wes—temple of the sun—grandiose, imaginative; Curtis—excellent plan of a house; Phyllis—stone carving; Ellis—cottage; Kenn—abstraction; Jay—Texas house; Johnny—house on Michaels ridge; Kay—4 abstractions; Henning—abstr; Gene—Vol. VI of the Autobiography printed; Howard—dairy for coöp community. He told David it was too symmetrical, & ∴ almost academic; showed great imagination in many ways; that he built up to complexity instead of down to simplicity.

Jack & Davy, went in to Madison—& the trial's postponed for a week & will be at Wausau, but all these delays mean that they're practically free men now.

Gathered asparagus. Traced. Letters from Julia, George, Blanche. Wrote to Julia & Florence.

About my plans, which FL looked at after tea, he said that I had a lot of common sense; that I took the school as it was & made an extraordinarily good thing out of it; that I had a lot of brains under this hair of mine; that now he knew I was busy during a lot of the time he couldn't account for me; that I was the surprise (David insists he said "prize") package of the box.

Jay & David talked politics in the pasture while I read Poliakov's "Russians Don't Surrender."

Traced for several hours. Played the recorder. Records—and we danced to them— just like old times.

THURSDAY, JUNE 10

Made 12 pounds of soap. Recorder. Piano. Gathered lettuce, asparagus, scallions, radishes. Washed and mangled laundry. Planned ménu. Traced Sheet 4—Schwartz House.

Letter from Burton—to be inducted tomorrow. I feel almost as resigned as he.

Visitors: George Dutton and ? Hebert—Dutton wants to buy a farm nearby; once came as an apprentice, paid $1100 and left the next day. Hebert always wanted to come, and is now in the army.

FRIDAY, JUNE 11

Made 12 more pounds of soap. Recorder & piano duets with Grace. Piano. Completed Sheet 4—Schwartz House—Improvements and Elevations. Gathered radishes and scallions. Tied tender new vines—pinky rose stems.

Read Alice Duer Miller's "The White Cliffs."

Judy's coming July 9—also Blanche. Letter from Muriel—cute as can be.

Ruby-throated humming bird on the wild columbine. Lilacs gone. Voluptuous pink peonies; the rose peonies just budding. Exquisite scent of yellow lilies. Luxuriant ferns. Soft pale green of white oaks. A thousand bird calls—jaybird especially.

Priscilla's **plans for the school** included "fields under cultivation," plantings, a library, and athletic fields, in addition to the classroom cluster. The curriculum would be structured not by traditional subjects but "integrated around a central core of pupil aptitude." The building, with "sound-proof construction," featured seating "on the diagonal for easy visibility" and of "adjustable height." The utility stack would provide audiovisual materials, such as "accessibly cinematic versions of books, or films seen as art medium in their own right, the news and its various interpretations, important talks, recording of poetry or plays . . ." Priscilla also provided plenty of "open book shelves, newspaper and magazine racks," "free rolling maps and charts," and "prints and abstractions to delight the eye." From the collection of the Taliesin Architects Archives, The Frank Lloyd Wright Foundation. Courtesy Elissa R. Henken, Jonathan T. Henken, and Mariamne H. Whatley.

George Dutton had briefly joined the Fellowship in 1933.

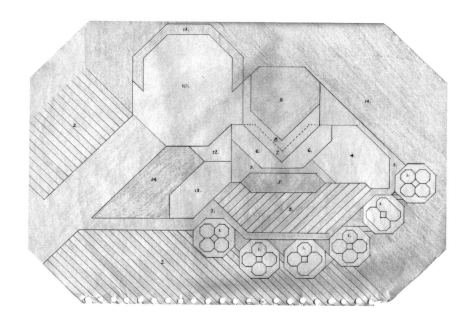

PRISCILLA'S PLAN FOR A SECONDARY SCHOOL, PREPARED FOR WRIGHT'S BIRTHDAY BOX, June 1943.
Key: 1. classroom cluster; 2. fields under cultivation; 3. walks and entrances; 4. lunchroom and after theater dining; 5. outdoor pool; 6. gymnasia—girls' and boys'; 7. dressing rooms beneath stands; 8. observation stands; 9. athletic field; 10. community center-auditorium-theater; 11. cooling pond; 12. offices and foyer; 13. library; 14. planting

SATURDAY, JUNE 12

Curtis' birthday, but the "U.S.A." we ordered hasn't arrived yet. Concentrated on gathering radishes swelling to the size of small beets. Studied mechanical drawing. Piano lesson. Recorder—and the group played at the picnic.

Picture for Wes's birthday—"Peter the First"—an unpleasant character even if Stalin is making him a national hero.

Picnic on beautiful site behind Mary Waterstuet's farm. We were conveyed picturesquely—Mr. and Mrs. in a rig; 11 of us in a carryall—with Wes, Svet, & Brandock in front looking just like old covered wagon day; 2 by horseback; 5 by truck; 3 by car.

A beautiful, tender, & "inarticulate" letter from Burton—a goodbye—and I his "truest friend of all." Also from Mom with license, and Hans quoting an extract from a below-the-level-of-genius letter by FL to Lewis about Hans—backbiting, of course.

Read two brief volumes of poetry—by Alice Duer Miller & Margaret Seiffert.

SUNDAY, JUNE 13

What a day for the kitchen—blazing hot, no help till 12:30; cream that wouldn't whip; humidity that turned crisp cookies limp. Howard didn't want to go in—horses; Henning neither—sheep; likewise David—a quick-tempered wife. After much quibbling, Howard finally came in, tho Johnny comforted me by saying that I had been wonderful in the kitchen with him, & did way more than I should have; later he said I had been in the kitchen a lot lately, but they're not complaining—the Fellowship benefits by it.

Lunch—roast chicken, hard boiled eggs, potatoes—baked, fresh greens—all for a picnic.

Dinner—baked ham; scallions, radishes & lettuce with Tal. dressing; asparagus, fluffy baked potatoes, coffee mousse & syrup, spice cookies, iced tea, & hot coffee for the Wrights. Compliments, plus one from Phil—"I hope I can do as well next time I cook."

MONDAY, JUNE 14

Burton was accepted for limited service—so air mail special delivery conveyed to me. I've cooked with a lump in my throat before.

Jay became new K.H. while Howard works on construction.

Sweet letter from Bonawit recommending my wisdom & coming here, & giving advice about the Fall.

Lunch: English beef stew, boiled potatoes, asparagus, scallions, radishes, lettuce (stewed strawberries and rhubarb).

Dinner: creamed asparagus & eggs; spaghetti with Napoli sauce; lettuce; mixed green salad w. Taliesin dressing; chocolate pudding (lemon pudding).

Amusing that Mrs. Wr. induced Jay by telling him that I would be the best cook to work for—Ruth would work him harder, and Phil and Grace were new.

Several free hours in one of which I wrote to Burton, remembering after I sealed the envelope, how much I still had not said.

TUESDAY, JUNE 15

Lunch: cold sliced ham, brabant potatoes, asparagus, (crème duchess & stawberries).

Dinner: Harvard beets, lettuce and potato salad, cottage cheese, fruit jello, poppy seed cookies (strawberry pie made by Iovanna).

Davy, Jack, Kay, & Wes left for Wausau today for the trial. Scher can't come, but they'll meet their substitute lawyer, Heisler, there.

Letter from Muriel asking us to dope out some puzzles.

Slept in the sun—evening walk with David.

WEDNESDAY, JUNE 16

Lunch: Meat loaf w. tomato sauce, asparagus, lettuce & potato salad.

Dinner: Cheese soufflé, mixed vegetable and cottage cheese salad, jellied beef bouillion, wax beans (asparagus), (cold sliced ham), strawberry short cake (strawberry pudding).

Wes phoned that Davy & Jack were given 4 years each, and fined $100 each. Is this their "comeuppance"?

Curtis thanked us for "U.S.A." by saying we had disturbed his sleep—but he said it with a smile. (David had put the book under his pillow, & tho he was uncomfortable, he didn't bother investigating till morning.)

Heisler, the lawyer, came back with Wes & Kay—& told us of a real rail-roading trial with Stone distorting evidence, & the only witness, a Miss McGill, head of the local draft board.

Francis Heisler (1896–1984) was a lawyer who specialized in defending conscientious objectors during World War II, the Korean War, and the Vietnam War. He helped change some of the CO laws, making it unnecessary to claim religious allegiance to the peace churches.

Phone call from Guggenheim Foundation asking FLLW to plan a museum for them. Read "Mediaeval Legends & Satires"—Shackford.

THURSDAY, JUNE 17

The Wrights left for N.Y. this morning about Guggenheim plans.

Hundreds of quarts of strawberries are coming in so fast we have to can or sell them.

Oriental peonies—purple petals with deep yellow centers in corner near studio; flaming orange oriental poppies with deep purple center on hill garden; deep shadowed fern.

A dispute at tea yielded the following superstitions about what the bob-white's call is: Mrs. Wr. —"bob-white;" Sister Maginel—"more wet"—a warning of rain; Iovanna—"But Daddy says it calls 'Frank Wright.'"

Lunch—roast beef; asparagus, mashed potatoes, gravy, greens, aspic & lettuce.

Dinner—baked beans, Boston brown bread (Jay says one of his mother's ancestors was reputed to have introduced it to America), sauerkraut, lettuce & frozen vegetable salad, strawberry chiffon pie with graham cracker crumb crust.

Read Phil Stong's "Stranger's Return."

Rumor hath it that the Spring Green American Legion is "laying for" Marcus when he returns.

Went walking with David & Jay in the evening—lovely sunset skies and cool breezes marred by mosquitoes so numerous your arms are black with them. But braved them with my pheasant's feather.

Read some plays in a collection of "American life & fantasy," but discovered I had read them before.

FRIDAY, JUNE 18

Lunch: Hungarian goulash, asparagus, boiled potatoes, greens.

Dinner: Macaroni, cottage cheese, lettuce & mixed green salad, cold fruit salad of

---

In 1939, the **Solomon R. Guggenheim Foundation** established the Museum of Non-Objective Painting for the purpose of exhibiting the extensive collection of modern art of Solomon Guggenheim (1861–1949). After operating the museum in rented space for several years, the foundation hired Wright to design a new, permanent home for the collection. The call to which Priscilla refers led to one of Wright's greatest works—the spiraling Guggenheim Museum overlooking New York's Fifth Avenue, completed six months after Wright's death in 1959.

Maginel Wright (1877–1966), Wright's youngest sister, studied illustration at the School of the Art Institute of Chicago, and became a graphic artist and prolific children's book illustrator. She had a daughter, Elizabeth (Bitsy), with her first husband, Walter Enright, in 1909, and later married Hiram Barney. She lived most of her professional life in New York but summered in Wisconsin with Wright. In 1965, she published *The Valley of the God-Almighty Joneses*, her memories of her family's farms in Wisconsin.

stewed strawberries, rhubarb, & grapefruit with whipped cream; maraschino cookies.

Very tiring day—baked bread, 42 weiner rolls, made cottage cheese, & tomorrow's salad dressings.

Read Stark Young's "Rose Windows," a play.

The boys picked strawberries all morning & evening after supper, & worked on the house or planted potatoes between times. Girls canned strawberries & asparagus. Sold so far about $140 worth of berries.

Kay saw Davy & Jack in the Madison jail yesterday and today. They seem high spirited, are eating the vegetables & cheeses she takes them with complaints about jail food, & are optimistic about Courtney's promise to carry their 2C appeal thru, which is now in the President's hands. Johnny's is in the same place—but he's off to Chicago on a brief vacation.

The Wrights phoned tonight, but we're ignorant of the measure of their success—just heard Gene's end, "Well, then, we won't say a thing about it."

Our swift creek is a stagnant swamp. The Oriental peonies & poppies are wilting; the wild iris is a paler blue; Henning wears netting from his hat brim to his ankles; Ted dons a sombrero; appetites lag—sumer is icumen in.

Attempted mothproofing & storing our clothes—but hard work & inertia are serious opponents.

Feel somehow as if Burton had died—how affection adds fears to those the world is already too full of.

Read clever, modern, brittle, tender yet sophisticated poetry of Ellen Glines—"Garden Untended."

A picnic is being planned for Saturday & Sunday—overnight, that is, to Baraboo, northeast of here, in the region of the Wisconsin dells. They say it is unimaginably lovely with clear waterfalls ending in fine streams for bathing and caves to go thru from one fall to the other. Sleeping bags & blankets are the order of the day—but I should also like a steel barricade of mosquito netting. Tales of Arab mothers who never bother to shoo the flies from their children's eyes seem much more pertinent now—it's not apathy; it's resignation.

Waited up quite late for David to return from berry picking—I've never seen anyone quite so bitten up. In the meantime, I was very domestic, and school marmish, going thru some of the thousands of pages David clipped from magazines with a far sighted view of Sunday and high school blackboards. It scarcely seems possible for me to return to teaching—certainly my attitude is changed. Will my methods be? How can I fit into the ballyhooing for war programs, the current un read literature about "after 1944, what?", or "the inside of the inside," or "the secret history of . . ."?

Lunch: beef and noodle casserole, brabant potatoes, asparagus, pickles.

Picnic Supper: weiners, buns, potato salad, vegetable salad, cottage cheese salad, strawberries, pickles, jams, peanut butter, brown sugar loaf w. coffee icing, coffee, milk.

A smooth, easy day until I spilled boiling water onto my leg instead of into the coffee maker, scalding my skin. Kay, Ruth, Jay applied first aid while I whimpered in agony until Dr. Wahl came, using Mrs. Wright's picrate ointment & lots of Kay's cheese cloth for a clumsy but necessary bandage. My fingers & arm were comparatively mild. David came in scratched & sweaty from baling hay and was very kind. I finally went to the picnic with enough dope in me to immunize me against anything, it would seem . . .

Ruth helped Jay serve; several people went bathing in the stream; Palestrina chorus around the fire, & then into sleeping bags & under blankets. And then the mosquitoes came in hordes, in armies, in legions. Citronella was passed around; we watched the moon rise inch by inch; we heard whisperings; frog croaks & swattings punctuated the silence; it was unbearably hot covered; absolutely unbearable otherwise. At 4 a.m. Henning tried to get enough people to fill a truck—& got enough to fill both. So we gathered our possessions by the moonlight that silvered everything but the insect life—and rode into the dawn, if not into the sunrise.

SUNDAY, JUNE 20

I slept till noon, but David is K.P. At one, Howard, Ruth, Curtis, Phil, & I went back to the scene of the crime to retrieve a pot of berries which Howard had left in a tree last night. Then we climbed up the steep sides of the gorge & down. I sat & wrote a letter to Daddy while the others climbed up the path the waterfall takes. My leg is incapacitating me for a while.

Then we saw Devil's Lake formed out of a crater at Baraboo, the Merrimac powder & explosives plant, & the Fellowship of Reconciliation Farm near Prairie du Sac.

Noted the horizontal terraces along steep hills—the cow paths which they make so they can graze, never walking straight up or down. FLW once said that a city's streets are always laid out along the cowpaths because they know the secret of contour walking. And cows go up to quite some height, too. When David & the boys were planting pines at Bryn Mawr, & had gone up as far as they thought they could, they looked up to the crest of the hill, & there was a cow looking down.

MONDAY, JUNE 21

Still find getting around quite painful, so confined myself to sedentary occupations—reading Skazki—Legends of Old Russia, tracing, fixing asparagus for canning, writing to the Board & Bonawit, piano & recorder playing.

Two very interesting guests—Mr. & Mrs. Graeffe. They're on their way to a small college in Nebraska where he'll be head of the joint music & arts department. Was at Olivet last session. Did research for Art Encyclopedia in West Africa—said that there music & poetry & the dance are one; you can't study one without including the others. They use not only half & quarter tones but eighths—very subtle & a whole group can sing each one a half tone higher—very textural effect. All their instruments are used for special occasions—e.g. one called the "saizsɘ" which is another name for woman—it is used only by lonely men who walk the streets at night, & is used as a charm against tigers, leopards, & all <u>feline</u> prowlers. She does a little weaving, & has lectured on it.

He also told us of German & British colonial official life. The British always dress for dinner; the Germans never—hence they have no social contacts with each other. But there was one German who had a dinner jacket, but spoke no English. Nevertheless he was always invited to their affairs. An English woman physician had a love affair by correspondence with an officer whose pictures were quite satisfactory, but who wasn't up to par when she met him. He wouldn't pay her return fare, & she had no money. At a dinner, she helped translate the above mentioned German's German into English thru an intermediary pidgin English interpreter—and married him.

Once a sausage necked German engineer beat a negro so that he was in the hospital for 3 months—he had carelessly left a valve open, & thus caused an explosion. He was fined in the British court—as was the negro—& he grinned because it was such an easy escape. The be wigged judge was so displeased that he insisted the fine be paid in exact coins. The German said he would donate the rest to charity. "That's fine; nevertheless I must have the exact farthing." Officially there is such a coin—but it's been out of circulation for years. It cost him untold expense getting it from London—explaining, locating—& for 6 months the judge held him on week by week tenterhooks—he would be exiled from the colonies if he didn't produce the farthing, about 3/4 of a cent.

Phil & Jay came in at night to talk & listen to records.

The Germans **Lotte and Didier Graeffe** were on their way to Doane College in Crete, Nebraska, where they both taught various subjects before moving on to careers at the University of Florida.

There was such a close, terrible, incessant lightening storm last night as made me afraid of lightening for the first time in my life. And then David accidentally jabbed his elbow in my eye—so I'm now writing with a half closed lid. I'm counting on a good poison ivy thicket for my right arm to make the picture complete. My scalded right leg is still difficult & frequently painful to get about on.

Piano. Recorder. Mangled laundry. But I'd love to be out in the garden! Listened for phone calls in the office for Gene—one from Davy's Dad saying his mother would be too emotionally harmed to see him, but chiefly berries & berry pickers. Wrote to Nat. Read.

Graeffe told us an amusing story about Henry Russell Hitchcock whom he knows. Russell went to Venice, where his bag was whisked away from him, & he was transported to a hotel on the "stinking" canal. The bag was there, strangely enough, when he arrived. Then he went out for some internal libation, & returned quite high. When he awoke in the morning, he was wearing his pink & green striped pajamas & a key. The landlord explained that he had come home, undressed, thrown his suitcase out the window into the canal, & then his clothes. Then after two hours of ringing, he understood the theft but could do nothing about it. So he ventured into the streets barefoot, but wearing his pajamas & his bushy red beard which made him look old and distinguished even at 23—and of course, two blocks down, met fellow Bostonians. They gave him what little they had, & then he sent several telegrams, "Please wire $50 immediately." One friend did, Graefes', and the others must have too. And then Russell traveled in China, etc. but never returned the money. This friend went to the Hitchcock household, lived there for 3 weeks, until he felt he had eaten $50 worth of food—and left. They are now still good friends.

David changed my bandage today—blood, lymph, & down to raw, very red flesh. The pain was as excruciating as the first day's. I took one of the capsules & sank into a completely drugged 6 hour sleep beginning just before tea, to awake & find the place completely deserted. It seems Jay, David, Phil, & Curtis were talking with the guests from supper till ten! They are fascinating guests.

Henry-Russell Hitchcock (1903–1987) was among the most influential architectural historians of the twentieth century. His 1932 collaboration with architect Philip Johnson on the International Style exhibition at the Museum of Modern Art and the corresponding book fed the myth of Modernism as a European movement and in so doing narrowed the definition of what was truly "modern" in architecture. No works by Wright were included in the exhibition or the book. Wright, modern before Hitchcock was born, never forgot the slight.

WEDNESDAY, JUNE 23

Tended the office and read & read & read, shifting from Giedion on architecture to Van Gogh's letters (which I completed), to Waxman's History of Jewish Lit. to Robinson's Poetry to Fletcher's Comparative History of Architecture.

Finally took to playing solitaire, sitting very bare legged, when the Catholic priest came in about berry-picking. Here's the basis for another Spring Green rumor.

My leg, however, gives no indication of improving. The Graeffes left today.

Wonderful air mail letter from Burton in the evening—pathetic and groping.

Phil came in to listen to some of our poetry & spiritual records. Kay gave me some magazines to read. Davy & Jack to be removed to Sandstone tonight.

THURSDAY, JUNE 24

Read & read again today with occasional visits from Ruth, Grace, Jay, Kenn (bringing a wasps' nest for Julia), & a new apprentice Molly Aich (Eck). She's from Georgia; her husband's designing air fields in South America (left last November); interested in ceramics; almost joined her friend in designing materials for pure silks & wools, owner of "The Weavers of Raeburn" on Madison Ave. in N.Y., employing 90 year old mountain women.

Read Robinson's "Roman Bartholow."

Chatted with Grace, Phil, Jay in Grace's room after supper—nice & cool.

Asparagus season over—spinach in. Also gooseberries & currants soon.

FRIDAY, JUNE 25

Curtis received notice that he is expected in a South Dakota C.P.S. Camp on July 16. Wonder if he can fight that so that Taliesin becomes his work of national importance.

Wrote to Frances Salzman while minding the office phone again. In the meantime, went thru 10 volumes of art published by Ernest Wasmuth and edited by Paul Westheim in Germany in 1921. Plates of old-Russian, Hittite, Greek plastiks, Islamite architecture, ancient Chinese "Kleinplastik," Japanese woodcuts, ancient Mexican, classic French paintings. Also completed Sigfried Giedion—very impressive history of & trends in architecture—the Charles Eliot Norton lecture of 1938–1939, "Space

---

Originally from Georgia, **Molly Whitehead Aeck** began at the Fellowship in 1943. An interior designer, she was the wife of Richard L. Aeck (1912-1996), who was at Taliesin between June and November of 1942. He worked for Pan American Airways in Columbia and Brazil during World War II. The couple established Aeck Associates, Inc., an architecture firm, in Atlanta. Their son, Antonin (Tony) joined the firm in 1971; Lord, Aeck, and Sargent, based in Atlanta, is the successor firm.

Time and Architecture, the Growth of a New Tradition." Excellent plates, & good chapter on Wright.

Letter from Muriel & strudel from Mom for Muriel's graduation. Also excellent letter from Hans comparing Taliesin to the Bauhaus, with the Bauhaus far superior because it practiced true democracy. This was only a weak imitation, which still might have succeeded had it been more democratic. Also says a new culture & a new politics could be founded on the inchoate Sons & Daughters of the Tavern, as the 19th © might have done with the Sons & Daughters of the Steerage.

Another restless, hot day—also read Robinson's "The Man Who Died Twice" & "Dionysius in Doubt." This leg of mine ought to leave me fat from inactivity but cultured. Still playing solitaire—my game must be 1 out of 10, & not a 1 out of 1000 kind.

Recorder, but I can't sit at the piano. Started a Sammartini Quartet with the "big group."

The girls are canning asparagus & spinach now, as well as strawberries, tho our allotment of canning sugar is practically all gone. The onions we planted when we returned after Easter, in the lower garden, were served for the first time today as scallions. And good soil beareth away the victory.

Curtis came in to talk in the evening while Jay, Phil, & David were likewise chatting down below the house. We discussed my plans for September; his course of action as regards the Hill City, S.D., Bureau of Land Reclamation Camp (irrigation & homesteads); why Egyptian architecture was as it was; the essential difference between Gropius & Wright (Gropius is German, urban, logical; FLLW American, rural, emotionally the artist & therefore with a logic of his own not apparent to the layman); Thomas Mann & his Egyptology; Massacio's dome; Giedion & Broadacre City; democracy at Taliesin; the fact that everything here goes by hearsay—Kenn's & Kay's release from the kitchen, Jay's wife, the chorus' desire for a vote, Svet's ordering music half of which Curtis already had because she thought she'd be leader, Kenn's quarrel with Wes because of the clash between the garden period & architecture; the difficulty of returning home once you've made your break with it, and so on. A rewarding evening.

Grace gave an order to David, & addressed him as "Davy." Kay screamed, "For God's sake, don't call him Davy." I sympathize with the way she must bristle about the name. Then David told me Davy had asked him in Jan. to change his name because he had priority rights. "But your name is Allen." "My grandfather was called Davy; my father was; & by God, I'll be." Insane?

Guest: a nearby H.S. principal who needed a lift to Madison.

Keeping my burn constantly moist with boric acid solution. Read two Greek plays—Sophocles—Ajax & Oedipus Rex, and a little of several other books, including biography of Carver lent by Molly.

Seems everyone had a wonderful picnic at the Fritz's—steaks, punch, & folk dancing—while David & I sat in this awful oven waiting for the movie—"H.M. Pulham, Esq.", one of Marquand's typical Boston in the rut studies.

I'm a little jealous of Grace who's done an 800 mile cycle-hostel trip in England.

Guests: Fred Benedict & Mr. & Mrs. Masselink.

I'm being fried between pain & ennui. G-D.

Kay gave me an evening gown of hers to try on—too big for her. What is this world coming to?

SUNDAY, JUNE 27

Sunned myself, talking to Jay & Phil & David. David took around some visitors, & used "heimische menschen." & discovered 2 were Palestinians, & we got an invitation to visit them in Madison.

Concert brief—chief attraction vocal duets with Mrs. Masselink & Gene. Then we played "21 questions"—I was Eleanor Duse & David, Clifton Fadiman.

Molly decorated Roosevelt's home in Warm Springs, Ga. About negroes, she summed up, "It isn't easy to overcome your background and training."

Talked with Herb Fritz about the Fellowship, his plans for industries in the Arena valley, etc. Interesting, too.

MONDAY, JUNE 28

Office duty. Letter from Mom, with checks for our anniversary—$5 from Julia, $10 from the Family; sweet letters from Bonawit, & the Henkens, & a book from George, which I finished this morning—"Suds in Your Eye"—very Lasswell—amusing, warm, good ideasy.

Read an exciting success story American biography, more exciting than a novel about "George Washington Carver" by Rackham Holt.

Get around more easily under my boric acid treatments. Maybe I'll walk easily in a week.

---

heimische menschen: Yiddish, used colloquially to mean "my people" or "my friends."

Eleonora Duse (1858–1924), an Italian actress, became an international sensation.

Franklin Delano Roosevelt's Little White House in Warm Springs, Georgia, was built in 1932. The house was Roosevelt's retreat and is where he died on April 12, 1945.

Last week's storm destroyed two barns nearby by lightening, & yesterday's destroyed our dam—it is now just a brimming creek.

Peas and chard are in. We all spent an hour after tea just hulling peas.

David's been with Howard, trying to learn as much about chickens as possible. What a man won't do for a soft boiled egg!

Met Alline at the train with Jay. Also Johnny & Gene home from Madison—and Gene said he felt as if he knew me now for the first time in a year. Strange. . .

TUESDAY, JUNE 29

Hulled strawberries for canning & shelled peas—ditto. Traced. Recorder group—Sammartini & ensembles. Cleaned room—new foliage, etc. Phil, Alline, & Jay visited us in the evening. Ironed and mended blouses.

WEDNESDAY, JUNE 30

How. caught a great horned owl with a 49 in. wingspread eating the chickens. Poor owl—its brains are dashed now. Shelled peas & hulled strawberries all morning for canning. Recorder. Proofread Preamble—Vol. VI of An Autobiography, Broadacre City—complicated wording, obscurantist as usual—a fine problem. Traced. Phil & Herbert Fritz came in for a short while in the evening. David's been "doping" chickens all day so they don't practice cannibalism. He's exhausted, & when he came in, he reminded me of Hardy's Diggory Venn, the reddleman. Gene called across the table as Johnny & I were laughing, "Is Priscilla still being charming as usual?" To which Phil replied, sotto voce, "David doesn't realize how much time he's spending with the chickens."

THURSDAY, JULY 1

Shelled peas again for canning. Gooseberries are being canned now. $10 check & letter from the Henkens reminding us we're married; letter from George Brewster; card from Nat—"It was a good day for me too. Otherwise how could I have met both of you?"; and Julia too sent her anniversary greetings.

Recorder group—Sammartini & Hayden, Purcell brief pieces. Proofread again—ennuiyant.

Mrs. Spaldorf of the printing office told Gene that when she was coming home from Madison early in January, she saw a glamorous looking girl wearing a hat trimmed with fur, pacing nervously, who got off at Spring Green, & was very

---

Alline Glass, the wife of fellow Jay Glass.

Diggory Venn was the reddleman in the 1878 Thomas Hardy novel, *The Return of the Native*.

ennuiyant: French for "tedious."

affectionately greeted by several people, among whom was Marcus Weston. It was shocking—people actually couldn't get off the train! And so I linger, a mysterious figure from the East, in the Spring Green brain—& Gene didn't disclose my identity, good boy!

Wonderful evening with the orchestra in the theater—Dvorak's Largo from the New World Symphony, selections from the Mikado, and Saint Saens Francaise Militaire. Ted & Kay do the oboe part on the recorder; Barbara on the flute & I on the recorder do the flutes; Ruth the clarinet; Ross Graves the trombone; Elizabeth Graves the French Horn; Svet & Henning violins; Curtis—viola; Kenn—bass fiddle; Grace—piano; Johnny—drums. Molly was the appreciative audience. It was really great fun with the strings calling us the whistle section, & I contending that a player is not to be judged by the size of his instrument. Of course, everyone wants to carry the melody, & Johnny gives an extra filip to his drums now & then just in case he should be forgotten.

FRIDAY, JULY 2

A volume of Pushkin & a very sweet, tired letter from my husband—anniversary greetings. And a card from Florence. And a dear letter from Judeth.

Tied up the tomato vines in the lower garden. Foot seemed to have a relapse after the morning's activities.

Completed tracing Sheet 3, Heating & Mat Plans for Bernard Schwartz House.

Tea party to celebrate our anniversary—beer, coca cola, salami, lettuce, white bread, pretzels, plums & cherries. Quite successful.

And David returned to the stupid little cannibalistic chickens, & I read Pushkin's lyrics, ballads, & narrative poems. Piano & recorder, too.

Phil, Jay, & Alline came in to chat in the evening, with interruptions for David to tuck in his brood.

SATURDAY, JULY 3

Shelled peas all morning; stemmed currants most of the afternoon. Read a little. A little recorder. Letters from Judy, & Harry Handler (sentenced to from 6 months to three years because of the fracas with the barber shop drunkards). Didn't see David all day—poor kid, he'll never have time for architecture now, with his learning about chickens, & Howard's being assigned to a CPS Camp August 3—unless he can delay it.

Picnic at Maginel's—good food, community singing, & folk dancing (how I hate to be an observer).

Then Jay, Alline, David & I joined Phil to meet his girlfriend, Florence Trench, in for the weekend from Minneapolis. The bus was due at 11:30. In process of parking, it was discovered by the state police that Svet's car had no 1943 license—summons for next Thursday; Phil had no driver's license, & none of the boys had their draft cards on them—warning about the $5000 or 5 years in jail. To make the evening completely successful, she didn't get off the bus when we had waited till 1:30.

SUNDAY, JULY 4

Movie after breakfast, "I Met a Murderer," left us all terribly depressed. I didn't see David all day, because it seems without saying it in so many words, they reposed all responsibility on him. Movies in Spring Green in the evening, & Nachreiners— families with children drinking beer, & trying to retrieve their lost lives. The ride was good tho, with fireflies so bright & casting so much light, as seen from the parapet, as if we were looking down at the stars.

MONDAY, JULY 5

Went to Dr. Hagerup in Dodgeville—he sloughed off the old skin, added tannic acid jelly, & told me to expose it to air in two days. He & his wife & Molly made a most entertaining conversation. He knew personally Knut Hamsun, who worked as a farmer here in Wisconsin and then as a street car conductor in Chicago, but soon left that occupation because his eyes were so bad he was always bumping into things, & forgot to collect fares—a total stay of one year. He's now turned Nazi, & Hagerup explains his "Hunger" & "Growth of the Soil" as the work of a man of 23 or 4. Also Bjorn Bjornsterne (father) & son of the same name who is an actor. And the Mayor of Narvik, twice condemned to death by the Nazis (one sentence revoked, & one escape) was his guest here.

While a flat was being fixed, we went on to Mineral Point, saw the County Fair grounds, the home of Gov. Dodge (about 1800), first territorial governor of Wisconsin, old lead and antimony mines, & Shake rag street, something like the set of How Green Was My Valley, where the women would come out & shake a rag to indicate to their husbands that it was time for dinner.

Nachreiners was a local tavern.

Dr. Trygve Alexander Hagerup (1893–1948), a physician and a member of Wisconsin's large Norwegian immigrant population, recounted tales of famous Norwegians: **Knut Hamsun** (1859–1952) was a writer, who engaged in pro-Nazi literary activities during the German occupation of Norway, for which he was tried, convicted, and fined in 1947. **Bjørnstjerne Bjørnson**

(1832–1910), a poet and playwright, was active in liberal and socialist political causes. His son Bjørnstjerne Bjørnson (1859–1942) was an actor. Theodor Broch (1904–98), **mayor of Narvik**, Norway, was captured by Nazis in 1939. He escaped through the mountains of Sweden and went on a speaking tour of the United States, to talk about what was happening in Europe.

Wes told us of a quick retort of Mr. Wright's. A Californian wanted to give an exhibit in architecture and asked FL if he minded being in the center of the exhibit with Neutra on one side and Schindler on the other. "Hell, why not? Wasn't Christ hanged between two thieves?"

Molly, Alline, Jay, Phil, Florence came in for an evening's visit. Good entertaining conversation.

TUESDAY, JULY 6

Molly told us the contractor for the Yemassee house couldn't read plans with hexagonal units, so he bought some chicken wire to help him.

Stemmed currants. Lightening, thunder, and a constant downpour allowed time for playing the recorder and tracing all of Sheet 5—Framing Plans For Bernard Schwartz House.

Orchestra in the evening—Gluck Air, Martini Romance.

Card from Burton, crumpled, pocket-worn, a week & a half old, arrived today—or rather, was put into our box today. It's his first day—"tired but amused."

Read Bemelman's "I Love You, I Love You, I Love You"—amusing.

WEDNESDAY, JULY 7

Recorder. Piano lesson. Traced Sheet 4—Second Floor Plan of Bernard Schwartz House. Wonderful letter from Bert Slanhoff in San Antonio, Texas, now a bombardier. Read Frances Noyes Hart's "Pigs in Clover," a charming travel book thru France. Phil, Grace, Jay, Alline came in for evening chat, nosh, and jazz.

THURSDAY, JULY 8

Laundered. Planned next week's ménus. Unveiled my ankle & exposed it to the healing influence of the air. Traced elevations, but was quickly bored. Jay, Alline, Phil visited & listened to records. Wrote to Nat. Cards from Dotty and Ada. Ennui, except for Curtis who received a letter from the draft board, & when David asked with concern what the news was, Curtis answered angrily, "I'll tell you when and if I choose to." Tzatzkele. I'm beginning to feel more & more as if warmth & emotional perspicacity are native only to Jews.

Architects **Richard Neutra** (1892–1970) and **Rudolf Schindler** (1887–1953) were both born in Vienna and both worked for Wright before establishing their own highly influential practices in Los Angeles. Both had difficult relationships with Wright.

tzatzkele: Yiddish for "little child."

FRIDAY, JULY 9

Still tracing elevations. Ironed clothes and mended some. Letter from Norman
Thomas verifying date of his arrival. Went to Spring Green with Molly to see about
materials for drying vegetables; to Dodgeville with Ruth to get a T handle valve.
Orchestra & recorder rehearsal. I feel dull & annoyed—my foot is uglier than sin. It's
quite definite that FL has signed the contract for the Guggenheim museum—and
Robert Moses is showing him the sites.

SATURDAY, JULY 10

Had a disgusting blow up with Svet in 3 acts. Act I—Kitchen with Molly, Phil, & Ted
as audience prompted by Molly's question, "Why doesn't anyone here like Mrs.
Wright?" Svet said I was responsible for "undermining & influencing, & malicious
gossip, etc., etc., etc. Act II—David, Gene, Svet, Burt in Svet's room—mutual & self
accusations; David defending me, not in my character, etc. Gene "had the feeling,
tho he never heard me himself," & it was surprising that I was that type when I was
otherwise so friendly & cooperative. References to inability to take compliments,
wise cracking, & intellectualizing. Act III—our room—Svet apologizing, everyone
apologizing, & Molly muffing it all by saying I wasn't the only one from who she had
heard unfavorable criticism. God, what stupidity.

   Piano. Shellacked drier for vegetables & then everyone discovered it should have
been varnished. Mostly read & moped.

   Letter from Judy; card from Dave & Frieda; & a Sears Roebuck catalog. Ah
wilderness were paradise.

   Picnic on sandbar to which I had to be carried across the water by Phil & Jay, and
back by Kenn. Movie was "Suspicion" which wears well. Phil, Jay, Alline, David & I in
a post mortem heavy conversation afterwards. Kenn went home to see his brother
on furlough.

SUNDAY, JULY 11

Johnny is my K.P. Dinner: Roast veal, brown sauce, tossed green salad, creamed
chard, mashed potatoes, strawberry mousse. Compliments, thank goodness.
Wes wanted to know whether the chard was his wonderful New Zealand spinach;
Mrs. Porter wanted me to tell her how I fixed the greens; Curtis said the last
course had to be taken lying down; Ted wanted to know what accounted for the

---

wilderness were paradise: Reference to a line from the
translation of Persian poet Omar Khayyam's (1048–1123)

"Love Poem." David also quoted this poem in his
December 25th letter (see p. 91)

wonderful consistency of the mousse; people in general said it was a good dinner. Guest was Jim Vickery, Grace's friend, a 4E sociologist, who is always where things are happening, as in the Detroit race riots. Concert: Nardini—Violin sonata, Sammartini's Sonata for 4 recorders.

MONDAY, JULY 12

Card from Florence Tabor; letter from Muriel.

Traced floor & roof plans—Sheet 1—of Yamassee cabins. Lunch:—braised pork chops, creamed chard, potato pancakes (lots of calls for the recipe—or is it a secret?). Supper—Italian spinach, macaroni & tomatoes with grated cheese, tossed salad, lettuce, jello frozen with the whipped cream.

Stupefyingly hot day.

TUESDAY, JULY 13

Lunch—cold roast veal; Italian spinach, dill boiled potatoes.

Supper—baked beans, gingerbread, cole slaw; apple sauce cake.

Read Robinson's "Cavender's House." Traced Auldbrass sheet 1 Roof & Floor Plan.

Yesterday, when I visited Molly, she told me about George Peabody, the Georgia philanthropist for whom Peabody College is named & best friend the Georgian negroes have—a personal friend of hers. He endowed Yadow at Saratoga Springs, N.Y., in memory of Mr. & Mrs. Spencer Trask, his best friends, & their 5 children. Trask was killed in a train crash; Mrs. Trask, Peabody's wife afterwards, died soon after her second marriage; their 5 children died of typhoid carried by typhoid Mary, their nurse. They used to say "see the sh yadows of the trees;" hence yadow. You are subsidized by a committee for a year at least, separate studios, any type of creative work, lunch brought to you in sandwiches & thermos so you're not disturbed; evenings are big affairs spent together. Louis Adamic is one of its products. Molly, thru the influence of her friend Margaret Peabody, was invited by

The **Detroit race riots** had just occured (June 20–22, 1943). The trouble started on Belle Isle and spread because of intense distrust between white residents and the growing African American population, who had arrived to work in Detroit's defense industry during World War II. In the end, thirty-four people were killed, hundreds injured, and stores and cars burned.

George Foster Peabody (1852–1938) made his fortune in railroads, electricity, and sugar beets. He gave away a considerable amount of money, with a focus on African American education in the South. His friends Katrina

and Spencer Trask had four children who all died young, though they could not have contracted typhoid from Typhoid Mary—Mary Mallon (1869–1938)—she was still a teenager and not yet working as a cook in the 1880s (the last Trask child died in 1888). Yaddo was the Trasks' estate in Saratoga Springs, which became a retreat for artists in 1926. Since then, Yaddo has housed over 5,000 artists-in-residence.

Louis Adamic (1898–1951), Slovenian-American author who wrote about labor issues from a left-wing perspective.

the committee to do designs, but she refused because she was going to be married. It's simply a place where once you've gotten some recognition, they give you a chance to do what you've always wanted to do.

Supper picnic out on sandbar in the river. Delightful & relaxing with everyone complimenting me on a perfect picnic supper. Swimming was warm & pleasant—friendly spirit. To movies to celebrate Glass' anniversary but it was closed—so Nachreiners & beer, cokes, & ice cream.

WEDNESDAY, JULY 14
Letters from Nat at Cape Cod, Helen & Leo (deferred till he recovers from phlebitis), & Burt in Camp Lee, Va., amply apologetic for delay, full of duties, & K.P. because someone at his table talked too loudly!

Lunch—roast pork, lettuce, spinach timbale, baked potato. Supper—rice parched with tomato sauce & cheese, cottage cheese, potato salad, cheese & crackers, & Henning bought a case of beer!

Traced Leigh Stevens' Auldbrass door schedule and door jamb diagrams. Wrote to Bonawit & Burt.

David, knowing I was recovering, kept the hors de combat en famille, by getting a deep gash in his knee with a metal lath. Everyone was helpless while he tried to do his own doctoring. After lunch, Wahl taped it together, hoping nature would take over the healing power of stitches.

Picnic supper on the sandbar again—quite delightful. When I got home, the room was full of Jay, Alline, and Phil again. I started tracing to give them a hint—but se hut gehelfen ve a toiten bankes.

THURSDAY, JULY 15
Lunch—pork chops, lettuce, chard ring, green beans.

Supper—tomato & cheese ring, peas epicurean, cole slaw, maple custard. Catsup cream dressing.

Mom sent a package with my jacket. Letter from Whites.

Recorder group with Svet—Moussorgsky Cossack Dance, Händel Sarabande.

Picnic on sandbar again—games, good food, good spirits.

Read Pushkin's "Boris Godunov."

David stayed in all day, leg outstretched, tracing.

---

se hut gehelfen ve a toiten bankes: Yiddish for "it helps like applying cups to a dead man," a reference to the ancient tradition of cupping a sick person to draw out toxins. Loosely translated, "useless, like trying to cure a dead man."

FRIDAY, JULY 16

Read Pushkin's "Mozart & Salieri," & "The Courteous Knight"—Plays.

David sweetly completed his anniversary gift to me with Hellman's Plays (all this happened on Wednesday) & I immediately read Days to Come, the only one with which I was unfamiliar—left me saddened, as she usually does. And Hemmingway's short stories which will be completely new to me, and Dorothy Parker's collected stories which easily bear re reading, but which David seems to have just completed with relish.

Orchestra rehearsal—I did my first long walking since my dear burn by walking to & from Hillside.

Johnny left Howard as K.P. while he accompanied his father to Ohio to look over his father's family's farm to persuade his father to sell it—he wants him to buy a farm in Wisconsin.

Lunch: peas epicurean, fried calf liver, baked potatoes.

Supper: cheese souffle, chard, tossed green salad, devil's food cake using syrup instead of sugar & lard instead of butter—∴ not too successful.

Letter with 3 pictures of herself from Julia; card from Gladys giving us Burton's address; very domestic brief epistle from Dave Wertman.

Briefly visited Glasses in the evening, tho his lack of cooperation in plans annoys me to the point of my showing it. Alline doesn't mind working for two, indeed!

SATURDAY, JULY 17

Letters from Judy coming indefinitely, & an embarrassing love letter about Julia from George Brody.

Lunch—spaghetti with Napoli sauce, lettuce with catsup cream dressing, creamed New Zealand spinach.

Supper—barbecued suckling pig, potato salad, cole slaw, pickles, jams, peanut butter, buns (after having baked 24 loaves of bread this week); I made 4 loaves of brown sugar cake before I discovered Mrs. Fritz would make the evening's dessert. David was sufficiently recovered to turn the pig on the spit for about 5 hours with Howard keeping the fire going, & Molly & Alline winding up as my kitchen help.

Movie was W. C. Fields' "Never Give a Sucker an Even Break," which was funnier this time than our marching in a 3 hour Broadway rain last time we saw it.

Wrights returned, too tired for the picnic which was good.

Curtis due to leave July 26. Marcus is assigned to Ann Arbor, Michigan Hospital.

SUNDAY, JULY 18

The Wrights are back. The contract is for a million dollar museum for non-objective art, sponsored by Solomon Guggenheim. Of the sites chosen, both Robert Moses' & Wright's favorite is near Fort Tryon Park overlooking the Hudson, the highest point in N.Y. with 8 acres of ground to convert into park. FL is to have the final say in the matter of building. His taxi fares cost $370 to say nothing of trips to Westport & Washington. He said the Baroness Rebay is a very forceful woman. He met her at two; had tea with her at three; & was at Dr. Otto Mayer's at four scheduled for a leech operation applied to the jugular veins, with appointments for first having all his dead teeth removed. Pretty soon ditto for Mrs. Wright. As they explain it, the scientific removal of blood, & injection of unknown valuable curative by leech, helps speed up the circulation intravenously. This swifter running blood helps remove some of the corrosions of coagulated blood that line the veins. Anyway, it seems to have worked with both of them—& sounds logical & simple.

The Guggenheim—Rebay—& servants contingent are coming here the last week in August with much bustling from now till then.

Spent the afternoon on Wes's hill under an elm (wonderful how transparent the leaves can be in sunlight, & the gold & green caused by casting their shadows on each other) writing, recorder ing, & reading.

Concert was fair; FL's conversation better. Said about Guggenheim "when you get a great man who's a Jew, he's better than most." Maginel—"We knew that thousands of years ago." "Who?" "Jesus Christ." "Oh, he was an Aryan." Other possible site is 5th Ave. & 54th Street, fronting 72 feet, right next to the church & practically back of the Museum of Modern Art. They seem quite stuck on 83 year old, gentle Solomon Guggenheim—different, of course, from most Jews. I feel tempted to greet him in the "Mama lushen." FL said he's going to declare from tomorrow on an emergency—obviously plenty of work & nix on play. "Sixty Families" says of the Guggenheim scholarships that thenceforth the recipient is known as a Guggenheim scholar, thereby giving value to "the socially & culturally sterile name Guggenheim."

The site at **Fort Tryon Park** was eventually rejected by Guggenheim and Wright as too far from the city. The Guggenheim Museum was built on Fifth Avenue between 88th and 89th streets.

Baroness Hilla von Rebay (1890–1967), a painter, worked with Guggenheim on his "non-objective art" collection and corresponded extensively with Wright

from 1942 to 1959 regarding the construction of the Guggenheim Museum.

mama lushen: Yiddish for "mother's language," i.e., "mother tongue."

America's 60 Families was published in 1937 by Ferdinand Lundberg to suggest the vast connections of wealth and business enterprises of America's richest families. The Guggenheim family was listed at number 13.

Also coming is Maurice Barret, here in the U.S. to lecture on the culture of France, & stuck because of the war. Carl Milles writes of him that he's the typical Sorbonne Parisian, highly cultured, & in a Frenchman that means the highest rung in civilization. He also added that he was as conceited as Dégas, that no one at Cranbrook liked him except Milles & his wife, Olga, but that they suffered him to stay because of what he was. Of course, he'll be a fellow here, not a guest of Mr. Wright's, whom he calls "the first American I met here."

MONDAY, JULY 19
Traced negro cabins—elevation—sheet 2—Auldbrass.
   Picked peas for 2 hours; picked chard, lettuce, radishes.
   Churned butter—plenty of arm muscle involved.
   Made coffee mocha and cheese straws for tea.
   Sylvia Brody announced birth of Elizabeth Ann.
   Curtis went home to see his folks before leaving for camp. Has to report on the 26th. Cheerful goodbye speeches to each other.
   Card from George Brody from Mexico & Ruth Charger.
   Read Pushkin's "The Stone Guest." —Quite a rebel—but one expects that in Europe's romantic period.
   Traced sofa and chest for Bernard Schwartz house.
   Phil, Alline, Jay came in to play records while David & I traced bravely on. It was a struggle.

TUESDAY, JULY 20
Weeded peas; picked lettuce, young new beets, raspberries in mosquito bombardment, gooseberries, & then washed them all like a good girl. Minty odor of tomato vines; complete camouflage of peas and their vines; the squeak of pea pods rubbing against each other; a grey & black spotted bird; the lovely creamy yellow & purple centered blossom of the mallow weed; the deep purple red of beet tops; the prickle of gooseberry branches; the delicate touch of the velvet weed leaf; the red-headed woodpecker seated on an iron fence-post; the sweet odor of pink clover; the insistent annoyance of the crow's croak.
   Blithe spirited letter from Jane Orlov.
   Traced additional furniture plans for Bernard Schwartz house—two plates.
   Prepared molasses cookies & iced strawberry tea punch for tea.

Maurice Barret was an architecture student at the University of Paris and studied at the Sorbonne. The French government sent him to the United States in 1939 to lecture at American universities about French culture.

Laundered. Read a little Pushkin. Wrote to Marcus & Sylvia Brody.

The Glasses, Phil, & we started walking—got as far as the studio, read the key sentences (to us, at least) in Davy's letter to Kay, "Your news about the Henkens is most encouraging. We envy your presence to appreciate their absence." It's filled with ominous portent, & had & still has us worrying, confused, perturbed. Further on, we met Herbert Fritz, jumped into his truck, & had refreshments at Stuffy's, so the evening turned out better than it would have, but was loaded with the blues for David & me—especially since Kay has warned Phil of associating with the left wing. Pretty shining brow. Pax vobiscum.

WEDNESDAY, JULY 21

Picked about 50 pounds of vegetables—radishes, onions, lettuce, New Zealand spinach, rhubarb, parsley, gooseberries. Saw a long legged sandpiper running in the road. Gooseberries should be picked in flexible armor. Washed vegetables afterwards—the kitchen's such a busy place—at 11, six of us were working in it— & not one was a canner; just washing, scrubbing, & piddling.

Phil told Mrs. Wr. he was unable, for physical reasons, to continue in the kitchen, but he'd be willing to relieve Howard of some of the responsibility, & she acquiesced, but also warned him of associating with some of the newer apprentices like the Henkens & Jay.

THURSDAY, JULY 22

Mr. Wr. told Phil if he was physically unable to do the kitchen work given him, he was unable to do any—& so might as well leave—that they had both made a mistake. Also said that he, like David & Jay, came here with the idea of getting as much as possible without giving anything—& that their day of reckoning would come soon too. Also had all 3 of our accounts out. Said Alline was here on false pretences—that she couldn't work, & he can't support a cripple. Also under the impression that I do no work. Rumors in the air; ominous undertones, whispers, accusations with no opportunity for defence or counter accusation. Kay & Burt (the not vicious) good ringleaders. David & I both had nervous indigestion, but that's minor. I'll probably turn into a paranoic. I jump every time the peacocks thud on the roof.

Traced 2 more plates of Schwartz house furniture. Picked chard, lettuce, beets, parsley, raspberries, washed vegetables.

Prepared raspberry muffins for tea.

Charming letters from Julia & Muriel.

Ten Brinks, Glasses, Henkens, Phil—farewell beer & cokes at Nachreiner's.

FRIDAY, JULY 23

Wednesday, a Uruguayan architect on a traveling scholarship, visited us. In a pronounced Spanish accent, he said his name was Jones. FL talked to him quite lengthily at tea, & then unable to contain himself, asked him how he arrived at the name Jones. "Oh, my grandfather was Welsh."

More news about us: Jay is the most despised person here—"They hate his guts." At first he was disliked for association with us; then for himself; & now dislike for him is transferred back to us. And to add more to the illogic of the situation, Kenn told David he made his worst mistake by giving up the chickens, & yet when he was on chickens, they thought he was loafing. But you can't fight back, as witness tea.

Mrs. Wr. came into the kitchen complaining about her teeth, & that she was going in to Dr. Kraus as soon as she could get a car. Then she phoned from town, asking me to take Tal in out of the rain, and not to serve Mr. Wr. any cream in his tea, nor any cinnamon roulettes—just graham crackers. Orders noted. Come tea. Svet, "Where's mother?" "I believe she went to town." "Oh, about her teeth, I suppose." Tal was taken in, but instead of wandering inside, we thought we'd take him to tea. Then, Mr. Wr. asked where his gnädige Frau was & Svet told him, evidently a secret from him, & he was angry at her going without her N.Y. doctor's instructions. She returned, & then these were the counts against me.

1. He wanted to know why she went to the dentist—dirty look because I was a squealer.

2. Thought I never took Tal in at all—dirty look 'cause I was irresponsible & "you didn't take care of him either."

3. offered her the biscuits. FL teased her, "Have them. They're good. I had three." Dirty look 'cause I was disobedient, even tho I said I had obeyed.

So they mount up, no matter what you do or don't do—a record of pettiness for people who boast of being above pettiness. And this is forced on us whether our natures desire it or not.

Of course, no one spoke to Phil, the outcast—complete social ostracism, except for us—& he didn't even quarrel with Mr. Wr. They parted amicably, & FL signed his book. "To Phil who made a brave try." Even sheep sometimes follow the unbeaten track.

We saw Phil off at Lone Rock—N.Y., Texas, & California.

Norman Thomas wrote he's coming Friday.

---

gnädige Frau: German for "kind, gracious wife," typically used as a form of address meaning "Madam."

FL signed ours & Bonawit's Autobiography, ours with the simple, "David Henken & Priscilla at Taliesin, 1942, Frank Lloyd Wright." Shipped them off.

Gathered beans, peas, lettuce, radishes, cabbages, onions. Shelled peas. Wrote some letters. Picked raspberries in the afternoon sun.

Movies—"Quiet Wedding"—amusing.

Took a long walk with Curtis & discussed our problems with him—nothing to do but lie low, & then get the jump on them & pack up & leave. He's disgusted with the whole business—everyone making much out of nothing, the cabals and intrigues, the trouble lovers, Kenn blurting out grievances in spite of his friendship, & Howard telling quick-tempered Wes what we tell him in confidence. Curtis has too much pride to ask for agricultural deferment, & believes they should make the first step—feels there is official indifference. Jay intends to leave in a few weeks, Alline this Tuesday—the undesirables are leaving. Taliesin is to be congratulated. Tears come too readily these days—needless ostracism for us, the least guilty of any offenders. Even the words "their reckoning will come" are Kenn's. This must be something like the fear of the Gestapo—you don't have [to] be involved in incidents any more—stories can be created by spontaneous generation. They even resent David's nerve in inviting Thomas—who the hell does he think he is to invite such guests?

SUNDAY, JULY 25

Went walking with Grace & Mollie—saw them make cheddar cheese from curds to loaf—simple processing but hard work. Picked myself for my soul's sustenance Queen Anne's lace, English mint, spearmint, & hollyhocks for room cheer. Traced bathroom & washing plans for Auldbrass negro cabins. Went swimming from our sandbar beach with Molly, Grace, Johnny, Kenn & Curtis. Grace is so far thoroughly accepted—so was I in the first month. Feeling completely miserable—more sniping—Burt advertising Phil was a swell fellow until he became cynical because he started hanging around the Henkens. David interested only in chickens because of the cooperative we may have—to Wes & cast abroad, via Howard whose momentary thoughtlessness can cause as much damage as deliberate viciousness. I feel surrounded. The news of Mussolini's overthrow, of Sicily's almost complete surrender, help minimize the abnormalities of our petty world. There is a life outside this cracked ivory tower. Cocktail party given by Svet & Wes for Curtis—knew I'd

Operation Husky, an Allied invasion, began July 9–10, 1943, and resulted in the Axis surrender of **Sicily** in August.

miss him too much to enjoy the cocktails, even tho they were good.

Evening concert excellent, Curtis leaving in a blaze of glory.

MONDAY, JULY 26

The flower shaped like a daisy, of beautiful lavender color with brown gold center is the rudebakia. Red English mint sprouts its new flower <u>thru</u> the brown center of another.

Picked peas, beans, lettuce, radishes, raspberries, & beets. Cleaned vegetables— but David's K.P. so it's O.K. Traced Sheet 3—Sections of Auldbrass negro cabins. Wrote letter to Burt in answer to his card & letter—such talk about rifle ranges! Helped Alline with tea. Piano & recorder. Alline, Jay, & Molly came in to talk & visit. All's quiet today.

Kay reports from her visit to Sandstone, that Jack is teaching drawing, & Davy is drawing up plans to reconstruct the complete heating, lighting, & plumbing plans. I can see the two cocksure pomposities strutting about importantly reconditioning the jail.

Curtis left for the Colorado C.O. Camp near Mesa Verde, looking forward to a "vacation." He goes by way of Chicago to Gallup, New Mexico by train, & then by bus to camp. David & I shall both miss him as one always misses a combination of sanity & friendship in an insane world.

TUESDAY, JULY 27

Picked peas, beans, lettuce, chard, radishes, onions, tomatoes, parsley. Cleaned the vegetables. Traced "Sheet—Mill 2—Sash Details of Caretaker's Cottage—Auldbrass, Yemassee." Served & washed dishes. Piano. Recorder. Orchestra rehearsal. Went swimming off sandbar across from Wes's meadow with Molly, Burt, Kenn, & Grace. Alline left for Ohio today to stay until Jay joins her in 2 or 3 weeks or until he makes up his mind about his course of action. Picked green apples & sat in the meadow, feeling almost at peace. If I don't turn into a paranoic, there's at least a good chance for manic-depression.

WEDNESDAY, JULY 28

Picked chard, onions, green peppers, peas, beans, parsley, & raspberries. Prepared peas & beans for canning over at Hillside. Guests—Dr. Lindemann of N.Y. School for Social Research, another professor whose name I didn't catch, & Mrs. Warmington, a friend of Curtis's. Too tired to pursue my "cultural life." David as K.P. reports Mr. X as a Mr. Kullen (Columbia School for Social Work) & dinner conversation in the little dining room as consisting of banalities & Lindemann's mathematical tricks which the home front did not catch on to.

THURSDAY, JULY 29
Picked chard, onions, peas, beans, parsley, raspberries, lettuce. Prepared vegetables. Helped can beans (80 quarts) & peaches (27) over at Hillside, & took a short time off to practice the piano there. Traced a little. Did some ironing. Bathed & washed my hair in the river—Mrs. Wright came along also to wash her hair—bathing in the nude—& Mr. Wr, lay on the sand in the sun while Twip took care of the discarded bathing suit.

It's amusing that they're all fussing about Thomas's coming, with a big dinner for him tomorrow night, & Sunday breakfast on Saturday. Mrs. Wr. is all excited about the "greatest man we've had here." Nu, & who's behind this invitation?—Herzele.

And in the meantime—Mussolini's in custody; "a democratic monarchy" is supposed to be re established; Germany invaded northern Italy; there are riots and insurrections against the Facists; Bulgaria, Rumania, & Hungary want to withdraw from the war;—The Balkans, chiefly policed by Italians under German command, will probably revolt as soon as the Italian troops are withdrawn.

FRIDAY, JULY 30
If there were ever any doubts in my mind, they're settled now. Howard & David planned to meet Thomas. FL's car can't be used—getting gas for it is illegal; the tires are bad; it should not be so far from home or they're liable to severe fine—yet he insists on using it to meet Thomas. He told David he thought David should not be the one to introduce Thomas to the Fellowship, & not to come along with him. Again the fear of the bad impression. He said he had important business to attend to anyway in the morning. Said David, "But the train arrives at 4:35." "Then I'll shift my business to the afternoon." David was good enough to work with Thomas in N.Y., but not enough to meet him here.

Letters from Pop Henken (referring to our last letter as hinting there was "etivas foil in Dennemark"), S.P. asking for David's annual $50; Harry Handler chirping with a jail sentence imminent; the Tabors on vacation with Sol's draft imminent, & Mom—sweet.

Picked peas, parsley, tomatoes, beets, radishes, & lettuce. Cleaned vegetables. Made a fractional indentation in the bottle room for more canning materials. But

---

"**Herzele**" is an affectionate Yiddish diminutive of "Herzl," David's middle name.

etivas foil in Dennemark: Yiddish for "something rotten in Denmark." Reference to Shakespeare's *Hamlet*.

what's the use? All our labor, & Kay's finishing touches—almost all 70 quarts of peas are already spoiled, & 20 cans of beans. But we don't talk about those things here.

Dinner was in the living room—formal clothes. Porters, Barneys, Graves, & FL announcing beforehand just which chair Thomas could sit so that he could answer the boys' "intelligent questions" because he wanted Thomas to leave with the impression that this was the most intelligent audience he had ever met. Thomas was extremely gracious, remembering to give David regards from Saurmy. He was full of facts & information—no jail or C.O. Camp or political leader or book or movie or magazine or piece of music that he couldn't discuss intelligently. Before the evening was over, however, it was obvious that he was here to relax & enjoy himself (Thursday at Yale, previous Sunday in Washington, Friday & Saturday—Taliesin, Sunday Milwaukee, Monday—Camp Walhalla, Michigan), & was polite, so that when Sister Jane exploded that she hoped we were fighting this war for internationalism, & brotherhood, he laughed, "I certainly hope so." He was not here to lecture nor to convert. However, toward the end of the evening, FL was sitting on the edge of his chair leaning over to listen to Thomas, spouting, relaxed.

Of course, Johnny & Bitsy disliked him because his plate didn't fit; others because David invited him; others because he was a "communist." God, what fools.

The only thing amusing was Kay's asking Grace who was coming—as if we all didn't know for weeks. Grace—Norman Thomas. Kay—Really! Who invited him? Grace—David. Burt—But he's a friend of Mr. Wright's too."

SATURDAY, JULY 31
David was able to speak to Thomas for an hour today with Mr. & Mrs. hovering, trying to break in, but uninformed. When Thomas mentioned Carlos Tresca, he replied to FL's ignorance, "Well, David here knows him, & so did a former apprentice of yours, Hans Koch." Wr. —"Hans was not an apprentice," explosively. And then he asked the perfectly asinine question, "What do you think of Sacco & Vanzetti, Norman?" They finally got him away for a walk. David worked on the combine.

I gathered & washed the days vegetables, slicing beans for brining, picking raspberries, & hurriedly planning a ménu.

Elizabeth "Bitsy" Enright (1909–68), Wright's niece, the daughter of his youngest sister Maginel Wright Enright. An accomplished author, she won the Newbery Medal in 1939. She married Robert Gillham in 1930, and they had three sons.

Carlo Tresca (1879–1943) was a labor organizer and a leader of Industrial Workers of the World.

Ferdinando Sacco and **Bartolomeo Vanzetti** were Italian immigrants, said to be anarchists, living in Braintree, Massachusetts; they were accused, tried, and hanged for murder in 1927. Many people thought they were innocent and unfairly accused; the hangings became a symbol of inequities in the American judicial system.

They all expected Thomas to leave on the afternoon train, but David surprised them by announcing that N.T. had expressed a desire to stay for the picnic.

The picnic was a howl. The kitchen car went up to George's hill (the farm of 30 acres $2000 which FL just bought—he was so persuasive to George about its beauties that he convinced himself) and all the others went, couldn't make the hill, & returned to Michael's farm, but on the way, they saw the Wrights at the theater, & stopped there. We started a fire, & when everything was going neatly, got a hurried call to go to the theater. When we got there—much running, much excitement, & Thomas was pulling weeds out of the flower garden. Then he spoke & we all sat around him, except Mrs. Wr. & family who was entertaining the Grassleys (Spring Valley—Thomas spoiled Wr's plans because they wanted to give his room to them). The clique sat far off, proud; the left wing sat around his feet. And pretty soon, FL begged, "Say, let me in on this conversation, too." And then he began boasting about his architecture. N.T. was amused because we gave him hot dogs after chicken, and said this was a good American custom—"Wasn't this the way King George was entertained?" I was kneeling on the grass, & answered, "See, I'm kneeling too." David says he gave me a look of appreciative "geschmach."

Picture was "Journey into Fear," an Orson Welles flop; undeveloped story and characters.

SUNDAY, AUGUST 1
Ten Brinks, Henkens, & Jay escorted Thomas back to Madison to get the 8:15 to Milwaukee. He wondered why the Broadacre City petitions varied in their wording about capitalism when presented to the politicians & non politicians. In discussing Silvio Gesell with David, he said he felt there was something wrong, but couldn't put his finger on it. David said, "Well, I think that re establishing the money system is not the answer to the whole economic & social set up, and besides, he sets up profit instead of service as the basis for reward." N.T. said, "By God, you've got it. That's just what I would have said."

When we returned, we found out via our faithful spy, Grace, that Mrs. Wr. began Sunday morning breakfast by announcing, "quick let's get over talking about Norman Thomas before the Henkens & Ten Brinks return." And they decided: 1. He was a great politician, but not a great man 2. He didn't have enough of the crusading spirit. (Why the hell didn't they invite him to lecture instead of to visit?) 3. He had the facts, but not the ideas. Anyone has to look at a yearly calendar to see that what this

---

geschmach: Yiddish for, literally, "tasty;" here, "well done."

royal family gripes about, he <u>does</u>, personally. And Johnny, Kenn, Burt, & Gene—the original-write-to-their senators kids.

Mr. Porter, however, told David this was one time he wished he had the use of his ears. FL came over to tell us in the evening, especially, that Thomas was intelligent, but he talked so darn much, he got all wound up in himself. Poor FL didn't have the center of the stage for a weekend, & couldn't get over it.

I was cook again. Lunch—tuna fish, scalloped potatoes, tomatoes, peas, rice pudding.

Dinner—lettuce, cucumber, tomato, & pepper salad, sweet corn, new boiled potatoes, Georgian string bean stew, rhubarb pie, coffee.

Mrs. Wr. riled me in the afternoon by fussing around with my pots, & then when I grabbed a napkin Kay had just put down, she turned on me, "That's the trouble with communism. No one has any respect for property. I never liked the communist life." And Kay smirked. I certainly want to get out of this in a hurry. And Molly, even more than I. To hear her compare Mrs. Wr. with a real lady, is to hear a study in black & white as only a nice Southern gal can do it.

And why all the fuss about dinner? 3 million dollars worth of the Evans family (a judge & his brother) were guests, & we had to put on the dog. Clara Bloodgood & 3 of her friends stayed too—21 guests. The Evans brothers wore slack suits. How could they know how real millionaires should act?

Concert was good, but FL put it on thick when he shook hands with the trio—orchestra conductor & concert master business.

MONDAY, AUGUST 2

Howard had a long talk with Wright before leaving for home today. Wr. didn't believe any of the accusations against Kay—"all accidents," nor did he believe the cliques were so bad, & besides Howard hung around with the "left wing" (again that phrase & now it's gone its merry rounds starting with Kay who had it from Mrs. Wr.) & that David & Jay were here to get all they could; that Phil was a psychiatric case; & Howard should give up his car (all apprentices must be dependent on the master), & that this is a democracy, & what Howard is asking for is <u>Communism</u>. Second time in 2 days—don't they know Thomas is a <u>Socialist</u>?

Henning's my K.P. Lunch—roast kid, tomato & radish salad, potatoes boiled in dill, creamed chard, (apple sauce).

Supper—wilted lettuce, baked cucumber with cheese relish, string bean stew, apple betty, (jello, squash, lima beans).

I kept on getting compliments all day on my cooking—Mrs. Wr., Wes, Ted, Molly who thinks I'm a "real cook," the best one here, etc.

Funny that all criticisms come to us in a round-about way—no direct attacks. Are they afraid we'll charge them with anti-semitism?

FL told us the other day at tea, that a client came once, and after waiting too long for Mr. Wright to emerge from his study, an apprentice came out and said, "Mr. Wright's too busy to be disturbed. He's busy killing flies."

TUESDAY, AUGUST 3

Lunch: pork chops, lettuce tomato cucumber kohlrabi salad, baked potatoes, buttered string beans Polonaise (stewed rhubarb).

Supper: cole slaw, buttered beets boiled in orange juice, macaroni & tomatoes, bread pudding with nuts & citron (scrambled eggs, peas, spinach).

Orchestra rehearsal: Rameau's Tambourin Dance was the only new piece—still a great joy.

Two prospective apprentices & their 3 year old son came for a while—Czerny is the name; habitat—N.Y. & Detroit.

WEDNESDAY, AUGUST 4

Lunch: hickory smoked spareribs in barbecue sauce (lamb stew), Italian spinach, Brabant potatoes, cucumber & tomato salad.

Supper: Sicilian salad, beans, sweet corn, (peas), apple pie.

Delightfully charming & amusing letter from Burton—quite cheered us both. He seems to be taking the army in his stride—like Greek or an intricate finger exercise to master.

Completed Maslow's & Mittelman's "Principles of Abnormal Psychology" & Lowndes "The Lodger," a mystery novel of abnormal psychology.

The prospective new apprentice who came & left Sunday was beginning to have his baptism by gossip today, with Gene's telling at breakfast how he said, "They called me Thunderbolt in two colleges, but I can't say why." Of course everyone disliked him on sight because he monopolized Sunday morning's breakfast conversation.

THURSDAY, AUGUST 5

Lunch: baked beans, gingerbread, cole slaw, baked turnips & onions, tomatoes & cucumbers.

Supper: creamed kid with sautéed peppers, tomatoes, & onions, buttered beets, Gurdjieff salad, stewed apples and rhubarb with whipped cream (carrots, cottage cheese).

Took a long walk with David. Letter from Curtis addressed to the Fellowship, telling of beautiful country & drab immediate surroundings. Read Huxley's "Antic Hay"—very much like "Point Counter Point."

FRIDAY, AUGUST 6

Letter from Jack says he's enjoying himself very much, & except for Taliesin there's no place in the world he'd rather be than Sandstone.

Warm, affectionate letter from Marcus, not yet having received ours—answers our questions (unasked), and proves his friendship & Curtis's. He is one thing for which we have to be grateful to Taliesin. Also letters from Steinleins (vacationing near Yale), Phil (beautiful picture post card of Mt. Rainier), and Judy, still hesitating about coming. The longer she has delayed, the more it coincides with my leaving—a very delicate situation. I answered Marcus in what was almost a fervent letter, including our unauthorized document of Jan. 23.

Lunch: cold roast pork, boiled cabbage, corn on the cob, green salad; (roast chicken, baked new potatoes, carrots, lima beans, corn, orange-cocoanut tapioca pudding). Baked 8 loaves of bread that are the pinnacle of my art.

Supper—cucumber-pepper-kohlrabi-tomato-onion salad with Taliesin dressing; grilled tomatoes, farmer cheese, creamed onions, chocolate pudding with whipped cream. And Johnny complained because we hadn't cooked any corn. I was unaware that 1100 ears were placidly sitting in the truck down below. Just an example of Taliesin inefficiency & there are many more.

5 rows of lettuce plowed under; ditto 2 rows of peas; ditto 3 of chard; 160 quarts of peas & beans spoiled; 150 pounds of pig inadvertently spoiled in the sun; vegetables picked, forgotten, & thrown to the pigs or chickens; 70 eggs going into 3 loaves of Baba, which is then rocked in a pillow so it won't settle; plows, rakes, hoes, wire rusting in weather of all sorts—and forgotten; berries neglected on the bushes; man power used to dress up a house instead of to repair it—all to show off for guests. Potemkin's false front and shabby rear.

And to add to the personality quotient: Mrs. Wr. crooking her fingers cat like when David served tomatoes in a "cafeteria bowl"—"I'm very mild & gentle, but a tigress when aroused." On complimenting her that she looked well, "But inside I am two orang-outans fighting each other, & they are tearing me apart. The Baroness Rebay wrote me that I am psychic. That means seeing inside people. You see how I know that inside myself I am two orang-outans fighting." "Some of my best friends are Lesbians."

Delightful orchestra rehearsal, to which I was accompanied by David. There is nothing to compare with the true amateur spirit. We played old: Martini Air, Gluck

---

Potemkin's false front is a reference to a story from eighteenth-century Russia in which Prince Potemkin would create fake façades of whole villages and hire peasants to act happy in order to impress Catherine the Great as she passed by.

Romance, Moussorgsky Cossack Dance, Rameau Le Tambourin, and new, Purcell—
Chaconne in G Minor.

SATURDAY, AUGUST 7
Lunch: Corn on the cob, onions & peppers smothered, salmon salad (tuna fish), boiled
cabbage (string beans), (boiled potatoes, Indian pudding), fresh vegetable salad.

Supper: in the tea circle—cold roast pork (cold roast chicken), potato salad,
vegetable salad with Taliesin dressing, corn on the cob, (lima beans, grilled
tomatoes), brown sugar loaf (cherries), watermelon.

Went swimming nude with Kay near the sandbar—washed my hair—delightfully
refreshing. Ran around on the sand till we were dry.

Read Pushkin's "Short Stories." Movie—"The Gay Sisters"—bad imitation in N.Y. of
"Little Foxes" family disintegration.

Another warm, wonderful letter from Marcus—with train schedules, & a most
cordial invitation to stay over night, and he signs it "wistfully."

SUNDAY, AUGUST 8
Wrote to Curtis. Traced. Practiced the recorder (Songs of Russia) under my favorite
apple tree—so low you can reach the apples while lying down. Went swimming
with Kay, Svet, Wes, the children, & Blusco. Concert good. Arne—Sarabande;
Dossek—Rondeau; Bach—Aria—all new. Crack of the day: Mrs. Wr. at breakfast,
referring to some former apprentices—"That's the way it is. We've always had a left
wing here." Someone should tell Mr. Wr. he need not resent finding in others what
he is—the left wing.

MONDAY, AUGUST 9
Traced Sheet 8—Revisions. Main House—Auldbrass and Sheet 22 Oboler House—
Plot Plan.

Garden: kohlrabi, radishes, lettuce, chard, tomatoes.

Helped can corn—about 9 bushels—36 quarts.

A wonderful letter from Thomas, full of praise for Broadacre City: "I don't think
that any kind of capitalism is worthy of Broadacre City or would bring out its
true value but on the other hand I do believe that a democratic socialism to be
worthwhile has to accept as basic the sort of decentralization & treatment of land,
resources & machinery which the Broadacre City plan incarnates." Needless to

---

"Little Foxes" was a 1939 play by Lillian Hellman.

say, Wes & several others have decided "he's a swell guy, after all"—this letter, & an editorial in the Call, saying someone ought to give the $30,000 to help build B. City—and a low breed becomes well bred.

Letters from Allene & that Storage Co. again—Oh, God!

Went swimming at sunset with Molly—a purple, orangey peace and a quiet horizon with a bright half moon.

Did dishes for Ruth—she & Howard were invited to dinner & theater in Richland Center by Henning (part of the be kind to left wingers program?) —and Gene, Wes, Svet, and Ted (Kay was invited but played the martyr for Mrs. Wright) went along to soften the blow.

TUESDAY, AUGUST 10

Thousands of yellow butterflies on the sand, hovering together like some abstract flowers or tiny sail boats—& then whooshing away. Yellow warbler on the broccoli leaves.

Picked beans, beets for canning, broccoli, turnips, washed vegetables. Read. Copied music. Washed beets for canning, but didn't can, actually—Wes was furious at Kay for not knowing how to turn on the drum of gas—& gave it to her thoroughly at tea, aided by Mrs. Wr., who after turned on Ted for reading. It was quite exciting. Picked lone left over summer squash at Hillside.

Went swimming with Kay. Crossed the river to the islands. Walked naked in the hot sun & cool breezes with the swift water swooshing around our knees—felt like an explorer on a Cyprian isle.

Joe Albano is a working-guest here for a month—has been here before. A Socialist, H.S. teacher of Fine Arts in an almost completely negro school, faculty half white, half negro, & negro principal. Knew Thomas was coming here. Helped me defend him (slightly compared to my violent effort) at breakfast when Svet "was disappointed in him—just a politician; no great creative ideas like Daddy Frank's." I explained the visiting guest angle, the polite heckler angle, her negligible apperceptive basis in Socialism as compared with that basis in Broadacre City. But it's no use arguing—she's a Wright which means stubborn, emotional, & besides she wasn't able to grasp her own point, much less mine. (Albano knows Maynard Krueger quite well, & was

Joseph Francis Albano (1906–1990) was not an official fellow, but was an occasional guest and worker at Taliesin. He studied with Mies van der Rohe at the Illinois Institute of Technology from 1944 to 1946. He began teaching architecture at the University of Michigan in 1947 and maintained a practice.

Maynard Krueger (1906–1991), a sociology and economics professor at the University of Chicago and a socialist politician, ran on Norman Thomas's ticket in the presidential race in 1940.

active in his campaign for Alderman in Chicago.) His aunt-in-law is Olgivanna's best friend in America, & politely told her that Gurdjieff stinks. It seems he was a cultured faddist who preyed on wealthy neurotic women. One of their exercises in self-discipline was to wallow in the mud—but gracefully. Taken either literally or figuratively, one sees the direct application to Taliesin. Its faults are therefore as largely—or more—imported as they are organic. On second thought, more.

Orchestra rehearsal quite dull—60 measures of rest for flutes in Purcell's Chaconne can be awfully tiring.

WEDNESDAY, AUGUST 11

Picked corn, tomatoes, lima beans, string beans, apples, potatoes. Cleaned vegetables.

Helped can beets & tomatoes—56 quarts. Put 30 gallons of garlic pickles into a stone crock.

Sweet letters from Nat & Muriel. Wrote to Muriel & Bonawit.

Joe says that judging from other visits here, talks with friends, & his wife's & aunt's opinions—this place has perpetrated a great fraud. It's impossible for Mr. Wr. to teach architecture because he can't—it's just an accident of birth. They take the boys' money, & use them for jobs for which other architects would pay them handsomely, or use them for menial jobs, so he & his family can live in baronial style. He also knows Heisler, Davy's & Jack's last lawyer for the trial—one of the foremost Austrian socialists & at the time a figure in European politics. His wife is Emma's friend (Joe's wife). They may both come up here for a weekend. Mrs. Heisler is a practicing psychiatrist, & she's interested in seeing whether conversation with the Wrights proves or disproves her theories about them—from his writings & reports of friends. She feels his complete indifference to other people would have ended in insanity if his genius did not redeem him. After all, no interest in World War I; depression affected him only insofar as his workmen preferred relief; likes Gesell because his theories would give him, Wright, unlimited money; World War II takes his boys away, etc., etc. No interest in world affairs until he was 40.

Joe's wife: Emma Naomi Krechefsky Albano (b. 1912), a socialist, union organizer, and artist married to Joseph Albano.

Friedy Heisler (1901–1997) was a psychiatrist and civil rights activist. She spent time talking with—and analyzing—several of the Taliesin fellows, as she discussed later in an oral history: "Dr. H: They [the fellows] used to come down from Wisconsin to see me . . . There were some who were very depressed . . . Several had their wives there. They were just scullery maids and doing all the dirty work. Not only that they never got paid for anything, but they never got any recognition for anything they did./Mr. H.: They had to pay to be at Taliesin./Riess [interviewer]: So they were in analysis with you just because they needed it to survive the experience?/Dr. H.: Because they got so depressed they could not function any more." (From the oral history of Friedy Heisler, Regional Oral History Office of The Bancroft Library, University of California, Berkeley, 1983.)

TALIESIN FIRSTS

1. Gather parsnips
2. Pick apples
3. Can apple butter
4. Can apple sauce
5. Can watermelon pickles
6. Can pumpkin
7. Can squash
8. Cut meats
9. Bake bread—whole wheat
10. Cook in large quantities
11. Bake pie
12. Bake cake
13. Make cottage cheese
14. Make sour milk
15. Grind apples for cider
16. Set up warp
17. Navajo weave
18. Trace drafting pen
19. Orthographic projection
20. Play Piano
21. Play recorder
22. Group concerti
23. Rake leaves
24. Plant potatoes
25. Weed garden
26. Tie vines
27. Plant onions
28. Use washing machine
29. Use mangle
30. Build a fire
31. Dye wools
32. Make skeins of wool
33. Saw wood
34. Hammer nails
35. Weave linen
36. Make sour cream
37. Pencil tracings

38. Weed quack grass and clover from strawberry patch
39. Draw colored perspective
40. Thin out radishes
41. Render lard
42. Weed dock, mallow, thistle, milkweed
43. Plant pine trees
44. Pick asparagus
45. Pick rhubarb
46. Pick scallions
47. Pick leaf lettuce
48. Shovel plaster
49. De nail laths
50. Chain warp for loom
51. Thread warp thru heddles
52. Make general plan for school
53. Make soap
54. Roll warp on loom
55. Pick strawberries
56. Can asparagus
57. Pick peas
58. Can peas
59. Tie tomato vines
60. Pick chard
61. Churn butter
62. Pick raspberries
63. Pick gooseberries
64. Pick beets
65. Pick New Zealand spinach
66. Pick parsley
67. Pick beans—wax
68. Pick boysenberries
69. Pick cabbages
70. Pick chokecherries
71. Pick green beans

72. Pick tomatoes
73. Pick green peppers
74. Bake scotch oatmeal bread
75. Can beans
76. Can peaches
77. Pick sweet corn —"Golden Bantam"
78. Pickle beans in brine
79. Dehydrate string beans
80. Pick carrots
81. Make farmer cheese
82. Pick cucumbers
83. Pick kohlrabi
84. Can corn
85. Dry parsley
86. Pick turnips
87. Pick broccoli
88. Feed the pigs
89. Can beets
90. Pick summer squash
91. Pick corn —"Country Gentleman"
92. Dig potatoes
93. Pick lima beans
94. Can Tomatoes
95. Can garlic pickles
96. Feed the chickens
97. Pick mint
98. Can crabapple jelly
99. Can mint jelly
100. Pick chinese cabbage
101. Pick golden table queen squash
102. Can apple compote
103. Can spiced apples

***

Mein Liebtsen, I still hope I did the right thing in leaving. You don't get a husband a dime a dozen and still a husband. Keep your dear lips shut and your ears open. And please remember—wherever you are dear it's my home. We have quite a day planned for me—Italian restaurants, Krueger, university. No reservations on trains—you trust to luck. So now I'm on my way. Libe [Love], Priscilla

A Broad-Acre Project (1954)

Priscilla J. Henken

This essay was originally published in the June 1954 edition of Town and Country Planning, *a British journal.*

The equation for the success or failure of an idea may be the ratio of the dream to the reality. Sometimes the dream is better than the reality; sometimes not. This is the story of a dream and its realization, and of the X factor in any idea—the individual human being.

Usonia Homes is a cooperative community of individually designed houses, with an acre of ground for each family, about thirty miles from New York City. Mr. Frank Lloyd Wright laid out the site plan and acted as consultant to preserve the integrity of the whole design. Even this idea, thus stated, owes its being to many sources. The Rochdale pioneers, all of the cooperatives and Utopian communities in England and America were its ancestors. Frank Lloyd Wright's vision of Broadacre City, with its emphasis on decentralization, on a "going forward to more intelligent use of man's heritage, the ground," and on the democratic ideal of freedom of the individual, was another forebear. Even the name was the gift of Samuel Butler, who in order to distinguish the citizens of the United States from other Americans on both continents, gave them the name of Usonians in *Erewhon* (U-United, S-States, O-Of, N-North, A-America, and I for euphony). Mr. Wright used the name to describe his house for the average American, or Usonian—that house whose principles have become a kind of ten commandments to modern architects everywhere. We use the name with his permission, for our houses embody the same general principles.

ORIGIN OF USONIA HOMES

Because he wanted a home of his own, because the ideas behind cooperatives and Broadacre City were in tune with his own social philosophy and because for him Mr. Wright's work represented the essence of integrity in architecture, David Henken, a young engineer, started to plan Usonia with his friends. There was as much parlor talk as there always is, and those content only to talk soon dropped out. David Henken apprenticed himself to Mr. Wright for two years, hoping to emerge sufficiently acquainted with the architecture to be an adequate supervisor of these houses. Then he and his friends got to work in earnest. In ten years, a few thousand families have been either mildly or intensely interested, but they were discouraged by the war, by high prices, by what seemed like a frightening isolation to the city-bred, by the long history of failure in cooperatives, and by the near impossibility of securing any financing. The banks had their counts against us too: the cooperative principle of nonracial or religious discrimination threatened a lowering of real estate values in certain communities; modern houses had no resale value as compared to conventional houses; and should the group dissolve, as was more than likely, there would be gargantuan disputes about the jointly owned water supply system, roads, and community lands.

Nevertheless, we incorporated in 1944 under the laws of the state of New York as a Rochdale Cooperative. Drawing a forty-mile radius from New York City for easier commuting, we finally located our "land" and purchased it in 1947. Surrounded on three sides by a pine-tree watershed that forms a permanent green belt, it is hilly, rolling, with pleasant little brooks, fine old trees as well as much new growth, stone fences which are remnants of ancient farms (our title search indicated that the land was originally the royal grant of William and Mary to Frederick Philipse), and abundant small wildlife.

THE FRANK LLOYD WRIGHT PLAN

Over the ninety-seven-acre site, Mr. Wright threw a circular geometric pattern. There are fifty-five circular plots—one for each house—of approximately an acre each. These touch neighboring sites only at contiguous points, and each group of six encircles another circular plot, which is used as a small park. The little triangular wedges that are left between circles remain the buffer areas of green. The land not used for home sites is allotted at present for planned-for playgrounds, vegetable gardens, a children's farm, swimming pool, community house, guest cottages, and ball courts. Winding roads skirt the edges of the sites or cut through community property. The cooperative dug its own well, built a storage tank and pump house, laid out the water and road systems, brought in electricity, and purchased the fire-fighting equipment and heating pipes.

Of the fifty families on which we planned, a number small enough to make a cohesive community, and large enough to share the financial responsibilities, thirty-three are living here now. They represent a cross-section of religious and political affiliation, and varied occupations: teachers, dentists, a lawyer, a doctor, engineers, architects, advertising executives, salesmen, business owners, chemists, journalists, decorators, and, of course, housewives. The ages vary from the middle twenties to the early sixties. The common denominator is the willingness to live cooperatively, and a feeling for modern architecture.

The houses are all different. That follows naturally from Mr. Wright's principles of organic architecture, which demand that each house be suited to the needs and personalities of the owners; that it be suited to the site; that it employ the products and technology of the times, using materials for their intrinsic worth and beauty with respect for the nature of the material; and that it reflect the creative integrity of the architect. The work of nine architects is represented.

Therefore even though standards of sizes, materials, and modules were established, and there are many features in common, each house is the only one of its kind, a work of art with the artist's signature. Each has been oriented, with sheltering eaves, to let the low winter sun stream in and keep the high summer sun out. Each has an open floor plan with few partitions, huge fireplaces, built-in furniture, and concrete floor slabs with radiant heating.

Many houses have been designed to allow for expansion as needs and incomes permit. In some cases only the shell was built, while wood walls gradually replaced cord-hung curtains for room partitions. The result is that houses are part of the site in that the outdoors is an integral part of the whole, welcomed in by the large glass walls, made one with the indoor planting, with interior walls flowing in subtle transition into terrace walls. These are houses with molded space, large free sunny areas contrasted with well-enclosed cozy rooms for a person's other moods; houses with great expanses of glass but so angled on the site that they have a great deal of privacy; houses scattered across many acres, yet subtly tied to each other by design, material, and the sense of belonging to that place.

FINDING THE MONEY

As anyone knows, finance is the rock on which most cooperatives founder. We almost did too. Basing our ideas on prewar costs, we aimed too high without realizing that houses would quadruple in cost. The banks would give no help for a long time; and no builder or architect in the country could make an estimate of postwar housing costs. We paid the initial expenses with a $100 membership fee and a $5 share from each member family. Each family agreed to pay $50 a month, which was put into a joint fund but credited to each member's account. When we were ready to purchase the site (at a tax foreclosure auction) for $20,000, we had already saved $1,200 apiece, or approximately $40,000. Besides the initial fees, each cooperator must have 40 percent of the anticipated total cost of his house in cash before construction can be started. Included in this 40 percent are $3,000 for site and architectural or other fees for his own house, which must be paid at the time the work is contracted for. The other 60 percent of costs can be covered by a long-term mortgage.

It all seemed so simple until we actually attempted to get money. We soon realized that if we really did want Usonia, we would be forced to finance the first houses ourselves, entirely out of our own pockets. With $120,000 in pooled cash that we had saved or borrowed from trusting friends and relatives, we decided in 1948 to build five houses as a pilot project. Soon two more were begun and then eight more families were given permission to go ahead with construction if they could get 100 percent of the financing on their own, since Usonia's pooled resources were too low to permit any more building. Meanwhile, all the families continued to save $50 a month in the cooperative fund.

A BANK BANKS ON THE FUTURE

With fifteen houses under construction, Usonia had jumped the financial and psychological hurdle, and in March 1950, Knickerbocker Federal Savings and Loan Association agreed to a group mortgage, with all the land and houses as security. Mr. Boecher, its president, said: "Here we have houses designed by Mr. Wright himself, and, as usual, twenty to thirty years ahead of their time. At the tag end of these loans we will be secured by marketable, contemporary homes instead of dated stereotypes, obsolete before they are started. We are banking on the future, not the past . . . Here we have a group that is setting a new pace both in cooperative ownership and architectural design. We think this will become an increasingly significant form of home ownership. We like it because we think group developments offer both the lender and the owner the maximum of protection against the greatest single factor in realty depreciation—that of neighborhood deterioration."

MUTUAL LOAN ARRANGEMENTS

Under the group mortgage plan, the bank writes a separate mortgage on every house, including those already built and "paid for." Usonia holds title to the land and the houses; members have ninety-nine-year leases renewable for their heirs, and make monthly payments to the cooperative for the principal and interest on their mortgages, maintenance of community properties, and community expenses. The co-operative, in turn, pays the loan association. However, each member family must agree to go on bond on his own leasehold so that if Usonia defaults on the group mortgage, each individual will be responsible for his own house and land. Since Usonia is the owner, when a member leaves he has to turn his house over to the cooperative, which may in turn "sell" it to a new member. If the house is sold at a profit, the withdrawing member will get back his equity in the house plus his share of the profit—a percentage that makes allowances for inflation by using the Bureau of Labor Statistics Index. If it is sold at a loss the owner must stand the loss alone. We haven't faced this problem yet, and don't anticipate it with any relish.

PROBLEMS AND PLEASURES

I often think of Usonia as a microcosm—a detail of the larger picture. If families quarrel in making simple decisions on the purchase of a refrigerator, imagine how much more violent the quarrel may become when thirty-three families, acting as one, must make decisions on road surfacing, or cost allocations after a siege of poor bookkeeping. There have been some disagreements among member families. Some, impatient with the cooperative practice of voting on everything, of sharing losses and responsibility, are urging private ownership.

But there is more that is good in Usonia: its community activities like the dance group and the children's day camp which even the neighbors enjoy; its integrated community plan, its architecture which has become a focal point for students and visiting foreign architects who have been told this is "one of the things to see." In the four years we have lived here, almost three thousand tourists have visited our house alone. When people wonder whether we mind this invasion, we can honestly say that we don't. Like the other families here, we enjoy showing our house and community. We are proud of what we have done. And as for the inevitable failures in the dream realized, Browning put it best when he said, "A man's reach should exceed his grasp, Or what's a heaven for?"

FRANK LLOYD WRIGHT AND DAVID HENKEN REVIEWING PLANS FOR USONIA, c. 1949
Photograph © Pedro E. Guerrero.

After Taliesin: Wright Way, Usonia Homes

Elissa R. Henken, Jonathan T. Henken, and Mariamne Henken Whatley

LIVING ON WRIGHT WAY

Our address—Wright Way, Usonia Homes, Pleasantville, NY—was a clear statement of the nature of one strong influence on our lives. As the three children of Priscilla Jussim Henken (PJH) and David T. Henken (DTH), we grew up absorbing stories of Frank Lloyd Wright and Taliesin as a core part of our family's history and folklore, as thoroughly embedded as the stories of our Bubbies and Zadies and their journeys from Ukraine to New York City. However, conversations about Frank Lloyd Wright were imbued with a different kind of respect, not the loving and warm respect for our grandparents, but with the deference shown to royalty. No one in our home referred to Wright, and certainly never to Frank, but always to Mr. Wright, Frank Lloyd Wright, or FLW. When Mariamne's elementary school classmate Andy Porter, a great-nephew of FLW, mentioned Uncle Frank, Mariamne was in awe that he could speak with such familiarity. Over many years we learned the names and stories from our parents, from their conversations with other former apprentices around our dinner table, and by dipping into books from their extensive FLW library. When we visited Taliesin as children, we finally were able to situate those stories in the Hillside drafting room and theater, in the farmland around Midway, in the Taliesin living room.

Growing up in a home designed by our father on the architectural principles he learned from FLW taught us a great deal about those principles through immersion. Our house nestled in a hillside and was protected from cold winter winds since the north walls were mostly below ground. The full-length windows in the living and dining rooms gave a full southern exposure and an uninterrupted view of the wooded acre below our house. In winter, the passive solar heating kept us warm while we looked out at snowdrifts on the terrace and, in summer, the overhangs blocked the hot sun, keeping the house cool without any air conditioning or fans. In winter, the dark red concrete radiant-heated floors were a perfect place to thaw out after snow shoveling or snowball fights, with kids and dogs jockeying for the best hot spots. In summer, the dogs came in to pant in relief on the cool concrete, where uninvited animals sometimes joined them. One hot summer day a garter snake slithered in past the dining room table and made its way to the indoor plant area filled with dirt where the concrete floor ended and which ran along both sides of the V formed by the full-length windows. The continuity of the huge house plants inside and the garden outside (inside the glass V) was reinforced by the presence of Lucifer, the snake who came to stay for many years, regularly surprising visitors and even our family as he draped around the air roots of monstera philodendrons. Other animals appeared in the V window, making them very easy to watch. Opossums occasionally hung on the trellis above the garden, and a skunk, less pleasantly, settled in for a while, limiting our movements, lest we scare it and get sprayed.

As expected in a Wright-style house, the living room centered around a large fireplace ("big enough to roast the architect") with a long, wide brick hearth that provided a perfect sitting area. We warmed pajamas there to be ready after a bath, toasted marshmallows and apples on long skewers, and practiced branding logs with the Henken Builds iron used to label tool handles. The fireplace was so core to family activity that when we were sick we were relocated to the couch by the fireplace until we recovered.

The warm tones of recessed lighting combined with clerestories at different levels and angles, skylights, and many large windows provided fascinating plays of light. The fire and candles could be endlessly reflected in glass. Reflections of the sun sometimes made it seem to be rising and setting at the same time. Easy access to the roof from the hill gave us an extra place to explore and the location for a fascinating tour of our house as we peered through skylights and clerestories for new perspectives on where we lived. Our father's studio was just a short walk up the hill on an outdoor concrete stairway. It was very unusual at that time to have a father who worked at home, especially since so many commuted into New York City. While he worked we could entertain ourselves with T-squares and triangles and long-pointed drawing pencils. Jonathan learned a great deal about architecture and building from hanging out with our father and his building crew. Under Jonathan's leadership, our childhood building projects were very complex and Usonian; he even cut and installed irregular trapezoids of plate glass for the windows and wired fluorescent lighting for our "museum," a structure that would instantly be recognized as Wright-influenced.

When friends visited us, they were usually amazed and confused by our house and often unable to find their way around the relatively small space. Conversely, as we each went off to college and to various later apartments and houses, we all experienced a strangeness in living in rooms that had only right angles; where the ceilings were usually at one level; where the walls went all the way to the ceiling and there were too many interior doors; where sunlight came in only through a few windows usually at the same height; where plants sat in pots—not built-in plant boxes; where walls were painted—not made of oiled cypress that would last forever; where a house perched on the land rather than seeming to grow out of it.

LEAVING TALIESIN AND LIFE AFTER

As children, the three of us loved to hear about Taliesin. Sometimes our mother would take her Taliesin diary out of the cabinet hidden behind the living room couch (a location we all knew but respected as off-limits) and she would read carefully chosen excerpts to us, to which our father would add his own commentary. For example, the description of the Halloween party in which everyone came as paintings involved a demonstration by DTH of how Johnny Hill posed when, dressed as an Egyptian pharaoh, he glided on roller skates across the room. However, we didn't read the diary until, long after our mother's death in 1969, Elissa photocopied and transcribed it. Some of it was familiar but there were many details and events that were new to us. Perhaps the biggest surprise and mystery was the abrupt end of the diary, followed by a list of "Taliesin Firsts" at the end of the second volume. None of us were aware of a third volume and the list at the end seemed to confirm the lack of any more record of her time at Taliesin. It was very unlike our mother to leave any work incomplete.

As far as we understood, PJH had taken a year's leave from teaching English in New York City high schools so that she could accompany DTH to Taliesin. He stayed on to continue his architectural apprenticeship when she needed to return to teach to provide family income. But if her departure were planned, why didn't the diary include details about preparations to leave, her departure, her return to New York?

In cleaning out our family home in 2006, we found a cache of letters that included many between our parents when he was at Taliesin and she was in New York, both over the Christmas and New Year's period of 1942–43 and after Priscilla's return in the summer of 1943. These wonderful letters gave us a view of our parents and their relationship before we were born. We also could read about Taliesin in our father's own words and get a sense of life in wartime New York City. The letters also held some hints as to what might have happened to precipitate our mother's rapid departure. Trying to understand that is obviously of personal interest to us. However, it also helps reveal some of the dynamics that made life at Taliesin such a contradictory set of experiences for many apprentices and indicates specific tensions our parents experienced there. A former apprentice, Curtis Besinger, discusses in his book, *Working with Wright: What It Was Like,* attitudes about our parents by some members of the Taliesin Fellowship:

> [T]here was a suspicion that the Henkens were government agents
> planted within the Fellowship to gather evidence against Mr. Wright
> and members of the Fellowship for their opposition to the draft and the
> war. Mrs. Wright seemed particularly concerned that the government

221

might attempt some sort of action against Mr. Wright since he was so outspoken. The Henkens also expressed opposition to the draft and the war, but their memberships in antiwar organizations were regarded as part of their cover.[1]

Given how much work DTH did to provide information and support for conscientious objectors (COs) and on other draft issues, this suspicious view of him is rather ironic. His expertise came from personal and political work. He had applied for CO status and always considered himself a CO (a 4E classification), even though the draft board never thus classified him. Our understanding when we were growing up was that, due to his poor eyesight and severe allergies, he had been classified 4F (physically unfit for service) but felt he should be given CO status so, in his usual principled—and often difficult—way, he was unwilling to accept the useful 4F classification. We may have been wrong about the 4F classification because, according to the diary, he had been classified as 3B (deferred by reason of dependency and occupation essential to the war effort) (February 1, 1943) and later as 2B (deferred because of occupation in a war industry) (May 1, 1943). In any case, on principle he wanted to be classified as 4E even though the classifications he had been given would have kept him from being inducted. It seems as though any issue related to the draft might have been a no-win situation for our parents at Taliesin; no matter what they did, it might be seen as "part of their cover." In addition, Besinger and others suggest that anti-Semitism, sometimes disguised by attitudes about "pushy New Yorkers," may have been a factor in making it difficult for our parents to work at Taliesin. Entries from the diary clearly substantiate the view that anti-Semitism was rampant there.

It is clear from the letters that PJH had not planned to return to teaching in the fall of 1943; they indicate that she did not have a job waiting for her and had to start looking for work when she returned to New York. Many letters refer to her discouraging job search and various temporary jobs, including one doing laboratory preparation for a class. Others refer to the difficulty of her decision to leave Taliesin, which entailed a separation from her husband, and to the reactions to her departure: "And I hate answering the perpetual Why are you so blue? What was all the excitement there? What did they do to you? It all seems very far away and silly,"[2] and: "I wonder if my leaving, with their half suspicions that the place was as much responsible as my mother's illness, could have anything to do with their being extra nice to you now. Are they apologizing? Are they trying to make amends? What is all this sudden concern and affection?"[3]

Several letters, such as the following, refer to the possibility of Priscilla returning to Taliesin:

Let's discuss this:

1. If I get a permanent job, you come to visit me for a week or two, and I'll join you in February.

2. If I don't, I'll join you in late November or December.

3. If the draft board intervenes, think fast, Mr. Moto.

4. If I do rejoin you, how long will you stay? Will you leave with me at the beginning of the year or will we have to make another wrench? I can't stand very much of that sort of thing.

5. Why do they want to know about my return? Do they think your staying depends on me? Or do they want a cook? Or do they dislike the idea of my skipping out on them? Or what?[4]

As this letter suggests, some people at Taliesin expected that she would return. We know of several apprentices who left under stressful circumstances. For example, a letter from DTH notes the story of another apprentice's sudden departure ("the Queen" refers to Mrs. Wright):

After a week of hell in the kitchen at the hands of the Queen, Henning decided to leave the Fellowship the same day he gave notice. The Queen hates him cordially. FLW told him he was leaving when we were shorthanded. Svet visited him at his farm imploring him to return. He replied that he couldn't stand living in a group where Svet & the Mrs. are typical of its womanhood.[5]

In another letter, DTH indicates that Henning's departure may have made his own life a little easier—at least for a while—through its effect on Mrs. Wright:

Tonight I am going to visit Henning, the Hermit, for a brief call. We will compare notes no doubt. His leaving had this one effect—the Queen is treating me so gently that I almost hate to hurt her with my news, but don't worry—nothing, and I mean nothing could keep me here.[6]

Trying to interpret comments in the letters in the context of diary entries and stories we had heard, it seemed likely to us that PJH simply had had enough of certain attitudes and behaviors of Mrs. Wright and some of her close circle. While Mr. Wright was almost always spoken of with great respect by former apprentices, even when they mentioned some of his less admirable behaviors, references to Mrs. Wright often evoked anger, sarcasm, and pain. We had all been able to piece together the portrait of a very imperious woman, who coddled her favorites, made life miserable for those out of favor, tried to manipulate the lives and romances of many in the Taliesin community, and even sent some apprentices into exile for petty "offenses." The diary shows evidence of these behaviors and the letters show even more. In his book Curtis Besinger described Priscilla as having "sharp wit,

intelligence, and perceptiveness" and as "delightful and charming company."[7] It is very easy to imagine that she had reached the limit of what she could tolerate from Mrs. Wright but still was reluctant to burn bridges. It seems reasonable that she would have used real circumstances (her mother's ill health) as
a plausible pretext for taking a break from Taliesin, with the expectation of returning at some later point. We do not know and are unlikely ever to know exactly why she left Taliesin suddenly and did not return. We also do not know exactly when and why DTH left.

After Taliesin, our mother returned to teaching in New York City, while our father continued his design work as the chief designer for Game Makers, Inc. At the same time, they worked together with an expanding group of friends and relatives toward their dream of a cooperative community with houses designed using principles of organic architecture. In 1948 the dream began to be realized, as the first house in Usonia was built, designed by DTH for his parents; FLW called it a "perfect jewel of a house." In 1949, we moved into our house, though it was not completed for many years after that, primarily for financial reasons, leading to many comments along the lines of "the shoemaker's children go without shoes." DTH designed thirteen houses in Usonia, including those built for his sister and brother-in-law, Judeth and Odif Podell, and for PJH's sister and brother-in-law, Julia and George Brody. PJH took time off from teaching to raise the three of us, while she also did secretarial and other work for Henken Builds, Inc. Additionally, she used her architectural knowledge to write several articles, one of which ("A Broad-Acre Project") appears in this volume, and to give guest lectures at architectural schools, such as Columbia University, on Usonia, Frank Lloyd Wright, and organic architecture. Eventually, she returned to teaching high school English, first substituting and later full-time teaching at Pleasantville High School, which all three of us attended. Even students not as biased as we were thought she was an excellent and well-loved teacher. Besides the knowledge of architecture, she also brought other skills from Taliesin, including weaving on a large loom set up in our living room, playing the recorder, and even cooking some Taliesin dishes, such as babka and paska cheese for Russian Easter.

DTH continued to do architectural design, not just in Usonia but throughout Westchester and neighboring counties, and occasionally in other states. He never went through the process of getting licensed as an architect, though we are not sure whether this was due to factors of time, stubbornness, or something else. He, therefore, needed other architects to sign off on his designs, which was sometimes frustrating for him. Later he worked as a campus planner. At the time of his death in 1985, he was working on a reconstruction of the FLW-designed Model Usonian

House, discussed below, for Tom Monaghan, a Frank Lloyd Wright enthusiast and collector, who was also then the owner of Domino's Pizza and the Detroit Tigers.

WORK WITH FLW: CHALLENGES AND REWARDS

Whatever the circumstances of their separate departures, our parents continued to have a good relationship with FLW, as evidenced in various ways. For example, there was a pleasant exchange of letters about the birth of Jonathan in 1945, and the Wrights sent a baby gift. There was also an invitation to visit Taliesin around the same time. Mr. Wright visited our home in Usonia. A favorite family story about one FLW visit was that a young Jonathan was whisked away from FLW's presence when he commented that he did not like "old baskets with white hair." Apparently Jonathan had heard workmen (possibly including apprentices), frustrated with trying to figure out some Wright plans, complain, "I wonder what the old bastard wants." This seems to contradict our view that Mr. Wright was always spoken of with respect. These same apprentices and workmen were likely to speak of FLW with respect outside of the circle of those who worked closely with him. However, they were able to vent frustrations and be more honest about difficulties of working with FLW among the inner circle.

Our parents were invited to Taliesin-related social events, such as a concert by Brandoch Peters, the son of Svetlana and Wes Peters. They were also invited to the opening of the Guggenheim Museum and to Mr. Wright's ninetieth birthday party; though Wright died before his birthday, there was a celebration of his life and work at Taliesin, which our parents attended.

Most significantly, there continued to be a professional relationship in several major ways: in FLW's involvement with Usonia; in FLW's employment of DTH and Henken Builds, Inc., for work on specific houses he designed, such as the Reisley and Serlin houses in Usonia; and in DTH's service in 1953 as the contractor for the construction of the FLW-designed Model Usonian House and Exhibition Pavilion, which were built, as part of a major retrospective exhibit of FLW's work (60 Years of Living Architecture), on the site where the Guggenheim Museum would later be located. Those experiences, while professionally exciting and fulfilling at some levels for DTH, were also extremely difficult in other ways. As we learned growing up, Mr. Wright believed and often stated that he was owed a living as an artist and, in his own words, as the world's greatest living architect. The diary and letters also mention that some apprentices were pressured to convince their families to provide funds to FLW. There are countless stories of unpaid bills to contractors, suppliers, workers, and local tradespeople, as well as cost overruns that clients were expected to accept. This made work very difficult for anyone who was overseeing the building of a design by FLW. Correspondence shows that DTH was frequently caught between clients frustrated by delays and cost overruns and FLW angered by clients who were withholding payment.

CREATING USONIA

When DTH returned from Taliesin in 1943, he and others began active planning for the community that he had dreamed of—a cooperative in the country, where people could raise their children in a healthy environment outside the city. FLW accepted DTH's invitation to play a key part in the architectural design and planning of Usonia. FLW's role would involve designing the overall site plan, designing some of the houses, and approving the designs of all the other homes before they could be built. DTH was the key member of Usonia communicating between the Usonians and Wright. Because there were some tensions over such issues as the usual cost overruns and slow payments, DTH had to serve as liaison and mediator, which put him in a difficult position, caught between demands and complaints from both sides. There were difficult conflicts around FLW's role in approving designs for houses to be built in Usonia; these arguments were a key part in Wright's angry withdrawal from involvement with Usonia. However, during the time he was involved, he designed the overall site plan, three homes (Friedman, Reisley, Serlin) that were built, and three buildings (two homes and a community center) that were never constructed. In addition, he had given feedback on the designs of many of the homes built in the first few years of Usonia.

As children, we loved our house and the wooded land around it. However, we all have painful memories about our "exile" from Usonia. Though our parents lived in our house on Wright Way until their deaths, they were voted out of membership in Usonia in 1955 owing to a complex series of disputes, some related to building costs. Our grandparents, Benjamin and Frieda Henken, resigned in solidarity, though they, too, continued to live in their house until their deaths. Interestingly, when Jonathan recently tried to find out what were the actual issues leading to this vote, the Usonians he talked to had only vague and contradictory memories. It was very hard for us to understand as children how our father could have been the man who dreamed of and founded Usonia and yet not be a member. The cooperative community seemed to us much less than cooperative; it felt hostile and we felt like outcasts. It was the loss of a dream for our parents. DTH used to joke sadly that he felt like Moses, having led the people to the Promised Land, but not being allowed to enter.

DTH's experience as an apprentice and architect was crucial in working on the Model Usonian House because the plans were basically rough sketches by FLW, which DTH would then develop into a working plan. Pedro E. Guerrero, the well-known photographer of FLW and his work, discussed the process in his book *Picturing Wright: An Album from Frank Lloyd Wright's Photographer:* "As the house progressed and the carpenters reached an undefined area of construction, Henken and Mr. Wright would huddle over a drawing and together would plot the next move. The entire effort to build the temporary Usonian model as part of the Wright retrospective exhibition was a "solve-as-we-go-along" project. The method was not only inefficient; it was expensive, so the house began to fall behind budget and over schedule." [8]

Working on the Model House was extremely difficult, as evidenced in this telegram that DTH sent to FLW on August 25, 1953:

> YOUR CHANGED PLANS AND OUR DELAY IN GETTING THEM CAUSED
> THREE DAY DELAY IF CHANGES ARE NECESSARY PLEASE RUSH THEM
> TO ME CARE OF HOLDEN OFFICE. ADDITIONAL DELAY FACTOR IS
> EVERY CHANGE MADE REQUIRES AMENDMENT FILED WITH NEW YORK
> BUILDING COMMISSION. [9]

Sometimes DTH had to fund payroll and pay suppliers out of his pocket, while waiting for Wright to provide required funds. In spite of the obstacles, the Usonian Exhibition House was completed by the deadline. Wright's responses to DTH's letters related to the model were often very unpleasant and insulting. For example, there are two letters dated November 16, 1953, from DTH to Wright. One letter begins with thanks to Wright for the "opportunity of building your exhibition house and pavilion. It was an experience I would not have missed—but don't think I could survive another." He acknowledges to Wright, "Naturally, you are the hero of the occasion. You deserve to be" and then continues, "But there are many small heroes, mostly unsung, even by you." [10] DTH then praises many groups, such as the apprentices, volunteers, and museum personnel, and individuals, who worked so hard, with personal sacrifices, to achieve a successful opening of the exhibit. The other letter pleads for FLW to send money to cover the expenses of the exhibition, as DTH points out that he had put all his money and what he could borrow into meeting those expenses. Mr. Wright's response to DTH on November 23, 1953, shows his irritation clearly: "DAVID: I WANT NO INSTRUCTIONS FROM YOU CONCERNING MY BEHAVIOR." FLW demands a full accounting of the funds he gave DTH, while also complaining about the museum's handling of finances. He concludes, "CUT OUT THE SOB STUFF." [11]

When FLW's letters are studied or published, they are often taken at face value and referred to as if they are a complete, accurate statement about what transpired; however, it is important to put all those letters in context. For the specific correspondence we refer to here, that context includes a man who is world-renowned as an architect having to deal with what he considers petty issues of money and acknowledgment of the contributions of many who gladly labored on his behalf. We know it is not appropriate to go into detailed arguments about who might be blamed for what, but we simply wish to show that for DTH, as well as for many others, working with FLW was a complex and contradictory experience, with the pleasure of learning from an architectural genius often offset by negative interactions. As children, teenagers, and young adults, we were exposed to very positive views of Mr. Wright; it was only much later that we became aware of some of the unpleasant experiences and started to understand the complexities. Our memories of the time of the Model House are mostly about the excitement and how much work had to be done under pressure, as our father stated the goal of "Out of the trenches by Christmas." However, we never heard criticism of FLW himself.

There is an interesting footnote about the Model House. After the house was dismantled, there was some hope that the pieces and plans would be purchased so that the house could be reconstructed elsewhere. In the meantime, these pieces were stored in our father's woodworking shop. In 1984, thirty years after it was dismantled—and assumed by most people to have been demolished—DTH donated the pieces of the house to WNET, a public television station in New York City, to be auctioned as part of their fund-raising efforts. As mentioned above, Tom Monaghan bid successfully. He hired DTH, who had most of the details in his head, as the plans were not complete, to oversee reconstruction. DTH was very enthusiastic about the project; he died in Ann Arbor while he was working on the plans for rebuilding the house. The rebuilding was never finished and the pieces were sold off at auction to benefit the Frank Lloyd Wright Building Conservancy in 1992.

TALIESIN FRIENDSHIPS

A lasting impact for many apprentices and their families was the establishment of long-term friendships, such as the ones our parents had, with other apprentices and those associated with Taliesin. From these friendships, we learned more about the complicated feelings they had about their Taliesin experiences. The following quotation from one former apprentice sums up some of the complex feelings among many of those who had spent time at Taliesin: "When one leaves The Fellowship and sees a little further than the petty obstacles (but none the less important because of their pettiness) one's love and admiration of Mr. W. grows. But then through letters, relating of injustices—all these bring back the muck of it all. Then one is torn by preserving and destroying in one single thought."[12] Time at Taliesin was a major formative experience for all those we knew who had been there. However, for many, the overall experience was often tinged with the sense of "injustices," whether petty or not, as in the remark quoted. Those who left under difficult circumstances often spoke publicly in glowing terms about their time at Taliesin.

Several of those mentioned in the diary remained close friends throughout our parents' lives. Eleanore Petersen, who was an apprentice at the same time and is discussed in the diary, left very abruptly. After PJH returned to New York, they stayed in close contact. Later Eleanore became a well-established architect and a frequent visitor to our home. The three of us remember her very lively and funny conversations about FLW and times at Taliesin. With a laugh like Carol Channing's, she always made us laugh, too. As with the others we knew, she was very respectful in discussing FLW though she had many unpleasant memories, particularly relating to her departure. Eleanore was one of the architects who worked with DTH and was very involved with his work at Nasson College.

Marcus Weston also became a close friend. Our father helped advise him on draft issues and how he might proceed. Besides being mentioned in the diary, his trial for failing to appear for induction is discussed in several letters. In a letter to our mother, dated December 23, 1942, DTH mentions, "By the way Marcus's statement which I helped him write appeared in yesterday's Capital Times."[13] In a letter on December 25, 1942, DTH mentioned that he also wrote the Fellowship's radio broadcast statement on COs. Our parents corresponded with Marcus; he found their supportive letters very important to his survival when he was on parole, working at a hospital in Ann Arbor. Our mother visited Marcus on a trip back to New York and this time together created a strong bond that continued to help support him through some difficult times. In the early days of Usonia, he lived with us, working as a draftsman for our father. As children we identified Marcus as someone who continued to be very important in our parents' lives after their time in Taliesin. Marcus wrote regularly to our mother until her death and has continued to maintain contact with us. Marcus still lives in Spring Green in a house he designed, where we had visited him and his family on a trip when we were young; at that time he escorted us on a full personal tour of Taliesin. Later, he refused to go to any Taliesin events because he was so upset that Mrs. Wright had ordered that FLW's body be disinterred from the family graveyard near Taliesin to be reburied at Taliesin West. Many others also saw this as a violation of Mr. Wright's wishes.

Pedro Guerrero got to know our parents in 1948 and became a close family friend for the rest of our parents' lives. Included among his many famous FLW photographs are a number that were taken in the early days of Usonia and at the construction of the model and exhibition pavilion.

Another lifelong family friend was Elizabeth Enright, known as Bitsy. Though she was not an apprentice, she was the daughter of FLW's sister Maginel Wright Barney and our parents got to know her at Taliesin. Our father had a crush on her that we all teased him about. Our mother agreed that he had good taste: "Bitsy is quite a gal, one for whom I would gladly change sexes."[14] Attractive, charming, and intelligent, she was a well-known children's book writer and illustrator, winning the Newbery Medal for *Thimble Summer*. Mariamne was so impressed by her that she announced in first grade that she planned to be a writer and illustrator like Bitsy.

There were a number of other Taliesin apprentices whose relationships with our parents continued after Taliesin. Curtis Besinger wrote to them from the CO camp where he was interned. Henning Watterson stayed in such close contact with our parents that he moved into their apartment in New York City. While we did not get to know Henning in the same way we did many others from Taliesin, we did hear stories of his misadventures, mostly involving experiments in dyeing. For example, he used to dry his freshly dyed fabric on our parents' clean linens, changing their color rather dramatically. Howard Ten Brink, another former apprentice and also a CO, remained a family friend. The three of us remember visiting him in his home in Michigan. Although Irene Buitenkant was an apprentice after our parents' time at Taliesin, our family and hers became good friends. It was impressive to us that she designed and then partially built her family's home. Having worked long into her pregnancy, she finally had to give up halfway through building the chimney. DTH let her "borrow" Nick Sardilli, the master mason for Henken Builds. After he started, she requested instead the apprentice mason, whose skills were closer to hers and, therefore, would make the rest of the chimney match her work.

When we started to discuss writing this essay, we realized that we shared many of the same memories, but each of us also had our own set. Going through these stories helped us understand more about our parents and the legacy of Taliesin. Our family life was deeply enriched by our parents' experiences at Taliesin, by their association with Mr. Wright, and by the continuing Taliesin friendships. On the other hand, the childhood joy of living in our house on Wright Way may be the best way for us to remember the role of Frank Lloyd Wright in our parents' lives.

1. Curtis Besinger, *Working with Mr. Wright: What It Was Like* (Cambridge: Cambridge University Press, 1995), 140-41.

2. Letter from Priscilla J. Henken in New York City to David T. Henken at Taliesin, Spring Green, Wisconsin, September 6, 1943. All letters © Elissa R. Henken, Jonathan T. Henken, and Mariamne H. Whatley.

3. Letter from Priscilla J. Henken in New York City to David T. Henken at Taliesin, Spring Green, Wisconsin, September 18, 1943.

4. Letter from Priscilla J. Henken in New York City to David T. Henken at Taliesin, Spring Green, Wisconsin, September 23, 1943.

5. Letter from David T. Henken at Taliesin, Spring Green, Wisconsin, to Priscilla J. Henken in New York City, November 19, 1943.

6. Letter from David T. Henken at Taliesin, Spring Green, Wisconsin, to Priscilla J. Henken in New York City, November, 1943.

7. Besinger, *Working With Mr. Wright*, 140.

8. Pedro E. Guerrero, *Picturing Wright: An Album from Frank Lloyd Wright's Photographer* (San Francisco: Pomegranate Art Books, 1994), 153, 155.

9. Telegram, David T. Henken in Pleasantville, New York to Frank Lloyd Wright at Taliesin, Spring Green, Wisconsin, August 25, 1953.

10. Letters, David T. Henken in Pleasantville, New York to Frank Lloyd Wright at Taliesin, Spring Green, Wisconsin, November 16, 1953.

11. Letter, Frank Lloyd Wright at Taliesin, Spring Green, Wisconsin, to David T. Henken in Pleasantville, New York, November 23, 1953. © Frank Lloyd Wright Foundation.

12. Letter from [unidentified fellow] at Taliesin, Spring Green, Wisconsin, to Priscilla J. Henken and David T. Henken in New York City, March 4, 1943. Used by permission.

13. Letter from David T. Henken at Taliesin, Spring Green, Wisconsin to Priscilla J. Henken in New York City, December 25, 1942.

14. Letter from Priscilla J. Henken in New York City to David T. Henken at Taliesin, Spring Green, Wisconsin, September 7, 1943.

Wisconsin, 1942

Sarah A. Leavitt

When the Henkens came to Taliesin in 1942, they encountered a rural state just beginning to change with the wartime economy. The population of Wisconsin at the time was just over three million, less than half the population of the Henkens' hometown, New York City. Agriculture remained the largest industry in the southern part of the state, with dairy farms and farms that produced grains—wheat, oats, rye, barley—leading the list. At the turn of the twentieth century, more than 90 percent of Wisconsin's farms raised dairy cows, and by 1915, cheese and butter were major state exports. Other industries in Wisconsin included logging and paper mills, mostly in the northern part of the state; lead mining; and, of course, beer making. The state's land grant university, the University of Wisconsin, was centered in Madison, also the capital city, located about forty miles east of the Wrights' home in Spring Green. Though Milwaukee, the state's largest city, was a diverse, bustling metropolis with a large immigrant population, the rest of the state retained a small-town or rural character. Wisconsin, in the mid-twentieth century, was known for, among other things, a cold climate, progressive politics, and its outspoken native son, Frank Lloyd Wright, who remains one of the most important, if controversial, cultural figures ever to hail from the state.

The Great Depression was hard on Wisconsin—as everywhere—in the 1930s. By the time the Henkens arrived there, wartime production had already moved into the state, employing many who had been out of work and nudging the economy away from reliance on agriculture. Priscilla noticed many of these changes, including the Merrimack Powder Plant near Baraboo, which later became the Badger Ordnance Works. Opened in January 1943 and in operation for fifty years, the plant was run by the Hercules Powder Company during World War II when it manufactured rocket propellant, smokeless powder, and EC powder (used in hand grenades). Priscilla also noticed the "soldier town" in Madison: the University of Wisconsin offered military training classes to students, radio transmission training for military personnel, and correspondence courses to soldiers around the world. Priscilla also observed the last of Wisconsin's old economy near Spring Green. Many of the state's hundreds of small cheese factories went out of business during World War II, soon after she visited: some were bought out by the government for the war effort; others failed when large corporations cut off their access to farmers.[1] The rural Wisconsin that Priscilla saw in 1942 would, in many ways, be gone soon thereafter.

In their year at Taliesin, the Henkens did not travel extensively throughout the state but rather stayed close to Spring Green, in the south-central part of Wisconsin. Thus they experienced the rural life of 1940s Wisconsin. The fellows made frequent use of the hills and streams around Taliesin for picnics and swimming. They shopped in local stores such as the Royal Blue, a Wisconsin grocery chain; drank beers at local taverns; and even went as a group to the Spring Green High School senior play. However, they spent most of their time on-site at Wright's complex. This was the rural, communal experience that the Henkens had sought, partially in preparation for their eventual move out of urban New York City. Each week there was a schedule of jobs around the estate, including cooking and cleaning but also construction work and farming. Priscilla spent a good deal of time weaving in the Midway building, completing Wright's designs for textiles that would then be displayed around Taliesin. She and other fellows also practiced the recorder and other instruments for their weekly concerts. The architectural drafting room at Hillside provided space for fellows to draw their own projects and to trace Wright's plans. The weeks at Taliesin were filled with literature, music, film, and political debate. The fellows were learning from Wright, but the lessons were not limited to architecture and showed a deep commitment to the idea that one could—and must— live a culturally rich life on a farm.

Along with other fellows, Priscilla took several day trips during her stay in Wisconsin. She visited the former lead-mining town of Mineral Point and saw some of the natural lakes and rock formations around Baraboo. On one occasion the fellows packed up sleeping bags and provisions, intending to spend the night near Wisconsin Dells, until they got chased back home by hordes of mosquitoes (June 19, 1943). Priscilla visited many of Wright's houses and buildings in the area, including the S. C. Johnson Wax headquarters and Wingspread near Racine, as well as the Jacobs and Pew houses and the Unitarian Church in Madison. On a day trip to the capital city, she walked along the lakes that form the town's isthmus and visited the State Capitol building. She admired the marble floors, the grand dome, and the "homey" nature of the exhibit labels in the Grand Army of the Republic Memorial Hall. That museum displayed Civil War battle flags and other relics, such as a piece of the wall from Camp Randall, the site of a Civil War encampment in Madison near the University of Wisconsin. Along with Wright's daughter Iovanna, Priscilla visited the State Historical Society, where she learned about Wisconsin's pioneer history and saw "Indian stuff." She also walked around the campus observing college life and ate at the Woolworth counter on the Capitol Square, apparently one of Wright's favorite stops in town (November 18, 1942).

As political progressives, the Henkens had much in common with the citizens of Wisconsin. Wisconsin was at the forefront of the progressive movement, passing legislation that regulated railroads and other corporations, established workers' compensation, limited hours for women and children working in factories, and enhanced forest and waterways conservation measures, among other reforms. Milwaukee had a socialist mayor for a good part of the twentieth century and embraced many of these policies. One law that set Wisconsin apart from other states allowed for same-day voter registration—Priscilla took advantage of this in November of 1942 when she voted the socialist ticket. In that election, Orland Steen Loomis, a progressive, was elected governor of Wisconsin (but never served because he died in December 1942), and Frank Zeidler was the socialist on the ballot. He lost but ran successfully for mayor of Milwaukee in 1948. The progressive party officially formed as a third party in 1934; the socialist party, also active in the state, proposed even more wide-reaching mandates.

Cheese making, tourism, and progressive politics aside, for Frank Lloyd Wright, the farms and towns of south-central Wisconsin were, simply, home. Wright's mother, Anna Lloyd Jones, descended from a family that had emigrated from Wales to south-central Wisconsin and that were prominent Unitarians. The large family settled all around the area; Wright's sisters and cousins lived nearby and often visited Taliesin. Wright himself lived for a time in Europe and in Asia and in cities, suburbs, and the desert. Spending part of every year in Arizona for the last several decades of his life, he had a special relationship with the light and landscape of that southwestern state, but Wisconsin, the place where his ancestors had lived and worked, always remained his touchstone. "I learned to know the ground plan of the region in every line and feature," he wrote of southern Wisconsin in his autobiography. "For me now its elevation is the modeling of the hills, the weaving and fabric that clings to them, the look of it all in tender green or covered with snow or in full glow of summer that bursts into the glorious blaze of autumn. I still feel myself as much a part of it as the trees and birds and bees are, and the red barns."[2]

By establishing his apprenticeship program in his native state, Wright ensured that generations of architects would take Wisconsin into their hearts. Many Taliesin fellows built houses in Wisconsin, including Edgar Tafel, Wes Peters, Marcus Weston, and John Howe. Though Priscilla and David Henken settled in a then-rural part of New York, they, like dozens of other fellows throughout the years, continued to visit Wisconsin after their apprenticeship had concluded. "You extended to us an invitation to visit at Taliesin, which pleased us greatly and which we should now love to accept," wrote Priscilla to Olgivanna Wright in the summer of 1945, several years after her departure from Spring Green. She mentioned that it would be nice to see the current fellows but concluded by expressing her wish to feel, again, the earth at Taliesin. "I hope it will suit your convenience because I look forward with a certain longing," she wrote, "to dig my toes into the garden soil."[3]

1. Wes Peters, a longtime Fellowship member, commented on the loss of Wisconsin's cheese factories during this period: "In and around the valley there used to be ten or fifteen cheese factories. They all folded. Most of them folded during the war because big outfits like Carnation came in and made deals with the farmers who served the factories" (Edgar Tafel, ed., *Frank Lloyd Wright: Recollections by Those Who Knew Him* [Toronto: General Publishing Company, 1993], 167).

2. Frank Lloyd Wright, *Frank Lloyd Wright: An Autobiography* (New York: Duell, Sloan, and Pearce, 1943), 167.

3. H075 D04, letter from Priscilla Henken in New York City to Olgivanna Wright at Taliesin, Spring Green, Wisconsin, June 2, 1945.

Film at Taliesin

Deborah Sorensen

> When the Taliesin Playhouse, latest addition to the Taliesin foundation
> near Spring Green, Wis., opens tonight at 7, another of Frank Lloyd
> Wright's visions will have taken definite form . . . . It is the only theater
> of its type in this part of the country, and probably the only one of its
> kind in the world.
> — Mary York, *Capital Times*[1]

In the months leading up to the opening of Taliesin's new Playhouse Theater on
November 1, 1933, apprentices worked to complete the transformation of the 1902
Hillside Home School gymnasium into a modern theatrical venue. This renovation
effort was the first building project undertaken by members of Wright's newly
formed Fellowship. Their hard work was soon rewarded, as the Taliesin Playhouse
quickly became a popular destination for cultured entertainment—in particular,
for its offering of foreign and domestic films otherwise available only in cities such
as New York or Chicago, if at all.

   Those who attended the theater's inaugural screening of selected shorts and a
German musical comedy *The Merry Wives of Vienna* (Die Lustigen Weiber von Wien,
1931) enjoyed the theater's warm ambiance: the wood paneling; moveable seating
for two hundred; curtains patterned in red, green, and blue; and arranged foliage,
which combined to form "a gorgeous color symphony."[2] But it was more than just
decoration; the theater was well equipped and included a 35-mm projector in an
overhead booth, a large screen positioned on the upper stage, and an integrated
sound amplification system that allowed one "to hear in the farthest corner as easily
as one can hear from the front seat."[3] The sound system actually stretched beyond
the theater, allowing music played in the projection booth to be heard throughout the
Hillside complex during working hours or public events.

   The fact that Wright chose the creation of a new theater as the initial building
project for the Fellowship signals his, and his wife Olgivanna's, commitment to
creating a home and studio in which the arts could play an active, driving force. Their
mission was not limited to family and Fellowship members. From its inception,
the Playhouse was intended to function as a public gateway to Taliesin and as a
cultural center for the Spring Green area, if not the entire region from Madison to
Milwaukee and beyond.

For 50 cents (one dollar would pay for a tour of the Fellowship's facilities), guests were treated to coffee or tea and cake, a musical performance, and the best entertainment that could be brought "from the four corners of the world via the new art of the cinema."[4] One has only to look at a sampling of films shown at the Taliesin Playhouse within its first few years to see that this was no exaggeration: Carl Dreyer's *The Passion of Joan of Arc* (France, 1928), Pudovkin's *Storm over Asia* (Russia, 1928), the "western premiere" of both Fritz Lang's *M* (Germany, 1931) and Leni Riefenstahl's *The Blue Light* (Germany, 1932), plus contemporary thrillers such as Alfred Hitchcock's *The 39 Steps* (UK, 1935) and documentaries such as *The Plow That Broke the Plains* (directed by Pare Lorentz, US, 1936). Award-winning Disney cartoons or foreign animated shorts rounded out each program.[5]

The significance of the diverse film programming offered at the Taliesin Playhouse cannot be overstated, with the *Milwaukee Journal* noting that "American metropoles boast of houses that provide such fare. For Spring Green it is a minor marvel and calls for a shout of congratulation, at least."[6] During the 1920s, a select group of noncommercial theaters devoted to the exhibition of older titles and foreign films, or "Little Cinemas," had emerged in the United States. Their numbers, however, were minuscule—only nineteen nationally in 1927—when compared to the dominant presence of studio-controlled theaters.[7] And of these few independent "salons of the cinema," many did not survive the costly transition to sound that occurred in the early 1930s.[8] Those that remained were almost exclusively located in large, metropolitan areas with diverse populations, such as New York's Cameo Theater, which became known for its regular offering of Russian films.[9]

Urban cinephiles also had access to independent, revival, or foreign films through a growing assortment of clubs, such as the original New York Film Society (founded in 1933), which held private, members-only events, or more grassroots organizations like the left-leaning Workers Film and Photo League, which sponsored screenings and distributed newsreels and Russian titles nationally through its film library.[10] The regional, university-based film programs that would play a pivotal role in the popularization of the "art film" in the postwar era had yet to fully form. So, while it may not have been an absolute fact, it was still without hyperbole that the *Capital Times* claimed the Taliesin Playhouse to be "the only theater of its kind."

Public screenings at the Playhouse took place on Sunday afternoons, usually at 3:00, and often included interpretation of the day's program by one of the apprentices.[11] Those called upon to introduce the Sunday program would have watched everything the night before, when the week's films were screened for Wright and his family, their visitors, and the fellows, following dinner at the Playhouse. Although theater operations were suspended on occasion, such as when the Fellowship decamped for Taliesin West in the winter months, these breaks lasted for only a few months. And when the Fellowship did remain in Wisconsin over the winter, not even the Playhouse's lack of steam heat prior to 1939 stopped its doors from opening each Sunday afternoon.

Playhouse films were advertised by homemade signs mounted on a post near the entrance to Hillside—prompting visits by curious motorists.[12] Films were also promoted through the Fellowship's newspaper column "At Taliesin," which was carried regularly by the *Capital Times* and the *Wisconsin State Journal,* and sporadically in at least five other regional papers between 1933 and 1938. When describing each week's program, the columns included quotes of praise by New York critics, listed any awards received, called attention to the musical score, or basically cited anything that could further signal the program as one-of-a-kind and educational.

The manner in which film, as "film art," was framed in the "At Taliesin" articles and other press surrounding the Playhouse Theater is worth noting. During this time, commercial titles cycled rapidly through diminishing tiers of theaters, with little hope (nor really even a perceived need) for "revival." The "At Taliesin" columns instead identified the films chosen for exhibition at the Playhouse as creative works worthy of study and repeat viewing. This position was all the more unusual given that these notices appeared not in publications already devoted to the art of the cinema, but within regular newspapers alongside ads for the latest studio pictures.

Curtis Besinger, who arrived at Taliesin in 1939 and was soon one of the fellows responsible for running the Playhouse projector, described in his memoir Wright's interest in film as "not only a means of acquiring information about the various cultures of the world, but of nourishing and developing one's own creative resources."[13] As such, the manner in which film was folded into the weekly ritual of activities at Taliesin would indicate that Playhouse offerings might have been as much, if not more, for Wright's personal pleasure and benefit than the ostensible goal of public outreach. One early member of the Fellowship, Yen Liang, voiced frustration over Wright's dedication to the Playhouse, stating "Mr. Wright, every week, pays from $15 to $25 for a picture. And the audience would often be only two or three people. They pay 50 cents. That amounts to from $1.00–$1.50—while we have no money to buy coal and other necessities."[14] Gene Masselink, Wright's personal secretary, was largely responsible for securing the weekly film rentals and would probably have disagreed with this assessment, as he enjoyed the film program. Cornelia Brierly later remembered that in 1938 Masselink had "great enthusiasm" about the bittersweet French drama *Un Carnet de Bal* (directed by Julien Duvivier, France, 1937).[15] Other fellows shared Masselink's enthusiasm and appreciation of the films shown at the Playhouse: John W. Geiger felt that there was "something presumptive and very satisfying about having your own private theater."[16]

As a film lover, Wright could be unflinching in his opinion of American filmmaking. In the 1939 article "Wright Thinks American Movies Are Flops," he stated bluntly, "Hollywood has missed its chance. It had the opportunity to create a new art form, possibly the best of the arts. The inventions were there, the machine was there, but the artist wasn't."[17] Following this rebuke, Wright went on to praise the French filmmaker René Clair, whose film *À Nous la Liberté* (*Liberty for Us*, 1931) was to him "the best film ever made. 'I've seen it 12 times. Of all the films we have shown at Taliesin, it has been voted the best."[18] The American filmmaker John Ford was also commended—with his films *The Informer* (1935) and *Stagecoach* (1939) placing fourth and sixth, respectively, on Wright's list of favorites.

Wright's eclectic taste in film is evident from the wide variety of specialty titles rented for exhibition at the Playhouse, through providers such as the New York–based Russian importer and distributor Amkino (later Artkino) and the Museum of Modern Art's Film Library (started in 1935), as well as through regional rental offices and several nontheatrical mail-order services. Early in the Fellowship's years, there was an emphasis on German films (mirrored by a thriving American market for German film at the start of the decade), but by the time the Henkens arrived in October 1942, Russian films dominated the international titles offered.

Russian film had long been favored by Wright and his wife, not surprising given Wright's personal interest in Russian culture, not to mention Olgivanna's fluency and personal experiences living there, as well as her training with the Russian spiritual leader George Ivanovitch Gurdjieff. Wright began collecting Russian films in 1932, the year the Playhouse opened, and he continued to purchase and rent Russian films well into the 1950s.[19] During a visit to Moscow in 1937, Wright was afforded an opportunity to meet the filmmaker Sergei Eisenstein, from whom he apparently received an uncut and uncensored print of a film, which was later returned.[20] He was also given a copy of the Russian cartoon *The Czar Duranday*, which Priscilla noted in her diary as being "in the exclusive possession of Taliesin" (February 7, 1943).[21] It was this cartoon that Wright took to Hollywood "in an attempt to save [Walt] Disney's artistic soul."[22] Disney was an artist whose work—other than the "pretentious" *Snow White*—Wright greatly admired and enjoyed offering as regular programming at the Playhouse Theater.[23] Popular titles, such as Disney's acclaimed *Silly Symphony* series, were no doubt a draw for visitors unfamiliar with the foreign films being shown, but they were also Academy Award-winning works from a recognized "genius."[24]

During Priscilla's stay at Taliesin, nearly half of the films shown were Russian or Ukrainian. Some of these, including *The Czar Duranday,* came from Wright's personal collection while others were rented from Artkino (often explicitly identified as such in Priscilla's diary).[25] Taken together they represent a diverse assortment, from fairy tales and documentaries to historical epics and musical comedies. No one type dominates, though many do feature the trials, both tragic and comic, faced by men in positions of power—such as *General Suvorov* (1941) and *The Czar Wants to Sleep* (1934). The latter is a satire about Soviet bureaucracy, with a lively score by Prokofiev, which Wright bought for his personal collection. The story was clearly one of his favorites, with Curtis Besinger noting that Wright "always left the theater . . . with his eyes brimming with tears from laughter, and saying to himself the last line of the film, 'It is difficult to be a czar.'"[26]

Another Russian film, Sergei Eisenstein's epic *Alexander Nevsky* (1938), made a strong impression on Priscilla, who came away from the screening with nothing but praise for the film whose "photography was beautiful—suitable for framed stills" (November 23, 1942). Within the month, she had also read Eisenstein's *Film Sense* (1942), which uses examples from *Alexander Nevsky* to help explain his concept of "vertical montage," or how "organic" film structure "achieves its total effect through the *composite sensation of all the pieces as a whole,*" a holistic idea not unlike Wright's own concept of "organic architecture."[27] He was a true fan of Eisenstein's work, showing the Russian filmmaker's work repeatedly. Eisenstein's personal career mirrored that of Wright in many ways, having skyrocketed to fame in the early 1920s, only to fall out of artistic and political favor in the 1930s, before returning to even greater form by that decade's end. When the two met in 1937, they were both entering new eras of professional success.

Although Russian films remained in heavy rotation while Priscilla lived at Taliesin, most were screened during the winter months—not during the Playhouse's busier, public summer "season," when more accessible Hollywood-produced movies held sway. This concession to popular taste was a shift from the more consistent foreign-film programming in place during the previous decade. Gasoline rationing may have contributed to this adjustment. The summer before David and Priscilla arrived, the *Capital Times* wondered how rationing might affect entertainment options in the area—observing that Taliesin would "no doubt attain a new status as a unique entertainment center for residents of Iowa, Sauk and Dane counties and workers from the Badger Ordnance works plant."[28] Offering revivals of successful Hollywood films would certainly have been a wise strategy for maintaining existing audiences and attracting area newcomers.

During Priscilla's wartime stay, she and David watched more than forty films and any number of shorts and cartoons. The Saturday night screenings for Wright and his apprentices provided a welcome dose of relaxation following the many hours spent in the fields, in the kitchen, and over the drafting board during the previous week. There is a remarkable sense of ritual about these evenings, as described in the diary. Priscilla documents each week's film faithfully, making note of titles and often her (or Mr. Wright's) opinion of the film. One film they both enjoyed was Sacha Guitry's farce, *Nine Bachelors,* which had been picked by two other apprentices—a choice that had incurred the wrath of Mrs. Wright (November 14, 1942). It would appear that the selection of films was, at least sometimes, open to input by the Fellowship and not completely controlled by Wright or Masselink's choices. Yet, given that many titles cycled through the theater again and again over the years—whether drawn from Wright's personal film library or as repeat rentals—it is clear that Wright and his apprentices drew on a sturdy list of favorites.

Lingering group discussions sometimes followed the Saturday night screenings, as with Alfred Hitchcock's *Suspicion* (1941), which prompted "heavy conversation," and Carol Reed's melodrama *The Stars Look Down* (1940), based on the A. J. Cronin novel of the same name (July 10, 1943). In the latter, following a horrible mining accident that sees the main character radicalized and recommitted to the cause of labor, the film concludes with a dreamy voiceover, intoning "And so, out of the darkness of the world that is, into the light of the world that could be, and must be . . . a world in which dreams are not empty, nor sacrifices in vain, a world of infinite promise, which the unconquerable spirit of man will someday forge into fulfillment." This is the "cloud-banked conclusion with hope for the future" that Wright, and all of the apprentices, felt was "no solution" (November 21, 1942). The western melodrama *The Parson of Panamint* (1941) provoked a similarly philosophical discussion about how Americans show "more interest in gold than in spiritual values"—a comment that Priscilla felt revealed more about the Fellowship's pretenses than the character of the nation (March 27, 1943). More often than not, though, Priscilla seemed to have genuinely enjoyed the weekly films. And when she encountered something that she might otherwise dismiss as "very obvious propaganda," such as the documentary about the Danube frontier, she still found something interesting in the film, observing that "some of the kerchiefed women & gesticulating men were so familiar, they might have been our relatives" (March 27, 1943).

When Priscilla left Taliesin in 1943, the Playhouse at Hillside had been screening films for Wright, his apprentices, and the public for nearly ten years. By that time, the theater was in competition for audiences coming from nearby Madison. The University of Wisconsin-Madison's burgeoning film community had welcomed the opening of the Fredric March Play Circle in 1940.[29] Within two years, that school's Union Film Committee was offering a subscription-based film series with classic titles drawn from the Museum of Modern Art's circulating film library—an entity whose educational mission was by then more established, actively supporting noncommercial film programs across the country.[30] The Playhouse would continue to serve filmgoers in the Madison area, but its role was less that of an art-house theater than an established cultural center devoted to the arts.

In terms of the Fellowship, an increasing amount of attention was being paid to Taliesin West in Arizona (1937–59), where films were shown in the stone "kiva"— the site's first permanent living area.[31] In the summer of 1942, a new projector was purchased for Taliesin in Spring Green that could be easily disassembled and transported to the Fellowship's winter quarters.[32] Frank Lloyd Wright clearly carried a love of film with him wherever he went—from Spring Green to Hollywood, from Moscow to Arizona. His taste ranged from obscure Russian cartoons to John Ford westerns. But for Wright simply enjoying film was not enough. He was compelled to create environments where film could be studied and shared as "sources of nourishment and inspiration."[33] The Playhouse Theater at Taliesin opened its doors to public screenings at a time when the appreciation of film history and form was only beginning to take hold in the United States. Wright's theater was remarkable, not only for its rural location and emphasis on international cinema, but also for how it enabled the weekly integration of film "art" into the lives of its patrons.

1. Mary York, "Frank Lloyd Wright Realizes Another Dream at Unique Theater Opening at Taliesin Tonight— Building Constructed by Apprentices from Native Materials," *Capital Times*, November 1, 1933.
2. York, "Frank Lloyd Wright." The size and luxuriousness of the Playhouse Theater is in keeping with the style of other intimate "little cinemas," which were often decorated with artwork and included lounges for coffee and conversation—contributing to the sense of intimacy and exclusivity deemed desirable for an emerging class of film devotees. For a lengthy discussion of the "little cinema" movement, see Barbara Wilinsky, *Sure Seaters: The Emergence of Art House Cinema* (Minneapolis: University of Minnesota Press, 2001), 46–62.

3. York, "Frank Lloyd Wright." See also David V. Mollenhoff and Mary Jane Hamilton, *Frank Lloyd Wright's Monona Terrace: The Enduring Power of a Civic Vision* (Madison: University of Wisconsin Press, 1999), 86. The inclusion of a 35-mm projector is impressive. A 1931 report on school use of 35-mm sound films noted that the so-called portable system required five trunks of space. Leo Douglas Graham Enticknap, *Moving Image Technology: From Zoetrope to Digital* (New York: Wallflower Press, 2005), 147.
4. Eugene Masselink, "At Taliesin, October 30, 1936." In *"At Taliesin": Newspaper Columns by Frank Lloyd Wright and the Taliesin Fellowship, 1934–1937,* compiled by Randolph C. Henning (Carbondale: Southern Illinois University Press, 1991), 219.

For comparison, in 1935, the average cost of a movie ticket was $0.13. Haidee Wasson, *Museum Movies: The Museum of Modern Art and the Birth of Art Cinema* (Berkeley: University of California Press, 2005), 225 n. 17.
5. Henning, "At Taliesin," 52, 64, 128, 97, 160, 210.
6. Walter Monfried, "Wisconsin as a Theater Haven—and Other Items," *Milwaukee Journal,* June 21, 1936.
7. Wilinsky, *Sure Seaters,* 47.
8. Wasson, *Museum Movies,* 40.
9. The Cameo had an average weekly attendance of fifteen thousand in the 1930s. Tino Balio, *The Foreign Film Renaissance on American Screens: 1946–1973* (Madison: University of Wisconsin Press, 2010), 35.
10. Wasson, *Museum Movies,* 41, 62–63. In terms of specialized

rentals, even though 16-mm film libraries expanded greatly during the 1930s—allowing well-worn copies of popular films and educational titles to circulate widely—in many ways this market was geared more toward schools, libraries, or other organizations that could better manage the necessary fees and equipment.

11. Henning, *"At Taliesin,"* 2.

12. Curtis Besinger, *Working with Mr. Wright: What It Was Like* (Cambridge: Cambridge University Press, 1995), 86.

13. Besinger, *Working with Mr. Wright*, 85.

14. Roger Friedland and Harold Zellman, *The Fellowship: The Untold Story of Frank Lloyd Wright and the Taliesin Fellowship* (New York: HarperCollins, 2007), 232.

15. Cornelia Brierly, *Tales of Taliesin: A Memoir of Fellowship* (Rohnert Park, CA: Pomegranate, 2000), 121–22.

16. John W. Geiger, "My First Summer at the Fellowship," *In the Cause of Architecture: Commentaries by John W. Geiger in Memoriam – Frank Lloyd Wright*. Retrieved December 3, 2011, http://jgonwright.com/ep01Fellows.htm.

17. Lloyd Lewis, "Frank Lloyd Wright Thinks American Movies Are Flops," *Milwaukee Journal*,

September 29, 1939, 2.

18. Lewis, "Frank Lloyd Wright," 2.

19. Bruce Brooks Pfeiffer, ed., "1933: First Answers to Questions by Pravda," *Frank Lloyd Wright Collected Writings, Vol. 3, 1931–1939* (New York: Rizzoli in association with the Frank Lloyd Wright Foundation, 1993), 139. Retrieved November 20, 2011, http://rosswolfe.files.wordpress.com/2011/08/frank-lloyd-wright-on-the-soviet-union.pdf.

20. The film is identified as Eisenstein's *Ivan the Terrible* (in Pfeiffer, "1933," 139), yet production on *Ivan* (Part I) did not begin until 1942 (completed in 1944). It is possible that Eisenstein loaned Wright a rough cut of *Bezhin Meadow* (1935–37), which was forced to halt production only a few months prior to Wright's arrival in Moscow. Jay Leyda, *Kino: A History of Soviet and Russian Film* (Princeton: Princeton University Press, 1960), 339.

21. Lewis, "Frank Lloyd Wright,"

22. Lewis, "Frank Lloyd Wright," 2.

23. Lewis, "Frank Lloyd Wright," 2.

24. Neal Gabler, *Walt Disney: The Triumph of the American Imagination* (New York: Knopf, 2006), 204.

25. Amkino was the sole distributor of Russian films in America between 1926 and 1940, when it was re-formed as Artkino. The

company's address was unchanged and key personnel also remained and assumed leadership roles. The longtime Artkino president, Nicholas (Nicola) Napoli, was later identified in the declassified, and controversial, Venona Project papers as a possible Soviet informant. James H. Krukones, "The Unspooling of Artkino: Soviet Film Distribution in America, 1940–1975," *Historical Journal of Film, Radio and Television*, 29: 1, 93, 109 n.7.

26. Besinger, *Working with Mr. Wright*, 87.

27. Sergei Eisenstein, *The Film Sense*, translated by Jay Leyda (New York: Harcourt, Brace and Company, 1942), 77.

28. *Capital Times*, June 7, 1942.

29. Patrick Callan, "New Cinema Continues 70 Years of Film Experiences at the Union," *Terrace Views*, March 1, 2011. Retrieved November 20, 2011, http://www.terraceviews.org/2011/03/01/new-cinema-promises-to-continue-70-years-of-film-experiences-at-the-union/.

30. "Study Group Will Present 3 Old Films," *Capital Times*, June 28, 1942.

31. Brierly, *Tales of Taliesin*, 49.

32. Besinger, *Working with Mr. Wright*, 86.

33. Besinger, *Working with Mr. Wright*, 85.

Food at Taliesin

Sarah A. Leavitt

In October of 1942, William T. Evjue, the *Capital Times* editor, dined with his wife Zillah Bagley Evjue at Taliesin. Writing about the experience in his column the following week, Evjue noted, "The Sunday evening supper with an informal program of music or discussion that always follows has long been a delightful Sabbath evening ceremonial at Taliesin. The food is served on small individual tables and is cooked by the young men and women of the fellowship who alternate at this job each Sunday evening." More impressed with the atmosphere of the meal than with the dinner itself, Evjue nonetheless pointedly observed that "much of the food served is raised on the premises."[1]

Food was both ceremonial event and arduous daily activity at Taliesin. Indeed, the Fellowship took as one of its main tasks the cultivating, preserving, cooking, and serving of food and drink to a large contingent of people. On the farm Taliesin Fellows raised cows as well as chickens, goats, and pigs. They planted and plowed rows of potatoes, lettuce, peas, rutabaga, corn, tomatoes, lima beans, beets, and chard and canned the vegetables, cooked them for dinner, or sold them to neighbors. They picked bushels of apples and made apple butter and apple sauce; picked watermelons and pickled the rinds. All of this work, spread among the fellows on a rotating basis, took a great deal of time. Writing many decades later, fellow Cornelia Brierly remembered that "Mrs. Wright taught all of us to cook," and that her fellowship experience included "constant cooking and baking."[2]

For most Americans in the 1940s, food traditions had strong ethnic and regional components. A typical meal included meat and potatoes, with the addition of homemade noodles or rice, and variations in vegetable preparation. Most Americans in this period, whatever their heritage, had limited access to foods from other cultures and regions. Restaurant dining, except in large cities, was for most limited to casual places like taverns and diners, lunch counters and cafeterias, and inns for travelers. Ethnic foods—such as the cuisines of Italy and China—had only begun to appear in cookbooks earlier in the century. At Taliesin, then, menus had considerably more variation than most American tables of the period. Olgivanna Wright was from Montenegro, a country in southern Europe, and her first husband had been Russian. The cuisines of those regions were well represented at Taliesin meals. Wright had lived in Japan, Italy, and Germany, and cuisine from those regions was incorporated into the cooks' repertoire as well. Fellows came from all over the world to Wisconsin, sharing their own food traditions.

The Taliesin Fellowship Cookbook, a collection of typewritten recipes with handwritten notes, such as "Mrs. Wright likes beets cut into smaller pieces," followed the Fellowship back and forth to their homes in Wisconsin and Arizona and served as a guide for the fellows in the kitchen.[3] As represented by the cookbook, the menu at Taliesin included regional preparations from across the country and the world. Among these dishes were brabant potatoes, a traditional New Orleans side dish of cubed, fried potatoes; bitki, Russian meatballs, usually breaded and fried, served with sour cream or cranberry sauce; and rote grütze, a German fruit pudding recipe of red berries cooked with sugar and cornstarch until thick and topped with cream. The fellows dined on sukiyaki, Japanese hot pot, usually sliced meat and vegetables cooked together in a broth; Franconian parsnips, a preparation native to a region of Germany, in which root vegetables were parboiled and then baked; and chicken timbale, a dish with eggs, akin to a quiche or soufflé. Processed foods were not a large part of the Taliesin menu, with most of the dishes prepared by hand by teams of fellows. However, Jell-O appeared on Taliesin tables often. Aspic and other gelatin-based preparations had been popular for refined diners for generations; Jell-O helped bring this type of food to a wider population. At Taliesin, Jell-O was served both as a side dish and with whipped cream for dessert. The menu was seasonal, varied, international, and ahead of its time; it was also traditional in many respects.

War rationing had only a limited effect on food preparation at Taliesin; for the most part, the fellows were able to continue cooking elaborate meals as a significant part of everyday life. Elsewhere during the war years, Americans were allotted tickets to purchase limited amounts of products such as butter, milk, and meat. The government encouraged home gardening to save produce for the troops overseas. In March 1942, the Wisconsin State Council of Defense warned residents that "we cannot expect to consume at the same level as before if we expect to win this war."[4] But like families all over America who planted victory gardens to ensure vegetables and fruits in the face of widespread shortages, farming, preserving, and cooking at home helped the Fellowship avoid shortages from strict rationing. Indeed, when Priscilla briefly returned to New York in December 1942, David sent, for distribution to their families and friends, a large package of cheese and butter which were plentiful in Wisconsin. As David explained, "The reason butter is included is because Eleanor wrote that her family hasn't been able to buy butter in more than three weeks. Realizing that our folks might have similar difficulty I took a chance & sent 4 trial packages . . ."[5] They continued to send fresh items back to New York; in January 1943, Priscilla wrote in her diary about sorting eggs to ship east

(January 16, 1943). Wartime limitations also affected what Priscilla could send from New York: she explained to David that because of the wartime shortages, his father had not been able to buy as much halvah, a traditionally Jewish treat made from sesame butter, as he had requested. "I'm sending you three boxes of Halvah, anyway—Give generously to the Wrights; serve some at tea; &. . . don't forget to save some for yourself."[6] The Fellowship was not immune to rationing: by the following summer, with supplies running low, Priscilla tried to make a devil's food cake with syrup and lard instead of sugar and butter, without much success (July 16, 1943). However, for the most part, the farm kept the Taliesin kitchen well stocked with fresh food.

Though food preparation was not the Fellowship's main focus, feeding dozens of people who depended on Taliesin for every meal was no simple task and demanded constant attention from the entire community. Indeed, farming and cooking took up much of the daily life of the fellows and their spouses. Picnics on the grounds were popular, but regular dinners were held in the Fellowship Dining Room at the Hillside School or at the main house. Dining at Taliesin was part of an elaborate ritual of gentility, with fellows summoned to the table by a series of bells and expected to dress formally for supper. The Fellowship ate as a group along with any visiting relatives, neighbors, or dignitaries—up to several dozen people at a time. Welcoming hundreds of invited guests—from prominent Wisconsin locals like the Evjues to traveling professors, antiwar activists, and experts in various fields—the dining room at Taliesin was a lively and interesting place, from the people at the table to the food itself.

1. "Mr. Wright's Pie. A Real American." *Capital Times*, October 20, 1942.
2. Cornelia Brierly, *Tales of Taliesin: A Memoir of Fellowship* (Rohnert Park, CA: Pomegranate, 2000), 10.
3. Recipe for Harvard Beets, Taliesin Cookbook, Collection of The Frank Lloyd Wright Foundation, Taliesin West.
4. "Suggestions to County Committees of Consumer Interests," (Wisconsin: State Council of Defense, State Advisory Committee of Consumer Interests, 1942); Wisconsin State Historical Society collections.
5. Letter, David T. Henken at Taliesin, Spring Green, Wisconsin, to Priscilla J. Henken in New York City, December 19, 1942.
6. Letter, Priscilla J. Henken in New York City to David T. Henken at Taliesin, Spring Green, Wisconsin, December 23, 1942.

Conscientious Objectors and Taliesin

Stephanie Hess

"That Marcus Weston who has become a national figure," wrote Priscilla Henken in her diary in January of 1943, "can hardly be the same who ran laughingly down cold corridors, played a hushed guitar, danced folk dances, rumbled uphill in a tractor, and chatted with us for long delightful hours (January 17, 1943)." The Henkens had met Marcus Weston only in the fall of 1942, mere months before his appearance in court as a conscientious objector (CO). They reacted strongly to his incarceration not only because they considered him a friend, but because his case resonated for them as a symbol of injustice on the part of their government. During the Henkens' time at Taliesin, the trial of Marcus Weston brought widespread attention to Frank Lloyd Wright and his antiwar beliefs. Though Marcus was neither the first nor the last CO at Taliesin—rather he was one of dozens of men in the Fellowship who took a stand against the war—his trial caught the attention of the local press and of the FBI in Washington, D.C., putting Taliesin at the forefront of a national debate on conscription during World War II.

In the 1940s, when a man registered for Selective Service, as required by law for men between the ages of eighteen and sixty-five, he could claim to be a conscientious objector and fill out a questionnaire, called Form 47, to prove his sincerity.[1] His local draft board would then evaluate his claim and assign him a classification number in one of these categories: (1) available for service, (2) deferred because of occupational status, (3) deferred because of dependents, or (4) deferred specifically by law or because unfit for military service. Whereas in earlier U.S. wars only members of the Mennonites, the Brethren, and the Quakers had been granted religious exemptions, the Selective Service and Training Act of 1940 had expanded this option, exempting any man "who, by reason of religious training and belief, is conscientiously opposed to participation in war in any form." However, Congress did not provide exemptions for Americans who opposed war on moral, philosophical, or political—rather than religious—grounds. Approved COs were designated 4E: "Conscientious objectors available only for civilian work of national importance."[2] These men could choose between noncombative roles in the military, such as the medical corps, or Civilian Public Service (CPS) camps, where they could work on soil conservation, reforestation, and agricultural projects; work as mental hospital attendants; or serve as subjects in medical experiments. About twelve thousand men with approved CO claims went on to work for the CPS program. For men whose CO claims were rejected by their local draft boards, the only options were military combat or prison. During World War II, approximately six thousand men chose to serve time in prison rather than to join the military.

Not all Taliesin fellows opposed the war. Nineteen members of the Fellowship were drafted into the armed forces and served overseas during World War II.[3] However, opposition to war was certainly a popular position at Taliesin and was supported by Wright himself. David Henken had filed for CO status before arriving in Wisconsin. Indeed, on his very first day, he announced his CO status to the Fellowship as a point of pride. He was a pacifist throughout his life and spoke out consistently against war as a matter of principle. Although David repeatedly applied for CO status, he was never granted it officially, receiving instead several different classifications during the war, including a 3B rating, a deferment for men with dependents, and a 2B, for work of national importance.[4]

On March 25, 1941, twenty-six members of the Fellowship submitted a petition, later known as the Taliesin Manifesto, to Local Draft Board #1 of Dodgeville, Wisconsin, going on record as "objectors to the compulsory military draft" during peacetime.[5] Several of these men went on to serve time in federal prison, including John Howe, Marcus Weston, and Davy Davison; others, such as Curtis Besinger and Howard Ten Brink, spent time during the war doing various jobs at CPS camps. Many CPS sites, run during the war by the Mennonite Central Committee, were former Civilian Conservation Corps (CCC) sites in western states, where men worked on dams and irrigation systems. Sandstone, Minnesota, where Marcus served his prison time, was the site of a federal penitentiary and the location for many COs during World War II. A community of pacifists formed there, and many had long careers after the war in peace and justice work.

Both David and Priscilla were taken aback by the political naïveté of the Taliesin fellows, especially in their handling of the CO issue. Marcus later remembered that David was "a little surprised to find himself among a group opposed to the war but so poorly informed about steps to take to achieve objector status."[6] Priscilla commented in her diary about the issue in January 1943: "Blunders! From the very first Marcus should have pleaded C.O., instead of taking Mr. Wright's advice that he hope for deferment on physical grounds—the same advice he gave to Curtis only a few weeks ago, and similar to that given Howard to declare himself necessary as a farm laborer. Then, none of the boys knew about form 47 till rather late to be demonstrative of one's conscience" (January 14, 1943). David tried to contribute his expertise, providing information, helping Marcus and the other fellows write letters, and putting them in touch with the War Resisters League (WRL), an organization that helped potential COs understand their rights during the war. The fellows' lack of political acuity became apparent during socialist Norman Thomas's visit to Taliesin in the summer of 1943, when they showed themselves uninformed and then criticized him (quite erroneously) for being a communist and for lacking ideas. "God, what fools," wrote Priscilla, exasperated (July 30, 1943).

The Henkens noted that not all of the apprentices claiming CO status were as committed to it as Marcus had been, but rather they were willing to claim other exemptions from the draft, most specifically as vital farm labor, working either Wright's farm or their own. At first, many fellows argued that they would be of more use to the United States as architects than as members of the military, particularly by constructing buildings during and after the war. Later, several fellows bought farmland and changed their status to argue for the importance of farm labor, rather than architectural practice, to American life. Neither of these tactics worked. On later review of their files, the FBI found that "there seemed to be a very definite and sincere opposition by each registrant to military service, but not upon any grounds that would qualify him for a 4-E Classification in the draft."[7] Priscilla was vexed by these machinations. "I'm full of malice," she wrote in her diary "when I think of Marcus, a real CO, in jail, and these draft-evaders becoming essential to the nation's agricultural work" (February 23, 1943).

Marcus Weston's case made headlines and became the center of an investigation by the FBI into Wright's antiwar views, the architect having long been seen as suspicious by many in the government. The federal judge in charge of Marcus's case, Patrick T. Stone, sent Marcus home in December 1942 to spend time with his parents and rethink his position. "I think you boys are living under a bad influence with that man Wright," said the judge in court. "I'm afraid he is poisoning your minds."[8] In response to Judge Stone's public accusation, Wright used his connection with newspaper publishers, especially Madison's *Capital Times* editor, William Evjue, to have an open letter published in newspapers across the country. Wright had always been strongly opposed to war, but now he came out publicly in support of conscientious objection. In the letter, Wright charged Judge Stone of "using the bench to sound off his prejudice against another man on mere hearsay."[9] He declared, "As for conscription, I think it has deprived the young men in America of the honor and privilege of dedicating themselves as freemen to the service of their country. Were I born forty years later than 1869, I, too, would be a conscientious objector."[10] Wright himself had strong and well-established pacifist views, but whatever the strengths of his political opinions, they seem often to have been echoed rather than understood by some members of the Fellowship.

Wright's case, though it was handled by the FBI field office in Milwaukee, came to J. Edgar Hoover's attention. Hoover corresponded with officials in Milwaukee in December 1942 and was told that Stone requested an investigation of Frank Lloyd Wright "for interference with war effort by counseling registrants to become conscientious objectors."[11] As part of the investigation, signers of the Taliesin Manifesto were asked about Wright's general influence over a long period of time; about the general atmosphere and conditions existing at the Fellowship; and specifically whether or not Wright intentionally influenced, aided, or counseled them to claim conscientious objection to the war. All answered that Wright's general influence and the atmosphere at Taliesin helped shape their convictions, but they argued it would be wrong to suggest there was any definitive attempt made by Wright to pressure them to avoid military service. Marcus Weston noted that "to accuse Frank Lloyd Wright or any one person of responsibility of my convictions is ridiculous and insulting both to me and to him."[12] As one of the original signers of the petition wrote in response to the publicity over Judge Stone's accusation, "My own feelings were that my work as an apprentice under Mr. Wright would enable me to perform greater service than as a member of a peacetime army. This was a conviction at which I had thoughtfully and independently arrived, after a long and troubled consideration of circumstances as they were at the time. As for 'influence,' I did not ask Mr. Wright's opinion, or the opinion of anyone else as to whether or not I should sign this paper."[13] The investigators concluded that the various Selective Service files from members of the Fellowship that they reviewed for appeal "seemed to present individual expressions of thought when the members claimed to be Conscientious Objectors."[14] Since the FBI unearthed no legal evidence of Wright's influence, Assistant Attorney General Wendell Berge confirmed that the facts did not warrant prosecution under the Sedition Statutes, and the investigation was closed.

Weston's case was part of a larger debate over the definition of a CO and about Wright's influence over a generation of young men. Although his military fate hardly concerned the rest of the country after the publicity waned, it served for the Henkens as a symbol of a flawed political system. Priscilla's despair about the case was clear: "Marcus was sentenced to 3 years in a federal penitentiary today. That's all that matters, no matter what else I write" (January 14, 1948)." From his prison cell in Dodgeville, however, Marcus wrote: "I do not regret my choice. I regret only that I had to make it and my stupid handling of the case. You now have a concrete example of the hardship you will have to endure if you stick to your principles. Even so, I still think I am better off than the boys who took the other course. This is war, and no one is going through it without great difficulties."[15]

1. Each registrant filled out a Selective Service Questionnaire (DSS Form 40). If a registrant signed "Series X" of that form, his local board would provide a Special Form for Conscientious Objection (DSS Form 47), which would become the basis for his Selective Service classification.
2. Selective Training and Service Act of 1940, (54 Stat. 885), passed by the U.S. Congress on September 16, 1940.
3. Robert McCarter, *Frank Lloyd Wright* (Princeton Architectural Press, 1991), 158.
4. See the recollections of David Henken's children, this volume; see also Curtis Besinger, *Working with Mr. Wright: What It Was Like* (Cambridge: Cambridge University Press, 1995), 141.
5. Report, Special Agent in Charge (SAC), Milwaukee, to Director, FBI, March 3, 1943, on Frank Lloyd Wright sedition investigation,

25-133757-6.
6. Writings of Marcus Weston, 2009.
7. Report, SAC, Milwaukee, to Director, FBI, March 3, 1943, on Frank Lloyd Wright sedition investigation, 25-133757-6.
8. "Judge to Ask FBI Probe of Architect Wright," *Washington Evening Star*, December 17, 1942. Included in the FBI file on Frank Lloyd Wright, 25-133757-1.
9. "Frank Lloyd Wright Denies Swaying Pupils against Draft," *Washington Times-Herald*, December 21, 1942. Included in the FBI file on Frank Lloyd Wright, 25-133757-3.
10. "Frank Lloyd Wright Demands Ouster of Judge in Draft Fight," New York Herald Tribune, December 20, 1942. Included in the FBI file on Frank Lloyd Wright, 25-133757-A. Frank Lloyd Wright was actually born in 1867, but he often changed that date when speaking to the press in order to appear younger than he really was.

11. Memorandum, SAC, Milwaukee, to Director, FBI, December 31, 1942, on Frank Lloyd Wright investigation, 25-133757-2.
12. Brief, Washington City News Service, to FBI Communications, December 21, 1942, quoting Marcus Weston re: Frank Lloyd Wright, 25-26701-4.
13. Redacted letter to the Taliesin Fellowship, January 27, 1943. Included in the Report, SAC, Milwaukee, to Director, FBI, March 3, 1943, on Frank Lloyd Wright sedition investigation, 25-133757-6.
14. Report, SAC, Milwaukee, to Director, FBI, March 3, 1943, on Frank Lloyd Wright sedition investigation, 25-133757-6.
15. Letter, Marcus Weston in Dodgeville, Wisconsin, to the Taliesin Fellowship at Taliesin, Spring Green, Wisconsin, January 17, 1943. Used by permission.

Taliesin's Place in Spring Green Folklore

Elissa R. Henken

I grew up hearing stories about Frank Lloyd Wright and Taliesin from my parents and family friends who had also been apprentices. My interest in these stories deepened when, as a folklorist, I recognized that they, along with clients' anecdotes and several legends, provided a wealth of folklore on Wright. I wondered what sorts of stories were told by people in Spring Green, Wisconsin, about their native but very unusual son. Therefore, in 1991 I collected local lore both from older residents who personally remembered Wright and from newer ones who had only heard about him. Spring Green folklore, which focused on three topics—the great tragedies, the alien nature of the Wrights and the Fellowship, and Wright's debts—demonstrates both how closely connected and how distant were the two communities of Spring Green and the Fellowship.

Memory of two Taliesin tragedies remains strong in Spring Green folklore, where slight variations in narrative underline that community's very different perspective. Members of both communities share the basic details of the 1914 tragedy when a servant set fire to the Taliesin dining room and attacked people with an axe as they tried to flee, killing seven, including workmen as well as Wright's mistress, Mamah Borthwick, and her two children. Both groups also include the heroic actions of the Spring Green carpenter William Weston, who, though himself wounded and having seen his son murdered, escaped to raise the alarm and fight the fire. With imagery limited to Taliesin, apprentices' stories report that the servant was caught the same or the next day and, as in the version we heard as children, that Weston bravely fought and subdued the killer. The Spring Green stories, however, stress the killer's alien character and the potential danger to the townspeople—reporting that he was black, from Cuba or Barbados, and that the hunt lasted several frightening days while nobody knew what sort of madman was loose among them.[1]

In the other major tale of tragedy—the accidental death in 1946 of Mrs. Wright's daughter Svetlana Peters and her infant son when her Jeep went off a bridge into the Wisconsin River— there is still greater divergence between the two sets of stories. The apprentices tell about Svetlana's other son, the toddler Brandoch, who escaped the crash and walked back several miles to Taliesin to tell the Fellowship. The Spring Green community, less involved with the family, mainly makes note of the bridge (one of many in the area) at which this took place, but there is no mention of the child's long walk home with his tragic news.

I knew some of the views held by the Fellowship about the local community, especially Mrs. Wright's condescending attitude, but what did the local people think about Wright and all the strange people he had brought into their midst? In the 1940s the reports at Taliesin indicated that some Spring Greeners considered the Fellowship a "free-love dive" and in June 1943 there was gossip that the Fellowship was building a landing field for the Japanese and that earlier two Japanese students from Taliesin had blown up the Spring Green Bridge (Diary, June 7, 1943). I hoped to learn from the townspeople themselves how they viewed the Fellowship. The two communities had kept a careful distance from each other, dealing with each other as necessary but never enjoying a close relationship. The town, for example, never hired Wright to design a building. The Fellowship and the community appear to have eyed each other warily and a bit condescendingly, with each side recognizing class as a complication in their relationship. The Spring Greeners confirmed that they viewed the Wrights and Taliesin as exotic. They described Mr. Wright with his flat, broad-brimmed hat, flowing cape, cane, and European cars and Mrs. Wright with her stark, pulled-back hair. They noted with some discomfort Mr. Wright's various love affairs, which gave credibility to views of the Fellowship as sexually loose:

> They thought Wright's life alone . . . they thought they were all like that. They lived in a secluded little group over there. They must be hiding something. And what kind of parties were they having anyhow?

It wasn't always that the Fellowship was perceived as bad, just very different. One person who went to school with some of the Fellowship children in the 1950s reported that even the foods they ate were different, noting in particular that they ate rice rather than potatoes. Another person commented:

> I think the people [in the 1940s] felt they were different—that the people felt different and the Wrights were different . . . They came from different worlds, they really did. They may have been living side by side but their dreams and aspirations were completely different.

The people who spoke with me made it very clear that the Fellowship and the local community did not mix socially, except on rare occasions, such as a time before World War II, when children were invited to see movies in the theater at Hillside. One woman said,

> He thought (maybe he didn't; he appeared to think) he was a step above everybody out there and we were all dirt farmers or, you know, people there to do what he needed done.

Her daughter described the situation a generation later:

> Taliesin did not want to associate with the locals. Period. And the people who did were breaking the rules.

Nonetheless, while the community felt that they were looked down upon by the Fellowship, they in turn looked down on the Fellowship and even pitied them. As one person summarized it, "They [the community] didn't have much use for him, and he didn't have much use for them." In the 1930s and 1940s, some townspeople thought the apprentices were the children of people in the cities, children who "weren't quite right" and were sent to Taliesin to be taken care of, but mostly they pitied the apprentices for the system in which they lived, having to do all the work while Mrs. Wright just sat back and ruled. As one person explained,

> There was this attitude about Mrs. Wright. It was supposed to be a communal group, but really a matriarchal community where Mrs. Wright was the head and everybody else was her minions. And also the stories about dressing up for dinner, and everybody working in the kitchen and everybody gardening and everybody taking their turn at the work—that just was very curious to us. We found that very interesting 'cause we were real interested in the social stratas 'cause we were all considered low; we wanted to know what everybody else was. . . . They all had to get dressed up and they don't sit down till she does. And she doesn't work in the garden. . . When Wes Peters married Svetlana [the second Svetlana, daughter of Stalin], [there were] a lot of comments on her leaving a communist country to join a commune.

Some townspeople felt sorry for the apprentices who were kept under such tight control that they weren't allowed out at night and would have to sneak out just to go into town. One person described giving a lift to a fellow who had crawled out of the bushes. Another person reported, "There was definitely the impression that if you were involved in the Fellowship you had to give up your life in order to believe everything that they believed, that you had to follow the party line."

Mrs. Wright's imperiousness, well noted by the apprentices, extended to the townspeople. The fourth-generation owner of the general store recalled:

> Mrs. Wright was somebody who didn't ask for things, she demanded them, and one day she decided that she wanted to give treats to the young people at Taliesin—candy, toys, stuff like that—and she called my father and told him to open the store. It was a Sunday. He said he decided he was not going to have Mrs. Wright tell him what to do, and he said, "No, today is my day of rest. The store will be open tomorrow." And she was so annoyed that neither she nor Mr. Wright ever came back to the store.

The most persistent stories in the community about Wright have to do with his constant state of indebtedness and with his belief that the world owes the artist a living. Every single person I interviewed mentioned this aspect of Mr. Wright. As one person reported,

They admired his architectural ability, but I don't think they cared for him as a person. Well, he didn't pay his bills. One fellow had a grocery store here and Mr. Wright came and made a big order. When they got it all sacked up and packaged and all, he said he didn't have any money to pay for it, so Fritz said, "Ok, Mr. Wright, we'll just put it back on the shelf." Mr. Wright, then and there, paid them.

There are many stories about whom he tried to get materials from, about bills still on the books all these years after he died, and other stories about the farmers who tricked him into paying in advance. Successfully getting paid for one's coal or lumber became a story of great victory, although Wright was accorded some grudging respect for his ability to get something for nothing.

The stories of his debts were, in fact, the one safe topic for the residents of Spring Green. One relatively new (twenty-year) resident said that the only thing she had heard about Wright was that he couldn't buy even a candy bar on credit in any of the stores. While Wright was alive and his presence generated all kinds of activity, the community was free to judge him as they pleased with the full range of emotions from admiration to disgust. However, I encountered an interesting problem as I did my folklore research. Since Wright's death, residents of Spring Green have become more and more economically dependent on the maintenance of his memory. I had great difficulty finding people who were willing to speak freely about the Wrights and the Fellowship. The only people who contributed without hesitation either were retired or earned their livings outside Spring Green, but the newcomers, especially shopkeepers, offered only the mildest of statements and apologia. One shopkeeper whose store specializes in Wright memorabilia, after bringing up the matter of Mr. Wright's debts, explained that it wasn't really that Wright didn't pay his bills; he was just very slow. Another said, "Oh, he'd never pay his bills, but that's so ridiculous; it's thirty years or so ago." Economically dependent on Wright and the tourist industry generated by his fame, members of the local community have become more protective of Wright's name and less willing to admit any disparaging views. As one of the women who knew the old stories said, "There's such an influx that have come into Spring Green from outside that see him in a different light, that never knew him personally." The once difficult and strange behavior of a neighbor has been transformed by time and economy into the harmless eccentricities of a genius.

---

1. Unless otherwise stated, all folklore was collected by Elissa R. Henken from residents of Spring Green in 1991.

ABOUT PRISCILLA AND DAVID HENKEN

Priscilla Jussim Henken was born in 1918 in New York City to Russian Jewish parents, Solomon Jussim and Kate Weiner Jussim. Her father was a milliner and was active in union organizing. Several of her earliest memories involved union meetings, including helping to sell busts of Eugene Debs in the back of the meeting hall. Her mother, Kate, had as a teenager worked as a bookkeeper in a garment factory, while also attending business classes and taking care of her widowed mother. Later, Kate did extensive volunteer work with Jewish organizations.

Priscilla's parents strongly emphasized education. After graduating from Seward Park High School, Priscilla enrolled in Hunter College, age fourteen; at that time she was the youngest student ever to enroll at the college. At eighteen, she received her bachelor of arts degree from Hunter. While in college, she also attended the Jewish Theological Seminary in New York, receiving a seminarian's diploma. She was awarded a master's degree in English from Columbia University a year after she graduated from Hunter. She then taught English in New York City high schools.

Priscilla married David Henken in 1938; she accompanied him to Taliesin in 1942 and returned to New York in 1943 to teach. She and David worked together closely in developing the ideas for their dream of a cooperative community, Usonia. They moved to their new house in Usonia, near Pleasantville, New York, in 1949, accompanied by their son, Jonathan (born 1945) and daughter Mariamne (born 1949). Their second daughter, Elissa Ruth, was born in 1952.

Priscilla put her architectural knowledge to good use, publishing several articles about Usonia and giving guest lectures on organic architecture at several universities. In addition to childcare and housework, she worked with Henken Builds, Inc., David's building company. Eventually, she returned to teaching, becoming an influential and popular English teacher at Pleasantville High School. She also taught at the women's state prison. She was diagnosed with breast cancer in 1966 and continued to teach even while receiving her treatments. She died in 1969 of metastatic breast cancer.

David Theodor Herzl Henken was born in 1915 in New York City to Russian Jewish parents, Benjamin and Frieda Ershovsky Henken. His father, who had been a forester in Russia, ran a candy store. His mother was a garment worker and a member of the International Ladies' Garment Workers' Union.

David graduated from Stuyvesant High School and enrolled in City College of New York (CCNY) at the age of fifteen. He graduated with a bachelor of science degree in mechanical engineering and a year later he received a master's degree in the same field from CCNY. From 1936 until 1942, when he left for Taliesin, he worked as a research and development engineer and a designer in the areas of packaging design and lighting for several companies. He decided to study with Frank Lloyd Wright as an apprentice at Taliesin to facilitate the realization of his dream of a cooperative community, an idea he had been working on since the late 1930s.

When David returned from Taliesin in 1943, he worked as the chief designer for a company that developed games. His primary work from 1947 to 1950 was as Coordinator of Design and Building for Usonia Homes, the community he had imagined and originated. He designed a large number of homes beyond the thirteen he designed for Usonia; his work appeared in a number of national and international architectural publications. His building company, Henken Builds, Inc., built many homes of his design and also some for Frank Lloyd Wright, including the Exhibition Pavilion and Usonian Exhibition House at the Guggenheim Museum site in 1953.

David eventually turned to campus planning, including work for Nasson College in Maine and Fiorello LaGuardia College and Pratt Institute, both in New York. He died in 1985 of a heart attack while working on rebuilding the Frank Lloyd Wright Model House in Michigan.

FILMOGRAPHY

Unless otherwise noted with an asterisk, all films were screened at the Hillside Playhouse during Priscilla Henken's stay at Taliesin.

Adventures in Toyland [Russia, unknown animated short]. Possibly *The Adventures of Bolvashka* [Russian: Priklyucheniya bolvaskhi]. Written and directed by Yuri Zhelyabuzhsky. Mezhrabprom. 1927.

Combined live action and animated short. A child fantasizes about the adventures of a wooden boy, Bolvashka, in a toy museum's workshop.

Alexander Nevsky [Russia]. Directed by Sergei Eisenstein and Dmitri Vasiliev. Written by Eisenstein and Pyotr Pavlenko. Mosfilm. 1938.

Historical drama. A Russian prince rallies his people against invading Teutonic knights at a lake near Novgorod. Hugely successful and significant production by the director of *Battleship Potemkin* (1925), for which Eisenstein received the Order of Lenin and widespread acclaim after several years of critical disfavor. Released in the United States in 1939.

All That Money Can Buy, also ***The Devil and Daniel Webster*** [US]. Directed by William Dieterle. Starring Edward Arnold, Walter Huston, and Jane Darwell. RKO. 1941.

Fantasy. Adaptation of Stephen Vincent Benét's book of the same title in which a farmer makes a deal with the devil to save his farm, only to need representation by Daniel Webster when he tries to avoid final payment. The film won an Academy Award for best music.

The Bear [Russia: Medved]. Directed by Isidor Annensky. Belgoskino. Written by Annensky (from a Chekhov one-act play). 1938.

Comedy. A land-holding widow duels with a pompous neighbor only to discover that they are meant to be together.

Crossroads [France: Carrefour]. Directed by Curtis Bernhardt. B.U.P. Française. 1938.

Mystery. A soldier returning from World War I suffers from amnesia, is blackmailed, and struggles to discover his true identity. Followed by the British adaptation *Dead Man's Shoes* (1939) and the MGM

version *Crossroads* (1942), starring William Powell and Hedy Lamarr.

The Czar Duranday, also ***The Tale of Csar Duranda*** [Russia: Skazka o Tsare Durandaye]. Directed by Ivan Ivanov-Vano. Mezhrabpomfilm. 1934.

Animated short. "Allegorical fairy tale about the triumph of the oppressed workers over their oppressors. The animation was beautifully drawn and had handsome patterns reminiscent of those of [Leon] Bakst and the [modernist Russian theater company] Chauve Souri" (Besinger, 87). Music by Dmitri Shostakovich. Shown multiple times at Taliesin, Wright's copy was destroyed in the 1952 fire.

The Czar Wants to Sleep, also ***Lieutenant Kizhe*** [Russia: Poruchik kizhe]. Directed by Alexander Feinzimmer. Belgoskino. 1934.

Musical comedy. Satirical treatment of the mad Emperor Paul I, in which a misunderstanding gives birth to the long-suffering, though nonexistent, "Lieutenant Kizhe." Based upon a story by Yuri Tinyanov, with music by Sergei Prokofiev. Shown multiple times at Taliesin, Wright's copy was destroyed in the 1952 fire (Besinger, 87).

The Forgotten Village [US]. Produced and directed by Herbert Kline. Written by John Steinbeck. Pan-American Films. 1941.

Docudrama. Mexican villagers distrust modern medicine and resist the efforts of a boy trying to bring aid for his sister and others suffering from typhoid.

The Frontier [Russia: Aerograd]. Directed by Alexander Dovzhenko. Mosfilm & Ukrainfilm. 1935.

Fantasy adventure. Pro-Stalin propaganda, depicts the conflicts surrounding the settlement of a Communist outpost/airfield in Russia's far eastern "frontier" lands. Shown multiple times at Taliesin.

The Gay Sisters [US]. Directed by Irving Rapper. Starring Barbara Stanwyck, George Brent, and Geraldine Fitzgerald. Warner Bros. 1942.

Melodrama. Three orphaned sisters struggle to keep their family estate and manage their romantic lives.

General Suvorov [Russia: Suvorov]. Directed by Vsevolod Pudovkin and Mikhail Doller. Mosfilm. 1941.

Historical drama. Biography of the legendary seventeenth-century Russian general, concluding

257

with remarkable scenes of the aging hero leading an army over the Alps; propagandistic elements clearly relate to the contemporary situation with Nazi Germany.

The Great Beginning, also **Member of the Government** [Russia: Chlen pravitelstva]. Produced and directed by Alexander Zarkhi and Iosef Kheifits. Lenfilm. 1940.

Drama. Centers on the struggles of a woman committed to the cause of collective farming and her ascent to the Supreme Soviet; starring the theater actress Vera Maretskaya, who received the Stalin Prize for her performance. (Identified in the diary as "The Great Awakening.")

The Great Man's Lady [US]. Produced and directed by William A. Wellman. Starring Barbara Stanwyck and Joel McCrea. Paramount. 1942.

Western drama. Melodrama told in flashback about a woman's many sacrifices for the man she loved, who abandons her following a misunderstanding and goes on to become a powerful city leader and respected senator.

Gypsies [Russia: Posledniy tabor]. Directed by Evgeni Schneider and Moisei Goldblatt. Mezhrabpomfilm. 1936.

Musical drama. A band of Gypsies joins a Soviet collective farm, despite several attempts at sabotage by the cruel Gypsy chief who is eventually arrested for his crimes.

Harvest [France: Regain]. Directed by Marcel Pagnol. Les Films Marcel Pagnol. 1937.

Drama. Love blooms between the last villager from a dying town and the mistreated girlfriend of a traveling grinder. Their devotion to one another and the land brings new life to the village. Released in the United States in 1939, it received the New York Film Critics Circle award for Best Foreign Language Film.

H.M. Pulham, Esq [US]. Directed by King Vidor. Starring Hedy Lamarr, Robert Young, Charles Coburn, Ruth Hussey, and Van Heflin. Metro-Goldwyn-Mayer. 1941.

Drama. A Back Bay Bostonian reminisces about his past, pondering his World War I experiences and how a romantic relationship was stifled by cultural differences. Although tempted to leave his wife

following a chance encounter with his past love, he decides to stay with his home and family.

I Met a Murderer [UK]. Produced, written, and directed by Roy Kellino. Starring James Mason and Sylvia Coleridge. Gamma Films. 1939.

Suspense. Henpecked British farmer kills his wife and then goes on the run. He forms a relationship with a mysterious novelist, who knows more about his unsavory past than he thinks.

Journey into Fear [US]. Directed by Norman Foster. Produced by Orson Welles. Written by Orson Welles and Joseph Cotton. Starring Joseph Cotton, Dolores Del Rio, and Orson Welles. RKO. 1942.

Suspense. An action-driven yarn in which an American munitions engineer working for the Turkish Navy is targeted by the Nazis but manages to escape multiple attempts on his life.

Laburnum Grove [UK]. Directed by Carol Reed. Starring Edmund Gwenn. Associated Talking Pictures. 1936.

Comedy. Bourgeois suburban family is shocked to learn that the head of their respectable family is not a paper-seller but actually a counterfeiter. Based on a play by J. B. Priestley. Released in the United States in 1941.

Louise [France]. Directed by Abel Gance. Starring Grace Moore. Société Parisienne de Production de Films. 1939.

Musical. Parents try to keep their seamstress daughter from becoming entangled with a bohemian composer, in this film adaptation of an opera by Gustave Charpentier. Moore performed the same role at the Metropolitan Opera in New York. Released in the United States in 1940.

The Magnificent Ambersons [US]. Written and directed by Orson Welles. Starring Joseph Cotton, Dolores Costello, Anne Baxter, and Tim Holt. RKO Radio. 1942.

Drama. After refusing her true love, a wealthy girl marries another and raises a spoiled son who destroys her happiness and squanders his family's fortune. This downfall is contrasted with the jilted lover's success and reconciliation with the bad seed who once blocked the man's union with the boy's widowed mother. Starring Frank Lloyd Wright's granddaughter Anne Baxter. Based on a novel by Booth Tarkington. Nominated for four Academy Awards. (*Rex Theater, Spring Green)

The Magnificent Dope [US]. Directed by Walter Lang. Starring Henry Fonda, Lynn Bari, and Don Ameche. Twentieth Century-Fox. 1942.

Comedy. In an attempt to revive his flagging business, a success coach manipulates a lazy dope into becoming more motivated and loses his fiancée in the process.

The Male Animal [US]. Directed by Elliott Nugent. Starring Henry Fonda, Olivia de Havilland, Joan Leslie, and Jack Carson. Warner Bros. 1942.

Comedy. A mild-mannered college professor's plan to read a controversial text to his class unexpectedly puts both his job and marriage at risk. Despite threats and personal obstacles, he stands up for free speech and wins out in the end.

Mozart, also *Whom the Gods Love: The Original Story of Mozart and His Wife* [UK]. Directed by Basil Dean. Associated Talking Pictures. 1936.

Historical drama. Biography of the famous eighteenth-century composer, focusing on his relationship with his wife, Constanze. Released in the United States in 1940.

A Musical Story [Russia: Muzikalnaya istoriya]. Directed by Alexander Ivanovsky and Herbert Rappaport. Lenfilm. 1940.

Musical comedy. Despite obstacles, a taxi cab driver finds recognition as an opera singer as well as true love. Starring the Russian opera singer Sergei Lemeshev.

Natalka, the Girl from Poltava [Ukraine: Natalka Poltavka]. Directed by Ivan Kavaleridze. Ukrainfilm. 1936.

Musical. A peasant girl is separated from a poor suitor, agrees to marry another, and is then reunited with her true love. Based on the 1818 operetta by Ivan Kotlyarevsky. A more well-received American version was released the same year by the Ukrainian nationalist company Avramenko Film Productions, which hoped to produce a series of films for American audiences based on works by Ukrainian authors.

Nazar Stodolya [Ukraine]. Directed by Georgi Tasin. Ukrainfilm. 1937.

Historical drama. Biography of Stodolya, a Ukrainian military leader who led a peasant uprising against the aristocracy. Based on the epic poem by Taras Shevchenko.

Never Give a Sucker an Even Break [US]. Directed by Edward F. Kline. Starring W. C. Fields. Universal Pictures. 1941.

Comedy. Bumbling Uncle Bill (Fields) encounters a variety of obstacles in his attempt to pitch a movie to an executive, is kicked out of the studio, and lands in the midst of yet more mishaps.

Nine Bachelors [France: Ils étaient neuf célibataires]. Directed by Sacha Guitry. Société des Films Gibé. 1939.

Comedy. Risqué farce in which an opportunistic man creates a match-making service between elderly French men and wealthy foreign women seeking a quick path to citizenship. Released in the United States in 1942.

Now, Voyager [US]. Directed by Irving Rapper. Starring Bette Davis, Paul Henried, Claude Rains, and Gladys Cooper. Warner Bros. 1942.

Drama. Boston spinster with a domineering mother finds confidence through psychiatric treatment and an illicit whirlwind romance, transforming her life and the lives of those around her. Academy Award for Best Music. (*Rex Theater, Spring Green)

Palm Beach Story [US]. Directed by Preston Sturges. Starring Claudette Colbert, Joel McCrea, Mary Astor, and Rudy Vallee. Paramount. 1942.

Comedy. Screwball caper in which a wife leaves her struggling architect husband to woo a multimillionaire, who in turn finances her husband's project and then marries her twin.

Parson of Panamint [US]. Directed by William C. McGann. Starring Charles Ruggles and Ellen Drew. Paramount. 1941.

Western. A new parson's efforts to reform the bad and to hold the good accountable triggers panic among the town's corrupt leadership, causing several deaths, an attempted lynching, and the town's eventual collapse.

Peg of Old Drury [UK]. Directed by Herbert Wilcox. Starring Anna Neagle and Cedric Hardwicke. Herbert Wilcox Productions for British & Dominions Film Corp. 1935.

Historical drama. Biography of the eighteenth-century stage performer Peg Woffington and her tragic relationship with David Garrick, a fellow actor and the stage manager of London's Drury Lane Theater. Released in the United States in 1936.

Peter the First, parts 1 and 2 [Russia: Pyotr Pervyy I, II]. Directed by Vladimir Petrov. Written by Alexei Tolstoy, Nikolai Leshchenko, and Vladimir Petrov. Lenfilm. 1937, 1939.

Historical drama. Grandiose biography of the famed Russian czar, Peter the Great.

Quiet Wedding [UK]. Directed by Anthony Asquith. Starring Margaret Lockwood and Darek Farr. Paul Soskin Productions. 1941.

Comedy. Meddling family members nearly derail a couple's plans for a "quiet wedding."

The Reluctant Dragon [US]. Directed by Alfred L. Werker. Narrated by Robert Benchley. Walt Disney Productions. 1941.

Animation. Comic, behind-the-scenes tour of Walt Disney Studios, in which the narrator is shown the process of animation while he waits for an opportunity to show Disney a book about a shy dragon.

Saludos Amigos [US]. Directed by Wilfred Jackson, Jack Kinney, Hamilton Luske, and Bill Roberts. Narrated by Fred Shields. Walt Disney Productions. 1942.

Travelogue/animation. Disney artists travel through South America and provide four short animated tales inspired by their trip. Nominated for three Academy Awards. (*New York)

Spring Song [Russia: Anton Ivanovich serditsya]. Directed by Alexander Ivanovsky. Lenfilm. 1941.

Musical comedy. A professor expects his daughter to study classical music but discovers that she is attracted to "light" operettas. He witnesses her success in this field. Released in the United States in 1942.

The Stars Look Down [UK]. Directed by Carol Reed. Starring Michael Redgrave and Margaret Lockwood. Grafton Films. 1940.

Drama. A scholarship student hoping to help the coal miners in his hometown is lured away from this goal by an ambitious woman. A tragic mine accident forces the young man to renew his commitment to

his original aspirations. Based on the A. J. Cronin novel. Released in the United States in 1941.

Suspicion [US]. Directed by Alfred Hitchcock. Starring Cary Grant and Joan Fontaine. RKO Radio. 1941.

Suspense. Shy heiress is romanced by a dashing gambler, who may or may not be trying to poison her. Joan Fontaine won the Academy Award for Best Actress.

The Talk of the Town [US]. Directed by George Stevens. Starring Cary Grant, Jean Arthur, and Ronald Colman. Columbia Pictures Corporation. 1942.

Romantic comedy/drama. A schoolteacher harbors an escaped prisoner, falsely accused of arson, and manipulates a visiting law professor into helping prove the man's innocence. Nominated for seven Academy Awards. (*New York)

Tanya, also ***The Radiant Path*** [Russia: Svetlyy put]. Directed by Grigori Alexandrov. Mosfilm. 1940.

Musical comedy. Romantic Cinderella story of a country girl's adventures in the big city. (Screened at Hillside during Priscilla's absence, December 1942—January 1943.)

Tulips Shall Grow [US]. Directed by George Pal. Paramount. 1942.

Animated short. Stop-motion "Puppetoon" showing a young Dutch couple's homeland coming under attack by a mechanical army of faceless "screwballs," symbolizing the German military, which had invaded the Netherlands in 1940. The Hungarian animator Pal and his wife fled Europe the same year. Nominated for an Academy Award in the category of Best Short Subject, Cartoons.

University of Life, also ***My Universities*** [Russia: Moi universiteti]. Directed by Mark Donskoy. Soyuzdedfilm. 1940.

Historical drama. Third in a trilogy of films by Donskoy drawn from memoirs of the author and social critic Maxim Gorky, showing the suffering of workers in late nineteenth-century czarist Russia. Parts one and two are *The Childhood of Maxim Gorky* (1938) and *My Apprenticeship* (1939).

Volga-Volga! [Russia]. Written and directed by Grigori Alexandrov. Mosfilm. 1938.

Musical comedy. Government officials are playfully lampooned in this American-style comedy celebrating rural life and work. Often cited as Stalin's favorite film. (*Screened at Hillside during Priscilla's absence, December 1942—January 1943.)

We Are from Kronstadt [Russia: My iz Kronstadt]. Directed by Yefim Dzigan with G. Berezko. Mosfilm. 1936.

Historical drama. A Bolshevic naval outfit defends Petrograd from encroaching White Russian counterrevolutionary forces during the Russian Civil War. Rousing picture was celebrated by the New York Times and well received in both Paris and London. Shown multiple times at Taliesin.

Wings of Victory [Russia: Valeri Chkalov]. Directed by Mikhail Kalatozov. Lenfilm. 1941.

Historical drama. Popular film biography of the Russian pilot Valeri Chkalov, who set multiple long-distance flight records. Depicts Chkalov's landing in Vancouver, Washington, following his record-setting polar flight.

READING LIST

This listing of books mentioned by Priscilla Henken in her diary includes a few works that Frank Lloyd Wright read aloud to the fellows. In addition to books that Priscilla or David owned and brought with them, there was an informal library at Taliesin, and various magazines, journals, and books freely circulated among the fellows.

Aeschylus. *Agamemnon.*
The Choephori.
The Persians.
Seven against Thebes.
The Suppliants.

Ameringer, Oscar. *Life and Deeds of Uncle Sam: A Little History for Big Children,* 1912.

Anderson, Sherwood. *Sherwood Anderson's Memoirs,* 1942.

Bayer, Herbert, ed., with Walter Gropius and Ise Gropius. *Bauhaus, 1919–1928,* 1938.

Beerbohm, Max. *A Christmas Garland,* 1912.

Bemelmans, Ludwig. *Hotel Splendide,* 1941.
I Love You, I Love You, I Love You, 1942.

Benét, Stephen Vincent. *The Devil and Daniel Webster,* 1937.

Benét, William Rose. *The Dust Which Is God,* 1941.

Bennett, Arnold. *Buried Alive: A Tale of These Days,* 1900.

Bragdon, Claude. *The Frozen Fountain, Being Essays on Architecture and the Art of Design in Space,* 1932.

Brooke, Rupert. *The Collected Poems of Rupert Brooke,* 1915.

Buchan, John. *Mountain Meadow,* 1941.
The Thirty-Nine Steps, 1915.

Burnett, Whit, and John Pen. "Immortal Bachelor: The Love Story of Robert Burns," *The Magazine of the Short Story,* November-December 1942, Vol. XXI, No. 98.

Chase, Ilka. *Past Imperfect,* 1942.

Dalí, Salvador. *Secret Life of Salvador Dalí*, 1942.

Dickson, Carter. *The Red Widow Murders*, 1935. *The White Priory Murders*, 1934.

Dos Passos, John. *U.S.A.*, 1938.
U.S.A. is a trilogy: *The 42nd Parallel* (1930); *Nineteen Nineteen* (1932); and *The Big Money* (1936). The three novels were first published together in 1937 and were released the following year in a single volume.

Duranty, Walter. *I Write as I Please*, 1935.

Eisenstein, Sergei, translated and edited by Jay Leyda. *The Film Sense*, 1942.

Eliot, T. S. *Collected Poems*, 1909–1935, 1936.

Erskine, Ralph. *A Paraphrase, or Large Explicatory Poem on the Song of Solomon*, 1743.

Fast, Howard. *The Unvanquished*, 1942.

Firestone, Clark B. *Coasts of Illusion: A Study of Travel Tales*, 1924.

Fletcher, Banister. *A History of Architecture for the Student, Craftsman, and Amateur; Being a Comparative View of the Historical Styles from the Earliest Period*, 1896.

Giedion, Sigfried. *Space, Time and Architecture: The Growth of a New Tradition*, 1941.

Giedion-Welcker, C. *Moderne Plastike: Element der Wirklichkeit*, 1937.

Glines, Ellen. *Garden Untended*, 1933.

Gloag, John. *Industrial Art Explained*, 1916.

Grahame, Kenneth. "The Golden Age," in *Woollcott's Second Reader*, 1937.

Gutheim, Frederick, ed. *Frank Lloyd Wright on Architecture: Selected Writings from 1894 to 1940*, 1941.

Hart, Frances Noyes. *Pigs in Clover*, 1931.

Hellman, Lillian. *Four Plays: The Children's Hour, Days to Come, The Little Foxes, Watch on the Rhine*, 1942.

Hemingway, Ernest. *The Fifth Column and the First Forty-nine Stories*, 1938.

Holt, Rackham. *George Washington Carver: An American Biography*, 1943.

Huxley, Aldous. *Antic Hay*, 1923. *The Art of Seeing*, 1942.

Isaacs, Edith J. R., ed. *Plays of American Life and Fantasy*, 1929.

Key, Ellen, with an authorized translation by Mamah Bouton Borthwick and Frank Lloyd Wright. *Love and Ethics*, 1912.

Lasswell, Mary. *Suds in Your Eye*, 1942.

Lawrence, Ada, and George Stuart Gelder. *Early Life of D. H. Lawrence*, 1932.

Lawrence, D. H. *David: A Play*, 1926.
The Man Who Died, 1931.
Mornings in Mexico, 1927.
Pornography and Obscenity, 1929.
Psychoanalysis and the Unconscious, 1921.
Reflections on the Death of a Porcupine and Other Essays, 1925.
Touch and Go: A Play in Three Acts, 1920.
The Triumph of the Machine, 1930.
The Virgin and the Gipsy, 1930.
The Widowing of Mrs. Holroyd: A Drama in Three Acts, 1914.

Lowell, Amy. *A Dome of Many-Coloured Glass*, 1912.

Lowndes, Marie Belloc. *The Lodger*, 1913.

Magnus, Maurice, with an introduction by D. H. Lawrence. *Memoirs of the Foreign Legion*, 1924.

Maslow, Abraham H., and Béla Mittelmann. *Principles of Abnormal Psychology: The Dynamics of Psychic Illness*, 1941.

Maugham, W. Somerset. *Cakes and Ale, or The Skeleton in the Cupboard*, 1930.

Mazzini, Giuseppe. *The Living Thoughts of Mazzini*, 1939.

McCullers, Carson. *Reflections in a Golden Eye*, 1941.

Mendelsohn, Erich. *Amerika: Bilderbuch eines Architekten*, 1926.

Meredith, George. *The Tragic Comedians: A Study in a Well-Known Story*, 1880.

Millay, Edna St. Vincent. *Fatal Interview*, 1931.

Miller, Alice Duer. *The White Cliffs*, 1940.

Monroe, Harriet, ed. *A Book of Poems for Every Mood*, 1933.

Moore, Olive. *Further Reflections on the Death of a Porcupine*, 1932.

Mukerji, Dhan Gopal. *A Son of Mother India Answers*, 1928.

Mumford, Lewis. *Technics and Civilization*, 1934.

Nathan, Robert. *A Winter Tide: Sonnets and Poems*, 1940.

Nehru, Jawaharlal. *Glimpses of World History*, 1934.

North, Arthur Tappan. *Raymond M. Hood*, 1931.

Parker, Dorothy. *Here Lies: The Collected Stories of Dorothy Parker*, 1939.

Pearson, Hesketh. *G.B.S. A Full-Length Portrait*, 1942.

Poliakov, Alexander. *Russians Don't Surrender: The First Eyewitness Account of the Russian Army in Action*, 1942.

Price, George. *It's Smart to Be People*, 1942.

Queen, Ellery. *The Chinese Orange Mystery*, 1934.

Rabelais, François. *Pantagruel*

Robinson, Edwin Arlington. *Collected Poems of Edwin Arlington Robinson*, 1929.

Rockwell, Kent, and Carl Zigrosser. *Rockwellkentiana, Few Words and Many Pictures.* 1933.

Rourke, Constance. *Charles Sheeler, Artist in the American Tradition*, 1938.
Davy Crockett, 1934.

Sandburg, Carl. *The American Songbag*, 1927.
Rootabaga Stories, 1922.

Seiffert, Marjorie. Various poems.

Seldes, Gilbert. *The Seven Lively Arts*, 1924.

Shackford, Martha Hale, ed. *Legends and Satires from Medieval Literature*, 1913.

Shaw, George Bernard. *The Doctor's Dilemma*, 1906.

Shridharani, Krishnalal. *My India, My America*, 1941.

Sophocles. *Ajax*
Oedipus Rex

Spaeth, Sigmund. *Words & Music, a Book of Burlesques*, 1926.

Sparks, William Sheppard. *Light on the Leaves*, 1937.

Steig, William. *The Lonely Ones*, 1942.

Stendhal. *Le Rouge et le Noir [The Red and the Black]*, 1830.
La Chartreuse de Parme [The Charterhouse of Parma], 1839.

Stong, Phil. *Stranger's Return*, 1933.

Stout, Rex. *Fer-de-Lance*, 1934.

Thurber, James. *The Middle-Aged Man on the Flying Trapeze*, 1935.
My World—and Welcome to It, 1942.

Trumbo, Dalton. *The Remarkable Andrew, Being the Chronicle of a Literal Man*, 1941.

Untermeyer, Louis. *Food and Drink*, 1932.

Waxman, Meyer. *A History of Jewish Literature from the Close of the Bible to Our Own Days*, 1930.

Westheim, Paul. *Indische Baukunst*, 1921.

Wright, Frank Lloyd. *Ausgeführte Bauten und Entwürfe von Frank Lloyd Wright*, 1910.
An Autobiography, 1932, 1938, and 1943.
"Broadacre City, the New Frontier," *Taliesin Magazine*, 1940.
Disappearing City, 1932.
Experimenting with Human Lives, 1923.
An Organic Architecture: the Architecture of Democracy, 1939.

Wyndham, Horace. *The Mayfair Calendar: Some Society Causes Célèbres, Famous Trials,* 1925.

Xenophon. *Hellenica.*

Yarmolinsky, Avrahm, ed. *The Works of Alexander Pushkin: Lyrics, Narrative Poems, Folktales, Plays, Prose,* 1936.

Young, Stark. "Rose Windows," published in *Plays of American Life and Fantasy,* collected by Edith J. R. Isaacs, 1929.

Zeitlin, Ida. *Skazki: Tales and Legends of Old Russia,* 1926.

PRISCILLA AND OTHERS WITH WRIGHT IN THE TEA CIRCLE, undated (1942-43).

LIST OF CONTRIBUTORS

Chrysanthe B. Broikos is an architectural historian and curator at the National Building Museum. She has coordinated the presentation of nearly 25 exhibitions since joining the curatorial team in 1998—including several of the Museum's signature shows (*Stay Cool! Air Conditioning America; On the Job: Design and the American Office;* and *Do It Yourself: Home Improvement in 20th Century America*). She is currently organizing an exhibition on disaster-resilient design. The intersection of architecture and photography is of particular interest to Broikos, who has collaborated with Bill Bamberger (*Stories of Home,* 2003) and MacArthur Prize grantee Camilo José Vergara (*Storefront Churches,* 2009). Likewise, she worked closely with the dean of architectural photography in Washington, D.C., Robert C. Lautman (1923–2009), whose archive is part of the Museum's Collection. Broikos holds a master's degree from the University of Virginia's School of Architecture and earned her undergraduate degree from Georgetown University's School of Foreign Service.

Elissa R. Henken earned her A.B. in Folklore and Mythology at Radcliffe College-Harvard University, her M.A. in Welsh Language and Literature at the University College of Wales, Aberystwyth, and her Ph.D. at the Folklore Institute at Indiana University. She now teaches Folklore and Celtic studies as a Professor at the University of Georgia. Her published works include two books on Welsh saints, one on the Welsh national-redeemer Owain Glyndŵr, and one, co-authored with Mariamne H. Whatley, on folklore and human sexuality. She has also published articles on Civil War legendry and developments in contemporary legend.

Jonathan T. Henken is a professional bagpiper and cabinet maker. After earning his B.S. in Oceanography from New York University, he developed his concurrent careers, using the knowledge of carpentry he developed growing up in Usonia. He serves as the Pipe Major of Mount Kisco Scottish Pipes and Drums, while also doing extensive solo piping; his work has been diverse,

including: being the Forbes Corporate and family piper; serving as the U.S. Piper for the Bank of Scotland; performing as a guest soloist with the New York Pops at Carnegie Hall and with the New Haven Symphony Orchestra; playing at curling matches, fashion shows, and social events, including the opening of the Alexander McQueen exhibit at the Metropolitan Museum of Art. He also has an animal rescue farm and restores, shows, and rides antique motorcycles.

Stephanie Hess is a Curatorial Associate at the National Building Museum. She served as assistant curator for the Museum's recent exhibition *Unbuilt Washington,* coordinating image and artifact acquisition. She has assisted with several exhibitions at the Museum in a similar role, most notably *Designing Tomorrow: America's World's Fairs of the 1930s* and *House of Cars: Innovation and the Parking Garage.* She also manages the Museum's library and exhibition archives. Hess earned a B.A. in history and ancient studies from St. Olaf College and an M.A. in museum studies from The George Washington University.

Sarah A. Leavitt is a curator at the National Building Museum where she has worked on exhibitions such as *House of Cars: Innovation and the Parking Garage* and *House & Home.* She previously held the position of Associate Historian & Curator at the Office of NIH History at the National Institutes of Health in Bethesda, Maryland and has taught women's history as an adjunct professor at American University. Her other research and museum experience includes positions at the consulting firm History Associates, Inc. as well as the Women of the West Museum in Boulder, Colorado and the Slater Mill Historic Site in Pawtucket, Rhode Island. Her book, *From Catharine Beecher to Martha Stewart: A Cultural History of Domestic Advice,* was published in 2002; other publications include articles on the home pregnancy test, on-line motherhood communities, and the television show *Veronica Mars.* Leavitt graduated from Wesleyan University and holds a Master's degree in Museum Studies and a Ph.D. in American Studies from Brown University.

Martin Moeller is Senior Vice President and Curator at the National Building Museum. He has organized exhibitions on diverse topics, including

Liquid Stone: New Architecture in Concrete; *Unbuilt Washington*; and *Reinventing the Globe: A Shakespearean Theater for the 21st Century*. He has also served as coordinating curator for the Museum's presentation of traveling exhibitions such as *Eero Saarinen: Shaping the Future*. Working independently, Moeller wrote the fifth edition of the *AIA Guide to the Architecture of Washington, D.C.*, published by the Johns Hopkins University Press in May 2012. Since 2007, he has been editor of *ArchitectureDC*, the quarterly magazine of the Washington Chapter/AIA. In 2009, he received the chapter's Glenn Brown Award, which honors an individual who has raised public awareness of architecture and its benefits to society. Moeller holds a Bachelor of Architecture and a Master of Architecture from Tulane University. He has served as an adjunct faculty member or guest critic at six schools of architecture. In the spring of 2010, he was a visiting scholar at the American Academy in Rome, researching the city's modern architectural history.

Susan Piedmont-Palladino is an architect, a professor of architecture at Virginia Tech's Washington-Alexandria Architecture Center, and a curator at the National Building Museum. Her most recent exhibition was *Green Community*. She is the author of several books, most recently *Intelligent Cities*, published by the National Building Museum. Previous books include *Green Community*, with Tim Mennel, *Tools of the Imagination: Drawing tools and Technologies from the 18th Century to the Present*, and *Devil's Workshop: 25 Years of Jersey Devil Architecture*, with Mark Alden Branch. A graduate of Virginia Tech's College of Architecture and Urban Studies and the College of William and Mary, Piedmont-Palladino writes and lectures regularly on sustainability, design education, and urbanism. A former president of Architect/Designers/Planners for Social Responsibility, she currently serves on advisory boards for the Oregon Museum of Science and Industry, the Green Hive Foundation, and the National Academy of Environmental Design.

Deborah Moore Sorensen is an assistant curator at the National Building Museum. Sorensen has worked at the Museum since 2002, managing several exhibitions and acting as co-curator of the 2010 traveling exhibition *Designing Tomorrow:*

American World's Fairs of the 1930s. In addition to curatorial work, Sorensen has contributed articles about architecture and film to NBM publications, such as "Bachelor Modern: Mid-Century Style in American Film." She has served as program curator for the museum film series since 2005, working on such programs as "Guys, Guns & Garages in 1970s Film," and has collaborated with staff at the American Film Institute Silver Theater and Cultural Center since 2010 to organize exhibition-related film programs, including the ten-part series "Things to Come: The City Imagined on Film." Sorensen earned her B.A. in the Liberal Arts/Film program at Columbia College and her master's degree in Museum Studies from George Washington University.

Mariamne Henken Whatley is Professor Emerita in the Departments of Gender & Women's Studies and Curriculum & Instruction at the University of Wisconsin-Madison, where she also served for many years as Chair of GWS and as an Associate Dean in the School of Education. She earned her A.B. in English from Radcliffe College, and her M.S. and Ph.D. in Biological Sciences from Northwestern University. She has taught and written extensively about women's health, feminist approaches to science, and sexuality education. She co-edited (with Nancy Worcester) five editions of a women's health text and co-authored (with Elissa R. Henken) *Did You Hear About the Girl Who. . . ? Contemporary Legends, Folklore, and Human Sexuality*.

272